THE DUTCH-AMERICAN FARM

The American Social Experience Series

GENERAL EDITOR: JAMES KIRBY MARTIN

EDITORS: PAULA S. FASS, STEVEN H. MINTZ,

CARL PRINCE, JAMES W. REED & PETER N. STEARNS

The Thomas Demarest House, Montville, New Jersey. Photograph by Harry Dorer. The Dorer Collection, Newark Public Library.

THE
DUTCH-AMERICAN
FARM

DAVID STEVEN COHEN

NEW YORK UNIVERSITY PRESS
NEW YORK AND LONDON
1992

Library of Congress Cataloging-in Publication Data
Cohen, David Steven
    The Dutch-American farm / David Steven Cohen.
        p.   cm. — (The American social experience series; 24)
    Includes bibliographical references (p.   ) and index.
ISBN 0-8147-1454-4 (cloth : acid-free paper)
    1. Farms—New York (State)—History. 2. Farms—New Jersey—
History. 3. Dutch Americans—New York (State)—History. 4. Dutch
Americans—New Jersey—History. 5. Farmers—New York (State)—
History. 6. Farmers—New Jersey—History. 7. Agriculture—New
York (State)—History. 8. Agriculture—New Jersey—History.
9. Farm life—New York (State)—History. 10. Farm life—New Jersey—
S451.N56C55 1992
630'.9747—dc20   91-32368
                                                                    CIP

For my mother,
Molly Gottlieb Cohen

Here I must say, a little anyhow; what I can hardly hope to bear out in the record: that a house of simple people which stands empty and silent in the vast . . . country morning sunlight, and everything which on this morning in eternal space it by chance contains, all thus left open and defenseless to a reverent and cold-laboring spy, shines quietly forth such grandeur, such sorrowful holiness of its exactitudes in existence, as no human consciousness shall ever rightly perceive, far less impart to another: that there can be more beauty and more deep wonder in the standings and spacings of mute furnishings on a bare floor between the squaring bourns of walls than in any music ever made: that this square home, as it stands in unshadowed earth between the winding years of heaven, is, not to me but of itself, one among the serene and final, uncapturable beauties of existence . . .

JAMES AGEE
Let Us Now Praise Famous Men

Contents

Illustrations

Tables

Acknowledgments

For the basic approach of this book, I owe much intellectually to folklorist Henry Glassie of Indiana University. It might be described as an application of his ideas to a topic he himself has never addressed. Different scholars who have studied the Dutch colonial farmhouse have come to very different conclusions about the defining characteristics of this house type. I found that Glassie's distinction between primary and secondary characteristics and his theories about the transformations of folk artifacts made sense out of what had previously been a confusing collection of contradictions. An indication that this approach was useful was that once it was applied to the subject matter, everything began to fall into place. Professor Glassie was kind enough to comment upon Chapter 2, when it was presented as a paper at a conference on New Jersey's architectural heritage sponsored by the New Jersey Historical Commission.

I am also intellectually indebted to a Dutch scholar whom I have never met—R. C. Hekker formerly of the Stichting Historisch Boerderij-Onderzoek in Arnhem. Without his thorough studies of the development of farmhouse styles in the various regions of the Netherlands this study would not have been possible. Unfortunately, little of his work has been translated into English.

I must also thank Charles Gehring, head of the New Netherland Project, at the New York State Library in Albany. In 1979 I took a course with Dr. Gehring at the Albany Institute for History and Art on reading seventeenth-century Dutch documents. He is perhaps the most qualified person in the country to teach that course, because his doctoral dissertation was on the structural changes that occurred in the Dutch language in New York after the English conquest. His translation project at the State Library is in the great tradition of E. B. O'Callaghan and A. J. T. Van Laer. It turned out that modern Dutch was more useful to me than seventeenth-century Dutch, but my friend Charles Gehring helped me in numerous other ways, such as suggesting articles and providing encouragement.

Several chapters of this book were given as papers at conferences; some of them were published as articles. Part of Chapter 1 was presented at a conference at the State University of New York at Binghamton in 1980 and was published under the title "How Dutch Were the Dutch in New Netherland?" in *New York History* vol. 62 (1981). Part of Chapter 2 was presented as a paper at a conference in 1980 in Trenton on New Jersey's architectural heritage, and another part of that chapter was presented at the Rensselaerswyck Seminar in Albany and again at Sleepy Hollow Restorations at an event sponsored by the New Jersey Historical Society. Part of Chapter 5 was presented at a conference in Albany on Dutch Families in the Hudson River Valley, and Chapter 6 was presented at a conference at the New Brunswick Theological Seminary and again as a talk at the Long Island Historical Society in Brooklyn. I am thankful to those people who commented upon versions of these papers, including Ronald J. Grele, Stefan Bielinski, and John Murrin.

There is another category of people who have supplied information and materials and ideas that have found their way into this study. They include Randall Herbert Balmer, Roderic H. Blackburn, Patricia U. Bonomi, Peter Christoph, Firth Haring Fabend, Joyce D. Goodfriend, Robert Grumet, Joseph Hammond, Bernard L. Herman, Field Horne, Richard Hunter, Paul Huey, William John McLaughlin, David Evan Narrett, Eric Nooter, Wilson O'Donnell, Ruth Piwonka, Oliver A. Rink, Herbert Rowen, Robert Blair St. George, Donald A. Sinclair, Ellen Snyder, Kevin Statton, Paul Taylor, Peter O. Wacker, Piet A. M. van Wijk, Charlotte Wilcoxen, Henk J. Zantkuyl, and Clifford W. Zink.

This book would not have been published had it not been for the generous support provided by New Jersey Historical Society's John A. Booth Prize with funds provided by the Florence and John Schumann Foundation.

Karen D. Gilbert prepared the index

Finally, I want to thank my wife Linda who spent many hours with me locating Dutch-American farmhouses on the backroads of New York and New Jersey.

Introduction

Having grown up in Bergen County, New Jersey, I wish I could say that I always have been aware of the red, sandstone farmhouses that dot what is today a mostly suburban landscape. I only began to notice these Dutch-American farmhouses when I visited home after taking graduate courses in American Studies and Folklife at the University of Pennsylvania. There I learned how to recognize house and barn types and to understand their significances in the study of local and regional history. Later, as a professor at Rutgers University in Newark, I observed my students undergoing a similar transformation, as they too learned how to "read" the landscape.

The literacy we learn in most schools usually is restricted to the written word. College courses in the liberal arts are for the most part in verbal arts; the Ph.D. is a degree based on words. When it comes to "reading" things, most of us are illiterate. For those of us who study the past, this kind of illiteracy distorts our understanding. When we base our conclusions about the past solely on written documents, we bias our conclusions in favor of those who kept written documents, namely, white, middle- and upper-class males.[1] Today, historians realize that important historical information can be learned from objects as well as words. Artifacts are now recognized to be "social documents."[2] "Artifacts, after all, are facts," wrote historian William B. Hesseltine, "and facts are the raw material out of which the historian constructs a narrative of the past."[3] As archeologist James Deetz noted, "the written document has its proper and important place, but there is also a time when we should set aside our perusal of diaries, court records, and inventories, and listen to another voice."[4]

Art historians have always recognized the importance of things. However, they have tended to emphasize esthetics and style, sometimes in a rather subjective manner. Usually, they look only at high-style architecture and furniture and attempt to construct stylistic periods (William and Mary, Queen Anne, Federal, Victorian), which they then relate to a *zeitgeist* or spirit of an age. The diversity of European peasant houses and American colonial farmhouses is reduced to a vaguely defined "medieval" architectural style.[5] Commenting on this "connoisseurship" approach to artifacts, folklorist Henry Glassie wrote:

> . . . some connoisseurs not only persist in treating the artifact as a unique wonder rather than as a material manifestation of culture, they even eliminate from scrutiny the things that do not measure up to their own taste. Maybe some of these things are "bad," but most of them are "good" things that the connoisseur has failed to understand. The decision to eliminate some artworks from study makes as much sense as would the choice by a historian to read only books with pretty bindings or to study only old documents calligraphed in a lovely hand.[6]

The problem results in part from two different definitions of culture. The art historian defines culture in the Matthew Arnold sense of "the best that has been thought and said."[7] The anthropologist defines culture as patterns of behavior, thinking, and artifacts. Subjective judgments about some things being more worthy of study than others disregard the fact that cultural patterns can be seen in all man-made things. Worse still is the tendency to generalize about the entirety of American culture based on data drawn solely from one level of culture (the fine arts) or one region of the country (New England or Virginia).

Folklorists and cultural geographers have been in the forefront of the material culture approach, which sees folk architecture as a central index of the forces that shaped American regional cultures. Folk architecture may be defined as a building tradition handed down from generation to generation of craftsmen, as opposed to buildings designed by professional architects and built from blueprints. Cultural geographer Fred Kniffen considered folk housing to be "a basic fact of human geography. It reflects cultural heritage, current fashion, functional needs, and the positive and negative aspects of noncultural environments."[8] Kniffen and Glassie collaborated in a ground-breaking study of the log cabin, in which they showed that rather than being the product of the American frontier, it was introduced to America from Germany and spread from the Delaware Valley, through the Great Valley of the Appalachian Mountains, and into the Midwest, following migration routes of the Pennsylvania Germans and Scotch-Irish.[9] What they showed, in effect, was that historian Frederick Jackson Turner was wrong. Rather than being the product of the frontier, as Turner claimed in his frontier thesis, it was more the product of an adaptation of European traditions to an American environment.[10]

Until recently, the Dutch-American culture area in New York and New Jersey has been given short shrift in the scholarly literature. Kniffen minimized its importance, stating that "the contributions of the Hudson River Dutch and the Delaware Swedes were lost in a sea of alien culture, so they do not constitute source areas."[11] Glassie paid little attention to the Dutch, except to mention the Dutch *kas* (clothes wardrobe), the Dutch barn, and a Dutch type of strap hinge. He writes that "the Dutch settled in New Jersey and many of their homes remain in the northern part of the state, but the material folk culture there is predominantely English."[12] It is true that the Dutch-American culture area was not a hearth region from which culture diffused into the interior regions as were New England, the Delaware Valley, Virginia, and the Carolinas. Nevertheless, the region had its own cultural identity that persisted well into the nineteenth century. While Glassie himself did not study the region in any depth, his approach makes sense of some perplexing problems about Dutch-American culture.

Just as there is a new approach to material culture studies, there is also a new approach to Dutch-American studies. The old approach, characterized by historian Langdon Wright (paraphrasing Herbert Butterfield) as the "Whig interpretation" of Dutch-American history, stressed Dutch contributions to democracy and religious toleration.[13] It is debatable, however, whether a colony in which the Dutch Reformed Church was the established church and the only religion that could be worshipped in public, in which there were large, tenanted patroon-ships and a company monopoly on the fur trade, and in which there was slavery, could be described either as tolerant or democratic.[14] As historian Thomas J. Condon has noted,

the great source collections of New York history have been ransacked to yield answers to such questions as whether New Netherland was more or less democratic, more or less religiously tolerant than her English neighbors in America. The answers obtained have depended for the most part on whether the point of view taken was Dutch or English. The result has been a curious concoction: one part myth, one part fancy, and one part history.[15]

In addition, Dutch historians have stressed the middle-class, urban, and commercial characteristics of seventeenth-century Dutch culture. The emphasis not only has been on a single class, but on a single province: Holland.[16] This approach has influenced Dutch-American historians, who have stressed merchants, towns, and commerce in New Netherland.[17] However, as historian Van Cleaf Bachman argues, this emphasis ignores the fact that a Dutch agricultural tradition did develop in New York and New Jersey and survived through the end of the nineteenth century.[18]

The new historiography of Dutch-American studies stresses other topics, such as structural changes that occurred in the Dutch language after the English conquest, the changes in Dutch family structure in America, the nature of Dutch-American agricultural towns, changes in Dutch-American religious institutions, and the relationship between the Dutch and other ethnic groups in colonial New York City.[19] At the same time historic archeologists have been excavating Manhattan Island and the Upper Hudson Valley and asking questions about artifacts, house types, and food consumption. The result has been an interdisciplinary inquiry that has dovetailed with the new interest in material culture studies.

This book attempts to present a holistic study of the Dutch-American farm in its cultural and historical context. My thesis is that the past emphasis on the single province of Holland and single class of urban merchants fails to explain the Dutch-American experience beyond the demise of New Netherland. After the English conquest, the Dutch urban merchants in America were quick to acculturate to English ways. It was in the agricultural traditions in the countryside that a distinct Dutch-American regional culture developed and survived through the end of the nineteenth century. Initially, Dutch cultural traits from various culture areas that crosscut the Netherlands were selectively adapted to the American environment. Environmental differences in New York and New Jersey resulted in new subcultures within the Dutch culture area that distinguished the upper Hudson Valley from the middle Hudson Valley, from northern New Jersey and Rockland County, New York, from western Long Island and Monmouth County, New Jersey. By the middle of the eighteenth century there occurred a major structural change in the culture resulting in a new Dutch-American culture, as opposed to transplanted adaptations of Dutch culture in America. This new Dutch-American regional culture was structurally closer to English culture than to Dutch culture. Dutch culture traits were still present, but they were survivals that gave the Dutch-American culture its distinctive identity.

I call this regional culture Dutch-American, rather than Anglo-Dutch, because it was structurally different from either Dutch culture or English culture. It was a regional subculture of American culture. The regional culture was like a dialect of a language. Americans spoke the English language, but in a way that differed from English spoken in England. Within American English there developed regional dialects, such as the Southern dialect, the Midland dialect, and the New England dialect. Thus, using this linguistic metaphor, the Dutch-American regional culture was a dialect of American culture. Thus, this book is not solely about the Dutch-American farm. By looking at the development of the Dutch-American farm we see the making of a regional American subculture.

In Chapter 1 I examine the European origins of Dutch-American settlers. I use genealogical and historical data to determine the places of origin of seventeenth-century Dutch settlers in New Netherland. I conclude that more than half of them came from places outside, but adjacent to, the present boundaries of the Netherlands and that most of them were either farmers, soldiers, or craftsmen. Then I survey the farmhouse types and settlement patterns in the places from which these emigrants came in order to determine the diverse culture areas that cut across the political boundaries of the Netherlands in the seventeenth century.

In Chapter 2 I attempt to define the Dutch-American farmhouse type in terms of Henry Glassie's distinction between primary and secondary characteristics. I argue that by defining the house type in terms of floorplan and framing one is able to distinguish between the Dutch farmhouse and the Dutch-American farmhouse. Using documentary and archeological sources, I show how a wood framing tradition common throughout continental Europe, but different from the framing tradition on the British Isles, and floorplans associated with specific regions of the Netherlands were adapted to an American environment in the Dutch farmhouse in America. I also show how by 1750 a new Dutch-American farmhouse type developed with a hybrid Dutch and English frame and with a floorplan that has been termed by architectural historians as English Georgian. I also demonstrate how secondary architectural characteristics, especially the materials used in construction, enable us to distinguish between the four subregions within the Dutch-American culture area in New York and New Jersey. Using estate inventories, I show the changes over three centuries in the interior use of space within these farmhouses.

In Chapter 3 I depict how similar cultural processes were at work in shaping the Dutch-American landscape. Three types of landholding patterns were introduced in New Netherland—the agricultural town, the isolated farm, and the tenanted manor. All three had prototypes in the Netherlands and corresponding types among the English. Fences were one of the main differences between the European and the American landscapes, being relatively absent in the former and highly visible in the latter. While the post and rail fence had a prototype in Europe, the worm or zigzag fence was a distinctly American feature on the Dutch-American landscape. The Dutch-American barn and the hay barrack were distinctly Dutch, or more accurately continental European, features. I show how the Dutch-American barn was an adaptation of a combination peasant house-barn found in the eastern provinces of the Netherlands and northern Germany and how the hay barrack was adopted from the grain-producing areas of the Netherlands.

In Chapter 4 I argue that there was a distinct difference in the Netherlands between the market-oriented, dairy-producing agriculture of the western provinces and the self-sufficient, grain-producing agriculture of the eastern provinces. The mixed agricultural tradition that developed in the Dutch-American culture area combined elements of both Dutch agricultural traditions. In addition, new crops were introduced in America as a result of cultural borrowings from the American Indians and the English in America. Even in the breeds of livestock there were cultural borrowings. Nevertheless, particular Dutch tools, such as the sith and mathook, and Dutch agricultural equipment, such as the hog plow and the Dutch wagon, continued to be used into the nineteenth century, contributing to the distinctive Dutch-American identity of the region.

In Chapter 5 I note that corresponding to the different agricultural traditions in the Netherlands were different family structures. In the eastern provinces, where the grain-producing farming predominated and the farm family lived under the same roof with the livestock, the extended family was the common pattern. In the western provinces, where dairy-producing predominated and separate farmhouses and barns evolved in the seventeenth century, the nuclear family was dominant. In America, the Dutch-American family tended to be the nuclear family, modified by the addition of children put out as servants in other families, farm laborers, and, through the early nineteenth century, slaves who lived in the household. The Dutch inheritance patterns of partible inheritance (that is, each child, both male and female, being given equal shares) and community property (that is, both the husband and wife owning property in common) were dominant in the seventeenth century in New York and New Jersey. By the eighteenth century, under English influence, these inheritance patterns were slowly modified into a Dutch-American tradition in which the husband alone owned the property. Equal division among male and female offspring continued, although in a modified form in which sons inherited real estate, reimbursing their sisters for its value, and one son inherited the family farm, while other sons were established on land purchased elsewhere.

In Chapter 6 I argue that unlike Washington Irving's stereotype of Dutch-American folklore and folklife as isolated, static, and outside the mainstream of American culture, a study of the authentic Dutch-American folk tradition shows dynamic changes similar to those in other aspects of the regional subculture. The English conquest of New

Netherland resulted in structural changes in the Dutch language in America, and two dialects of Dutch developed in New York and New Jersey that were comparable to the subregions in architecture. There were also cultural borrowings from the neighboring English both in Dutch-American folk music and folk dance. Distinctive traditions associated with the yearly cycle (New Year's, Pentecost, Christmas) and the life cycle (marriages, funerals) also changed in response to the English presence. Nevertheless, pre-Reformation and even pre-Christian traditions and beliefs and references to the European social structure in folk songs survived through the end of the nineteenth century in America. It is not surprising that the most distinctive Dutch traditions survived longest in the rural areas. What is surprising, however, is that some of these traditions survived longer among the Afro-Dutch slaves and free blacks than among the Dutch-Americans themselves.

In the conclusion I attempt to clarify the meaning of the term Dutch-American by looking at some recent research into the changes that occurred in the mid-eighteenth century in the Dutch Reformed Church. At about the same time a structural change was occurring from Dutch farmhouses to Dutch-American farmhouses a religious revival known as the Great Awakening was sweeping through the English colonies. In the Dutch Reformed Church there was a schism between those who participated in the revival and those who did not. One faction favored the establishment of an American Coetus, and the other wanted continued loyalty to the Classis of Amsterdam. While the division was eventually healed, the alignments in this so-called Coetus-Conferentie schism corresponded with the Whig-Loyalist division during the American Revolution. I argue that the structural change from Dutch to Dutch-American in architecture, the latter which misleadingly has been called English Georgian, is comparable to the Americanization of the Dutch Reformed Church that occurred during the Great Awakening. Like the religious revival, this new style of architecture crossed ethnic, religious, and political boundaries integrating various groups in the American colonies into an intercolonial movement. Also like the Great Awakening, this new farmhouse type represents a separation from European tradition and the emergence of an American tradition. Yet despite the reintegration of Dutch-Americans into a newly developing American culture, regional and ethnic diversity continued in the form of Dutch cultural survivals that gave the regional subculture its identity. In this sense, the Dutch-American farmhouse becomes a symbol of the emergence of an American regional subculture.

CHAPTER I

Origins

European historians have stressed the urban, middle-class character of the Netherlands. "The solidarity of the Dutch people," wrote Johan Huizinga, "springs from their bourgeois character. Whether we fly high or low, we Dutchmen are all bourgeois—lawyer and poet, baron and labourer alike."[1] According to Pieter Geyl, the "Holland regent class is not only the most important political factor, but also the most notable social phenomenon in the Netherlands throughout the seventeenth century and beyond."[2] The emphasis has been not only on one class, but one province: Holland. Again, Huizinga said it best:

Though we, who are attached by ties of memory, kinship and love to all parts of our country, cannot forget the beauty and goodness of incomparable Friesland, noble Guelders, the prosperous and pious medieval towns on the Ijsel, we must remember that, seen from Holland itself, the Republic looked like a flimsy embroidery round a strong and colorful central pattern.[3]

This myopia is reflected in the common misconception that the name "Holland" refers to the entire country, not just one province. Even Simon Schama, in his recent study of Dutch culture in the golden age, admitted that his generalizations about the Dutch national culture were based on evidence taken from "the middling sort" *(brede middenstand).* "It described a culture that was predominantly urban, surprisingly literate for its time; one that nourished a market for prints, engraved histories, poems and polemics." Schama took issue with Huizinga and Geyl by stating that "at the center of the Dutch world was a burgher, not a bourgeois."[4] But this is only a slight shift in emphasis from economic values to civic values.

American historians writing about the Dutch in New Netherland have been influenced by this orientation. Alice P. Kenny stressed the "Dutch patricians" of Albany, who, she argued, emulated the traditions, values, and behavior of the wealthy merchants of the Low Countries. She stated that "the colonists who settled in towns—particularly New York, Albany, Schenectady, Kingston, Brooklyn, and New Brunswick—recreated the way of life of Dutch burghers."[5] Social historian Donna Merwick argued that "the strong town tradition of the Low Countries" led to a distinctive social history in New Netherland "that exalted town life over rural existence."[6] This contrasts, she said, to the weaker town tradition of the English. Thomas J. Condon argued that the Dutch were more interested in the fur trade than in planting agricultural settlements. Since the commercial spirit was essentially the same in Virginia and New England, the history of New Netherland, he argued, "is not the story of the gradual development of a distinctively Dutch society in the New World but rather the story of why such a society did not take shape."[7] He concluded that "the end result in New Netherland was a combination of the forms that developed in Virginia and New England, which can be explained by historically conditioned factors rather than by exclusive ethnic or regional concepts."[8] Architectural historian Alan Gowans divided architecture in New Netherland into two types: the urban houses of the merchants and the rural houses of the farmers. The urban houses, he argued, "reproduced those of the rich burghers of Amsterdam and Haarlem and Delft who first financed and governed the New Netherland settlement," but the rural houses were "not, like the urban type, an expression of Dutch (or Flemish, or any other) national traditions transplanted to the New World."[9]

None of these scholars looked at the social and geographical backgrounds of the seventeenth-century Dutch settlers in New Netherland. It is only then that one gains an understanding of the cultural processes that shaped the distinctive Dutch-American culture area in New York and New Jersey. I have determined the places of origin of more than 900 settlers who immigrated to New Netherland in the seventeenth century, as revealed in ships' passenger lists, genealogies, collections of colonial documents, and ethnic and local histories.[10] The data include those people in the New Amsterdam in 1660, Rensselaer-swyck from 1630 to 1657, on ships arriving between 1654 and 1664, and who founded Dutch families still residing in New York and New Jersey, whose place of origin was known.

These 900 settlers represent a significant part of the total Dutch population in New Netherland. In 1647, Director General Stuyvesant estimated the population, excluding the three English villages on Long Island, as 250 to 300 men capable of bearing arms. In 1673, the Dutch population including women and children was estimated to be 6,000. The first census for New Jersey was not taken until 1726, but based on the number of people swearing oaths of loyalty to the English government, it is estimated that the total population of East Jersey was 548 during the period 1665 to 1668 and 1,955 in 1673. Using the estimate of Captain Mathias Nicolas, Secretary of the Province of New York, that the average family size in East Jersey was 5 individuals, our data represent about one-half the families in New York and New Jersey.[11]

The names of the ships' passenger lists constitute only part of the overall data, but these lists provide the previous occupations of the emigrants in their place of origin. These were not necessarily the same as the occupations they assumed in New Netherland. There were 177 individuals who immigrated between 1654 and 1664 for whom occupations are indicated. Of that number, one-third had been farmers, more than one-quarter had been soldiers, and another quarter had been craftsmen. The remainder were farm laborers, servants, fishermen, and laborers (see Table 1).[12] While several of these people became the founders of wealthy families in New York and New Jersey, their social class in the Old World was more humble. Certainly, they were not from the ruling, regent class.

Historian Oliver A. Rink studied 102 immigrants to Rensselaer-swyck between 1630 and 1644, whose occupations were reported to public notaries in Amsterdam. He found that 38 percent had occupations associated with agriculture and 14 percent were either carpenters, masons, wheelwrights, or carpenter's apprentices. Rink notes that the

TABLE I

Occupational Backgrounds of Immigrants to
New Netherland 1654–1664

	Number	Percentage
Farmers	59	33.3
Soldiers	49	27.7
Craftsmen	45	25.4
Laborers	10	5.6
Farm laborers	8	4.5
Servants	4	2.3
Fishermen	2	1.1
Total	177	100.0

Sources: "List of Passengers, 1654–1664," Holland Society of New York. *Yearbook* (1920): 5–28; Rosalie Fellows Bailey, "Emigrants to New Netherland, Account Book, 1654–1664," *New York Genealogical and Biographical Record* 94 (1963): 193–200.

agricultural category was probably larger, because many of those listed as servants or laborers were probably under contract to do agricultural work.[13]

The same has been shown about the social origins of seventeenth-century emigrants from England to America. Mildred Campbell compiled data on 10,000 individuals who left for America from the port of Bristol between 1654 and 1685. She found that 36 percent were yeomen and husbandmen, 22 percent were artisans and tradesmen, and fewer than 1 percent were gentlemen and professionals. She concludes that there were twice as many farmers as skilled workers and five times as many farmers and skilled workers as laborers.[14]

One observes the same phenomenon when one looks at the social origins of the first ancestors of some of the wealthiest Dutch families in New York and New Jersey. Philip Pietersz Schuyler, the founder of the influential Schuyler family of New York State, was the son of a baker. He immigrated in 1650 and married Margareta van Slichtenhorst, the daughter of the Director of Rensselaerswyck. Schuyler became one of the wealthiest men in the colony. Frederick Philipse, who became the landlord of Philipsburgh Manor, was the son of a slater. He himself was a carpenter. He immigrated in 1647 to New

Netherland, where he married Margaret Hardenbroeck, a wealthy widow. Oloff Stevensen van Cortlandt, the landlord of Van Cortlandt Manor, came to New Netherland in 1673 as a soldier. Dirck Jansen Dey, the founder of one of the most wealthy and influential Dutch families in New Jersey, came to New Netherland in 1641 also as a soldier employed by the Dutch West India Company.[15]

There was one important exception to this pattern. Kiliaen van Rensselaer, a director of the Dutch West India Company and patroon of Rensselaerswyck, sent his eldest son, Jan Baptist, to New Netherland in 1652 to be director of his patroonship. When Jan Baptist returned to the Netherlands in 1658, his younger brother, Jeremias, replaced him as Director-in-Residence of the colony.[16] Jeremias founded the American branch of the van Rensselaer family.

Notwithstanding this exception, the social origins of the founders of the wealthy Dutch families in New York and New Jersey indicate that they were clearly not from the merchant class in the Netherlands. This does not mean that they didn't model themselves after the merchant class, once they rose to social prominence in America.

A study of the places of origin of the settlers in New Netherland refutes the past emphasis on the single province of Holland.[17] Of the 904 persons in our sample, almost half (445) actually came from places outside the Netherlands (see Table 2). The largest group (about 37.5 percent of the non-Dutch emigrants) came from Germany, mainly either from places adjacent to the Netherlands (Aachem, the Duchy of Cleves, East Friesland, Westphalia, Bremen, Hamburg, and Oldenburgh) or from places further up the Rhine River (Cologne, Bonn, Hesse, Baden, and the Lower Palatinate).[18] For example, Wessel Wesselse ten Broeck came from the town of Wessen near Munster in Westphalia, Meyndert Barentszen came from Jever in Oldenburgh, and Pieter Claesen Wyckoff came from Norden, a town near Ems in East Friesland.[19]

The next two largest contributors of colonists from outside the Netherlands were France and the Spanish Netherlands, each with approximately 14 percent of the non-Dutch immigrants to New Netherland. Many of the emigrants from France were French Huguenots from the cities of Calais and La Rochelle and the provinces of Picardy and Normandy. Some of them fled first to the Palatinate region of

TABLE 2

Places of Origin of 904 Family Heads Who Immigrated to New Netherland
(New York and New Jersey) in the Seventeenth Century

The Netherlands (N = 459; % = 50.8)		SOUTH HOLLAND (N = 45; % = 5)	
NORTH HOLLAND (N = 142; % = 16)		Delft	2
Alckmaer (Alkmaar)	3	Dort (Dordrecht)	3
Amsterdam	90	Gorcum (Gorichem, Gorkem)	7
Barcom (Blaricum)	2	Ter Gouw (Gouda)	3
Edam	4	Leyden	13
Haerlem (Haarlem)	6	Rotterdam	5
Hilversum	3	Schoenderwoert	6
Hoorn	11	Other	6
Medemblick	2	FRIESLAND (N = 25; % = 3)	
Naerden	8	Harlingen	5
Other	13	Workum	3
GELDERLAND (N = 88; % = 10)		Other	17
Aernheim (Arhem)	6	DRENTHE (N = 22; % = 2)	
Beest	8	Meppel	5
Betawe	2	Ruinen	2
Buren	5	Other	17
Doornyck (Doornik)	2		
New-kerk (Niewkirk)	13	NORTH BRABANT (N = 16; % = 2)	
Newenhuys	2	Breda	7
Putten	2	's Hertogenbosch	3
Thillerwarden (Thillerwaerd)	4	Other	8
Tiel (Teyl)	7	OVERIJSSEL (N = 21; % = 2)	
Tricht	2	Deventer	3
Wagening	7	Hasselt	2
Other	26	Kampen (Campen)	5
UTRECHT (N = 68; % = 8)		Oldenseel (Oldenzaal)	2
Amersfoort	15	Steenwyck	5
Breuckelen	3	Swoll (Zwolle)	3
Bunnick	4	Other	1
Hilversam	2	LIMBURG (N = 7; % = 1)	
Houten	6	Maestricht (Maastricht)	2
Leerdam	5	Other	5
Loosdrecht	2	ZEELAND (N = 18; % = 2)	
Maersen (Maarssen)	2	Middleburg (Middelburgh)	6
Soest	3	Veere	2
Westbroeck	2	Vlissingen (Flushing)	3
Ysselstein	3	Other	7
Other	21		

GRONINGEN (N = 7; % = 1)
Spanish Netherlands (Belgium)
(N = 63; % = 7)

WALLOON PROVINCES (N = 30; % = 7)

Avesnes	2
Liege	3
Hainaut (Henegouw)	2
Tournai (in Hainaut)	3
Valenciennes	7
Artois	5
Richebourg (in Artois)	2
Other	18

FLEMISH PROVINCES (N = 31; % = 3)

Antwerp	5
Leeuwen (Leuven, Louvain)	2
Bruggen (Bruges)	4
Iperen (Ypres)	2
Other	18

BRUSSELS (N = 2; % = .2)
Germany (N = 167; % = 18)
EAST FRIESLAND (N = 20; % = 2)

Embden (Emden)	9
Norden	4
Other	7

OLDENBURGH (N = 23; % = 3)

Oldenburgh	12
Jever	8
Other	3

WESTPHALIA (N = 18; % = 2)

Munster	5
Other	13

BRUNSWICK-LUNEBURG (N = 6; % = 1)

Brunswick	3
Wolfenbuttel	2
Other	1

Calemburg (N = 2; % = .2)
HESSE (N = 12; % = 1)

Darmstadt	7
Other	5

BADEN (N = 3; % = .3)

Mannheim	2
Other	1

BRANDENBURG-PRUSSIA (N = 7; % = 1)

Magdeburg	2
Other	5

BAVARIA (N = 5; % = .6)

Nurnberg	4
Other	1

BREMEN (N = 18; % = 2)
HAMBURG (N = 7; % = 1)
HANOVER (N = 2; % = .2)
OSNABRUCK (N = 2; % = .2)
COLOGNE (N = 3; % = .3)
CLEVES (N = 5; % = .6)
AACHEM (N = 2; % = .2)
BONN (N = 5; % = .6)
LIPPE (N = 2; % = .2)
LOWER PALATINATE (N = 2; % = .2)
THURINGIA (N = 2; % = .2)
WURTEMBURG (N = 2; % = .2)
POMERANIA (N = 2; % = .2)
SAXONY (N = 4; % = .4)
OTHER (N = 13; % = 1)
France (N = 64; % = 7)
PICARDY (N = 10; % = 1)

Amiens	2
Calais	4
Other	4

NORMANDY (N = 9; % = 1)

Dieppe	2
Other	7

SAINTONGE (N = 4; % = .4)

La Rochelle	3
Other	1

PAYS DE VAUD (N = 8; % = 1)
PARIS (N = 3; % = .3)
LANGUEDOC (N = 2; % = .2)
OTHER (N = 28; % = 3)
Schleswig-Holstein (N = 60; % = 7)

Barlt	2
Dithmarschen	11
Flensburg	4
Holstein	26
Husum	2

TABLE 2 (*Continued*)

Lubeck	7	Vesteras	2
Nordstrand	2	Varberg (in Scania)	2
Schleswig	3	Other	8
Other	3	*Norway* (N = 47; % = 5)	
Denmark (N = 11; % = 1)		Bergen	5
ZEALAND (SJAELLAND) (N = 4; % = .4)		Fleckero	3
Copenhagen	2	Frederikstad	3
Other	2	Sant	3
JUTLAND (N = 5; % = .6)		Sleewyck (Sleviken)	2
OTHER (N = 2; % = .2)		Other	31
Sweden (N = 24; % = 3)		*Poland* (N = 3; % = .3)	
Gotenborg	4	*Other* (N = 6; % = .7)	
Stockholm	8		
		TOTAL = 904	

Germany prior to coming to New Netherland. For example, Abraham and Jean Hasbrouck were brothers from Calais, who came to New York in 1678 by way of the Palatinate, Rotterdam, and England. They were two of the original patentees at New Paltz. David Demarest (Des Maree) was born in Beauchamp, near Amiens, in Picardy. He fled to Middleburg in Zeeland, then to Mannheim in Germany, prior to coming to America in 1663. Other French Huguenots came by way of the Netherlands. For example, Jacques Cousseau was a merchant from La Rochelle. He immigrated to New Netherland by way of Holland in 1658 and subsequently lived in New Amsterdam and then in Harlem. Still others were Waldensians—members of the brotherhood known as the *Pauvres* of Lyon, founded by Peter Waldo in the twelfth century. During persecutions in 1655, they fled to Holland and then to New Netherland to settle on Staten Island and Long Island.[20]

In the sample of emigrants from the Spanish Netherlands (Belgium), roughly half (30) came from the Walloon provinces (Hainaut, Namur, Liege, Luxembourg, Artois, South Brabant) and half (31) from the Flemish provinces (West Flanders, East Flanders, Antwerp, Limbourg, North Brabant). In fact, several leaders of the colony were originally from the Spanish Netherlands. Peter Minuit, Director General of New Netherland from 1626 to 1632, was the son of Walloon refugees who settled in the town of Wessel in Westphalia, Germany. And Cornelis Melyn, the patroon of Staten Island, was a Fleming originally from Antwerp, who came to New Netherland in 1638.[21]

Approximately 14 percent (60) of the non-Dutch immigrants to New Netherland came from Schleswig-Holstein, at that time part of Denmark. Laurens Andriessen van Boskerk, for example, emigrated from Holstein about 1654, settling first in New Amsterdam and then in Bergen County, New Jersey. Jan Pietersen Slot (Sloat) was also from Holstein. He immigrated to Amsterdam and then to New Netherland, where he took up residence in Harlem. Another 2.5 percent (11) came from elsewhere in Denmark. Perhaps the most notable was Jonas Bronck, after whom the Bronx was named. He was the son of a Lutheran pastor from Thorshavn on the Faroe Islands. He came to New Netherland in 1639 and obtained a large tract of land in what is today known as the Morrisania section of New York City.[22] Another 11 percent (47) of the non-Dutch immigrants came from Norway. There were economic ties between Norway and the Netherlands in the seventeenth century. Norway supplied the Netherlands with lumber, and many Norwegians and Danes joined the Dutch fleet.[23] Two brothers, Arent Adriessen Bradt and Albert Adriesse Bradt, came from Frederikstad, Norway, to settle in Rensselaerswyck. Albert Bradt built a mill a few miles south of Albany. He was known as *de Noorman* (the Norwegian), and the stream on which he built his mill was called *de Noorman's Kill* (today known as Norman's Kill).[24] Approximately 5 percent (24) of the non-Dutch immigrants came from Sweden. Together, the Scandinavian countries contributed 32 percent (142) of the non-Dutch immigrants to New Netherland.

Of those colonists who came from the Netherlands, the largest number (90) came from the city of Amsterdam. But they represent only about one-fifth of the total number of immigrants from the Netherlands. Even when those from Amsterdam are included, the number of individuals from the province of North Holland was only 31 percent (142) of the total Dutch immigrants. Several came from Hoorn, the seaport on the Zuider Zee, including David Petersen de Vries, onetime patroon of Staten Island and Vriesendael, and Jan Pieterse Haring, one of the original shareholders in the Tappan Patent. Approximately 10 percent (45) of the Dutch immigrants came from South

Holland, including Pieter Gerritse van Alen from Rotterdam, who settled in the Saddle River Valley of Bergen County, and Peter van Ecke, a planter from Leyden who immigrated in 1657. Rutger Jacobsen, the founder of the Rutgers family, came from Schoonderwoert, a village near Utrecht, in South Holland. He started out as a farmhand, became a foreman at Rensselaerswyck, and then became a prominent man in Beverwyck (Albany), and also owned a house in New Amsterdam.[25]

About 15 percent (68) of the Dutch colonists came from the province of Utrecht. A significant number (15) came from the town of Amersfoort. Wolphert Gerritsz van Couwenhoven came from Couwenhoven, an estate near Amersfoort in the province of Utrecht. He was hired by Kiliaen van Rensselaer to supervise the establishment of farms and the purchase of cattle in Rensselaerswyck. Cornelis Anthonisz van Schlick was a carpenter and mason from Breuckelen, in the province of Utrecht; he immigrated in 1634 and settled in Rensselaerswyck. The province of Zeeland, along the coast in the southwestern corner of the Netherlands, contributed about 4 percent (18) of the sample of Dutch immigrants. They came from places such as Middelburgh and Vlissingen (Flushing). Claes Martenszen van Rosenvelt, the founder of the Roosevelt family in America, came from the town of Rosenvelt in the province of Zeeland.[26]

Almost 20 percent (88) of the Dutch settlers came from the province of Gelderland, through which the Rhine River flows on its way across the eastern Netherlands. Newkirk (Nykerck, Niewkirk) contributed the largest number (13), but individuals came from Arnhem, Beest, Buren, Thillerwarden, Teyl, and Wagening. For example, Arent van Curler, the commis of Rensselaerswyck from 1642 to 1644, came from Nykerck; and Gerrit Gerritse, the founder of the van Wagoner family, emigrated from Wageningen in 1660 and settled in Communipauw (now part of Jersey City).[27]

Lesser numbers came from the provinces of Friesland, 5.4 percent (25); Drenthe, 4.8 percent (22); Overijssel, 4.6 percent (21); North Brabant, 3.5 percent (16); Limburg, 1.5 percent (7); and Groningen, 1.5 percent (7). But taken together, they represent 21.3 percent (98) of the total Dutch immigrants—more than those who came from the city of Amsterdam—and included some very important people. Pieter

Stuyvesant was born in the province of Friesland, and Epke Jacobse Banta, founder of the Banta family of Bergen County, came from Harlingen in Friesland. Steven Coerte van Voorhees and Joris Dircksen Brinkerhof both came from the province of Drenthe; and Dirck Storm and David Ackerman both came from the Mayory of Bosch ('s Hertogenbosch) in North Brabant. Also from North Brabant was Adriaen van der Donck, the owner of Colendonck (present-day Yonkers). And finally, Gerrit Hendricksen, the founder of the Blauvelt family, was born in Deventer in the province of Overijssel. He worked as a shoemaker in Nykerk, before coming to New Netherland in 1637.[28]

What conclusions can be drawn from these data? First, the emphasis of both European and American historians on the urban merchant tradition in the Netherlands does not explain the origins of the Dutch settlers in New Netherland. Most of the immigrants were farmers, soldiers, or craftsmen, even among the ancestors of the families that gained great wealth in New York and New Jersey. Second, the emphasis on the single province of Holland has masked the fact that the majority of the Dutch immigrants came from other provinces. And, third, almost half of the immigrants to New Netherland were not from the Netherlands, but from places adjacent to the Netherlands. We tend to think in terms of political boundaries instead of ethnic and linguistic boundaries, and political boundaries changed frequently during the seventeenth century. Only when we look at the cultural boundaries and how they relate to the places of origin of the Dutch settlers can we understand the cultural processes that shaped the Dutch culture area in New York and New Jersey.

In 1965 the anthropologist Conrad Arensberg called for a reconceptualization of European and American history using the culture area concept.[29] Arensberg stated that the culture area concept is based on folk culture ("the Little Tradition"), rather than on elite culture ("the Great Tradition"). "Obviously the successive historic Great Traditions of civilization and ecumenical religion—Classical, Christian, Moslem, Jewish, Catholic, Protestant—which are conventional names for the people's cultures, or the successive epochs, Hellenistic, Merovingian, Renaissance, Victorian, cannot be abandoned," Arensberg wrote.

They will continue to recapitulate a great deal of the institutional, social-organizational, and value data of varying cultures and areas which the anthropologist must use since they identify much for him. The anthropologist's work, nevertheless, has taken him as with the folklorist, far below these historical rubrics, where much older continuities may run and little traditions still flourish and are constantly renewed. For us in comparative ethnology, the problem of useful classification exists precisely in the discovery at the folk-level of patterns which, because they straddle the expected, conventional high cultural divisions of institutions and ethnicities, throw them together in world-wide perspective or isolate elements of continuity unsuspected in the apparent great successions of epoch on epoch and people on people.[30]

Arensberg suggested a trial formulation of European culture areas. He wrote that Europe generally was characterized by a mixed agricultural complex, consisting of clean-cropped fields which were left fallow in the winter and hoofed livestock that were fed on grassland fodder. The fields yielded hard grain for bread, and the livestock provided manure, milk, and meat. Within this larger European culture area, Arensberg differentiated between four smaller culture areas: the Atlantic Fringe, the Northern European Plain, the Mediterranean Lands, and the Alpine Climax. The Mediterranean Lands and the Alpine Climax need not concern us. On the Atlantic Fringe, grain was less important than the kitchen garden, and fresh milk and meat were important in the diet. Grain was prepared as griddle breads and porridges. In the "wheat villages" of the Northern European Plain, fresh milk and meat became progressively less important as one traveled from west to east, from Germany into Poland and Russia. The diet consisted of preserved cheeses, sausages, beers, and oven-baked breads. The boundary between the Atlantic Fringe and the Northern European Plain cut across the Netherlands, with the Frisian and Holland coasts within the former and the Drenthe Plateau within the latter.

Audrey M. Lambert, a geographer at the London School of Economics, developed a more refined formulation of culture areas for the Netherlands. He noted that throughout history and prehistory the Low Countries have been a frontier, where different cultures came in contact with each other. This pattern was established by the close of the Bronze Age (circa 1100 B.C.), when there occurred a prehistoric migration from Germany. These people have been called the Urnfield folk, because they cremated their dead and buried them in urns. By 700 B.C. a distinction could be made between the northern and southern Urnfield folk. Some scholars believe that these two prehistoric groups were the ancestors of the Saxons and the Celts, respectively. About 300 B.C. a third group, known as the proto-Frisians, began to settle in northern Friesland and Groningen, where they lived on man-made mounds, known as *terpen*, and raised cattle. By the time of the Roman conquest, Julius Caesar noted that the lower Rhine was the boundary between the Germans and the Celts. After the withdrawal of the Romans (between 260 A.D. and 270 A.D.), another Germanic tribe, the Franks, invaded the region. During the Early Middle Ages, the Frisians, the Saxons, and the Franks established their respective culture areas.[31]

By the end of the seventeenth century, Lambert noted, five rural settlement types developed, each with its own landholding pattern: (1) the *brinkdorp*, (2) the *kransesdorp*, (3) the *waldhufendorp*, (4) the *terpdorp*, and (5) the *geestdorp*.

The *brinkdorp* was a nucleated, agricultural village, in which all the farmsteads were clustered together in the town along the village green (the *brink*). The arable lands (the *essen*) were divided into blocks and alloted to individuals, but they were farmed communally in a manner similar to the open-field system in England. The meadows, usually located along the brooks, separate from the village and the fields, were used as pasturage. Farther away were the uncultivated lands, which were originally wastelands. This settlement type and landholding pattern were common on the Drenthe plateau in the eastern part of the Netherlands.

In nearby Salland, Twente, and the Achterhoek, the early settlement type was similar to the nucleated villages and large, communal fields of Drenthe. But as private ownership replaced communal tenure, a more dispersed, secondary settlement type developed. This was the *kransesdorp*, which literally means "ring village." Individual peasants enclosed small pasture lots *(kampen)* and located their farmsteads around the open field thereby forming a circle of farmsteads with the arable fields in the center. In some cases the *kransesdorp* was a primary settlement pattern; here the arable land was divided into strips and located near their respective farmsteads, instead of being scattered like the *essen* of the open-field system.

Under the feudal system, introduced in the late eighth and ninth centuries, when the Carolingians subjugated the Saxons, large estates, modeled after the Frankish pattern, were introduced to this region. They consisted of the *curtis* or *hoofdhof* (the residence of the lord's bailiff), which was the chief farmstead, surrounded by a ring of peasant holdings (the *hoeven*). Later, squatters carved out isolated *kampen* in the valley wastes for flax cultivation. "Thus by the later medieval times," Lambert summarized, "Salland, Twente, and the Achterhoek formed a region where *kransesdorpen* were interspersed with the scattered farms belonging to the *hoeven* of large estates and the *kamphoeven* of individual reclaimers in the wastes."[32] A similar settlement and landholding pattern developed in the hill country of the Veluwe and in eastern Utrecht. The *brinkdorpen* and *kransesdorpen* were also spread by early German migrants into the great river lowlands of the Rhine and the Maas.

In North Brabant and North Limburg the terrain consists of marshy brook lands *(broeklanden)* in the valleys and peat bogs on the plateaux. The bottom lands *(beemden)* in the valleys were reclaimed as pasturage, and plowlands *(akkers)* were located along the slopes of the valleys. The unimproved wastes on the plateaux were often separated by woodlands. The early farmsteads were clustered in the valleys between the *beemden* and the *akkers*. Later settlement followed the *kransesdorp* pattern. On the plateaux the settlements were more dispersed, with either arable lands, divided into blocks separated by meadow *kampen*, or hamlets, consisting of a few farmsteads and their *kampen*, or isolated farmsteads with their arable land and pastures. Good agricultural land in North Brabant was scarce, and the initial settlement pattern consisted of large rectangular plots located near the homesteads. As the population increased, smaller plots were the rule. Thus, the *akkerland* in North Brabant tended to be more irregular than the *essen* in Drenthe.

The *waldhufendorf* was a type of nucleated village, found on the plateaux of South Limburg, where the Frankish influence was great. The farmsteads formed enclosed courtyards along the streets of the village. In some cases, the villages were located in the valleys, where the meadows were situated along the streams, orchards on the lower slopes of the plateaux, and the arable land on top of the plateaux. In other cases, the villages were located on the plateaux, and the farmsteads along a line separating the plowlands from the arable *essen*.

The *terpendorp* (literally, "mound village") was established by the Anglo-Saxon and Anglo-Frisian peoples who settled along the coasts of Groningen and Friesland. The early *terpen*, built in pre-Roman and Roman times, were small, man-made mounds, accommodating a hamlet or an isolated farmstead, surrounded by small block-shaped fields. In Groningen, the *terpen* tended to be larger, consisting of a radial arrangement of farmsteads with their yards converging toward the center of the *terp*, where there was usually a fresh-water pond. Also located on the *terp* were small garden plots, orchards, some arable land, and often a church. The pastures for the livestock were located near the village mounds, and the hayfields were farther away in the marsh.

The *geestdorp* was the settlement type common on the western coastlands, which were sparsely settled by Germanic people in the fourth century A.D. The terrain nearest the coast is known as the "Young Dunes," and farther inland are the so-called "Old Dunes," which consist of low ridges with sandy soil (the *geestlands*), separated by narrow clay or peat flats. The farmsteads were located on the *geest*, along a circular track or embankment that surrounded the arable, open fields. Each field was divided into strips. The church was located at one end of the *geest*. Farther inland the swampy wastes were used as common grazing land for livestock. These wastelands consisted of rich peat bogs, which were later reclaimed by the construction of drainage ditches. The resulting pattern of drainage ditches and enlongated, arable plots was known as the *opstrekkende landerijen* (literally, "raised fields"). Eventually, new hamlets developed along these reclaimed lands in the bogs. The farmhouses faced each other across the dike, and stretching behind each farmhouse was its own narrow strip of reclaimed land. The fens were used for tillage and pasturage, and the peat as fuel.

On the islands and mainlands at the mouths of the Rhine, the Maas, and the Schelde rivers, there was a variation of this settlement and landholding pattern. There were a few *geest* villages, such as Domburg, Ouddorp, and Oostvoorne, that antedate the Carolingian period. The towns of Middleburg and Souburg on the island of Walacheren were located on ridges; the town of Duivendijk on the island of Schouwen was located on a man-made mound known as a *vliedberg* (literally, "refuge mound"), which was smaller and steeper than the *terpen* in Friesland and Groningen. Similar mounds were constructed in the ninth century in Zeeuws-Vlaanderen on the mainland. By 1000 A.D., after the Viking raids ended, the landholding pattern in Zeeuws-Vlaanderen changed to the reclaimed land pattern of the western coastlands farther north. However, the land reclamation here was organized by abbeys.

Lambert summarized the various settlement and landholding patterns as follows:

The wide variety of settlement types and forms, ranging from large nucleations to isolated farms, from round *terp* to elongated dike villages, and of field patterns, varying between the hedgeless expanses of the open-field *essen*, to oval *geest-gronden*, the ditch-bounded *opstrekkende landerijen* to tiny tree-ringed *kampen*, was an expression of the interplay of a wide range of influences. Factors such as the limited technical ability of the immigrants; the relative proportions of the different types of land available and their positions in relation to each other and the water-table; whether the settlements and their fields were established by communal or individual effort, and, lastly, the tenurial circumstances under which the land was occupied and the extent of lordly influence upon landholding, all played their part in the evolution of a pattern of fields, farms, hamlets, and villages which was to survive, in large measure, down to the present day.[33]

These seventeenth-century landholding and settlement patterns were related to different agricultural traditions. Lambert distinguished between the market-oriented arable agriculture and cattle raising on the clay soils as opposed to the self-sufficient agriculture on the sandy soils.[34]

On the Drenthe plateau, where the *brinkdorp* was common, rye was the main crop, because the climate was too damp for wheat, barley, or millet. The remainder of the arable land was planted in buckwheat, small plots of pulses (peas, beans, and lentils), and vegetable gardens near the farmsteads. Sheep were more important than cattle, because sheep are better manure-producers and manure was the main fertilizer. Cattle were limited to plow oxen and some dairy cows to supply the family with butter, milk, and cheese. A similar self-sufficient agriculture was the rule in Twente and the Achterhoek, where the *kransesdorp* was found. Farmers also grew rye and buckwheat and kept some cattle to supply their own dairy needs. On the sandy soils of the great rivers, self-sufficient agriculture was also prevalent.

Since the sixteenth century, the *geestdorpen* in the province of Holland had a predominantly pastoral economy. Because livestock raising requires less labor than arable farming, there was a labor surplus. There was also a surplus of animal products, but a shortage of grain. Hay was vital to maintain the livestock during the winter months. By the seventeenth century, Holland was producing "industrial crops" for urban markets, such as dairy products in Gouda, hops for breweries in Gouda and Delft, hemp for cordage, sailcloth, and nets and flax and dyes for the linen industry in Haarlem. Also, horticulture became important, especially fruits, vegetables, and exotic flowers, such as tulips.

In the *terpendorpen* in the clay districts of Groningen and Friesland in the seventeenth century, cattle raising was dominant. Trade ties were established with Holland, supplying dairy products for butter and cheese making. As the arable land in Drenthe began to produce a surplus, trade developed with Groningen in which grain was traded for dairy products. On the loess-soil plateau of South Limburg, mixed arable agriculture predominated, including the production of grain, meat, and milk products.

These different agricultural traditions correlate roughly with different types of farm architecture. R. C. Hekker, formerly of the Stichting Historisch Boerderij-Onderzoek in Arnhem, divides the Netherlands into five culture areas, based on types of farmhouses, barns, and hay barracks: (1) the Frisian House Group *(Friesehuisgroep)*, (2) the Aisled-House Group *(Hallenhuisgroep)*, (3) the Compartmented House Group *(Dwarshuisgroep)*, (4) the Zeeland Barn Group *(Zeeuwse-Schuurgroep)*, and (5) the Flemish Barn Group *(Vlaamse-Schuurgroep)*.[35] These culture areas extend beyond the political boundaries of the Netherlands into adjacent provinces in the Spanish Netherlands (Belgium), France, Germany, and Denmark.[36]

The Frisian House Group culture area included not only Friesland, but also North Holland and northern Groningen in the Netherlands, the northern part of East Friesland in Germany, and the west coast of Schleswig-Holstein. The Frisian House Group was characterized by a combination dwelling and barn, with an interior, central grain pile *(tas)*. The threshing floor *(deel)* occupied one side aisle, and the cow stalls *(stallen)* were on the other side aisle. A variant of this farm house type was the *stolp*, in which the entire structure had a pyramid roof. Another variant common in Friesland was the head-neck-torso arrangement, in which the barn and house were connected by a narrow dairy.

Scholars once termed the Aisled-House Group the "Lower Saxon Peasant House" *(Niedersachsiches Bauernhaus)*, but today there is some doubt whether this house type correlated with the ethnic and linguistic boundaries of the Saxon people. Like the Frisian House Group, the Aisled-House was a combination dwelling and barn. But unlike the Frisian barn, the Aisled House had a wide, longitudinal aisle down the center, which was used as a threshing floor. On either side of this central aisle were cow stalls. One variant of this farmhouse type, found in Gelderland between Westerwold and Achterhoek, was the *loshoes* (literally, "open house"), in which there was no partition between the dwelling and the barn. Nor was there any chimney, and smoked meats were hung from the rafters. Thus, this structure was a combination farmhouse, barn, and smokehouse. This farmhouse type is found in the Netherlands in the provinces of Drenthe, Overijseel, Gelderland, and South Holland and outside the Netherlands in East Friesland, Oldenburg, Schleswig-Holstein, and Mecklenburg. Linguistic evidence reinforces the architectural evidence that this culture area spilled over the border with Germany. According to William Z. Shetter, since the Middle Ages the local dialects of this part of the Netherlands "were closely similar to the dialects spoken farther to the east, in what is now Northern Germany. . . . The local dialects of the eastern part of the country still merge with the local dialects of Germany."[37]

The Compartmented House was found in the Netherlands only in the province of Limburg, but its culture area included most of the eastern (Walloon) provinces of the Spanish Netherlands and the Middle Rhine region of Germany, including the Lower Palatinate. This house type was once known as the "Frankish Courtyard," but like the Lower Saxon Peasant House, there is doubt about the accuracy of this ethnic identification. In the Compartmented House Group, there was a separate farmhouse, byre (cow shed), and barn. The barn was of the "midstrey" type, which was similar to the English three-bay barn in floorplan, but not in framing. The door was on the side of the barn, and a transverse threshing floor divided the two bays, used for hay and crop storage. The farm buildings were arranged around a rectangular barnyard. Sometimes the byre and barn were connected to form a closed courtyard.

The Zeeland Barn Group and the Flemish Barn Group, while having different barn types, were similar in some ways. Not only are these two areas adjacent to each other, but they were both settled later than the abovementioned regions. As a result, the farm architecture in Zeeland and Flanders was derivative. Both regions had Compart-mented Farmhouses, built of brick, with either tile or thatched roofs. The farmhouses in both regions had one of two basic floor plans. The two-room floorplan consisted of a multipurpose room for living and cooking *(woonkeuken)* and a hall *(opkamer)*. The four-room floorplan consisted of a kitchen, hall, parlor *(zitkamer)*, and bedroom *(slaapka-mer)*. By the late seventeenth century some of these houses also had an entrance corridor *(gang)*. Both had a garret or attic and one or more cellars. However, there were major differences between the Flemish barn, which had a threshing floor along one side aisle, and the Zeeland barn, which had one or more transverse threshing floors. Both had wood frame construction and thatched roofs. Originally, the barns were connected longitudinally to the farmhouses, but in the late sev-enteenth century separate barns and farmhouses were built in both Zeeland and Flanders. Rather than maintaining the longitudinal ar-rangement, the detached house and barn were oriented around a rec-tangular barnyard.

Dutch architectural historian Piet van Wijk notes that changes in the function of the *hallehuis* in the seventeenth century resulted in differences in its form in the eastern provinces as opposed to the western provinces in which it was found. In the eastern provinces, where arable farming was the rule and manure was important to fertilize the sandy soils, the central nave was made wide to allow for a large threshing floor. The cattle faced the central nave, which was a position not suitable for dairy farming. In the dairy farming areas in the western provinces, the threshing floor was not needed. The large barn door was replaced by a narrow door through which could be brought hay from the barracks, and the anchor beam was lower to allow for more room in the loft for hay storage.[38]

These traditional farm structures continued in use through the early twentieth century. In 1892 L'Abbe J. Lemire described a typical Walloon farmstead *(cence)* and a typical Flemish farmstead *(hofstede)*. The *cence* was an example of the Compartmented House Group. Outside the courtyard were a drinking trough, wood pile, and bake house. The entrance to the courtyard led directly into the barnyard, in the center of which was the manure pile. The dwelling formed one side of the courtyard, its entrance facing the barnyard. Inside the house, there were two large rooms—the common room and the hall. Behind these two large rooms were smaller bedrooms. In the rear of the house were a kitchen, pantry, and a stairway to the cellar. The farmhouse also contained a lumber storage room, another storage room for livestock provisions, and a stable for two horses. Across the courtyard from the dwelling was a barn with a transverse threshing floor and two bays for crop storage. At either end of the barn were a cart shed and a coach house. On the front side of the courtyard was a byre with a cow shed and a calf shed. On the rear side of the courtyard were a shed and small barn with pig sties, the privy, a transverse threshing floor, a crop storage bay, a hen house, and a husking room.

The *hofstede*, located in the vicinity of Cassel and de Steenvorde in Flanders, consisted of sixteen hectares (about forty acres) of land, twelve hectares (about thirty acres) of which were cultivated and four hectares (about ten acres) in pasture. At one end of the barnyard was the farmhouse with a garden in front. The front door entered into a corridor, to the right of which were two large rooms—a common room and a hall. On the left side of the corridor was the parlor. To the rear of the house were four bedrooms, a wash room, the stairway to the cheese cellar, and the stairway to the butter cellar. Attached to the rear of the house was a kitchen and to the side were dugout bins for lumber and charcoal. Off to the side of the farmhouse were the bake house, the flax house, and silo. In the barnyard itself were two dung piles and a drinking trough. A stable and a barn formed the other two sides of the barnyard. The stable consisted of a stall for two horses, the servants' quarters, a manure pile, a cow stall, and a calf stall. The

barn had two pig sties, a privy, the chicken coop, a transverse threshing floor, and two bays for grain storage. Attached to the barn was a
husking shed, and behind the barn a cart shed.[39]
    The Aisled-House Group was still being used in the mid-twentieth-
century. In 1955, John and Dorothy Keur described a typical farmhouse in their study of Drenthe community. It measured fifty to
twenty-five feet wide by fifty to eighty feet long. The wattle and daub
walls were five to seven feet high in the barn and ten to twelve feet
high in the dwelling. The thatched roof was twenty to thirty feet high.
In the dwelling there was an open hearth in the center of a clay floor.
Pots were suspended over the hearth on adjustable hooks, and smoked
meats hung from the rafters. The living space was undifferentiated,
being used for multiple purposes as kitchen, parlor, and bedroom.
Closet beds were built into the walls. In the largest farmhouses there
were additional rooms, such as bedrooms and a parlor, and the hearth
was located against one wall with an overhanging canopy hood and
chimney. In the barn, the cows were kept on the one side of the central
aisle, and the horses, sheep, and pigs on the other.[40] This living
arrangement was basically unchanged since the Middle Ages.
    Thus, the Netherlands in the seventeenth century was divided into
several culture areas defined by landholding and settlement patterns,
type of agriculture, and farmhouse and barn types. The boundaries of
these culture areas extended beyond the political boundaries of the
Netherlands. When we correlate these culture areas with the places of
origin of the seventeenth-century settlers in New York and New
Jersey, we see that 680 and 904 settlers in our sample came from one
or another of these culture areas—210 (32%) from the Frisian culture
area, 360 (53%) from the Aisled-House culture area, 51 (7%) from the
Compartmented-House culture area, 41 (6%) from the Flemish-Barn
culture area, and 18 (3%) from the Zeeland-Barn culture area. However, some of these culture areas had a greater influence of the architecture than the number of settlers they supplied.
    The origins of the Dutch-American farm can best be explained by
the cultural process of "selective adaptation." In this process culture
traits were selected from certain of these culture areas that cut across
the Netherlands and adapted to a new environment in America. This
process was shown by historian Sumner Chilton Powell in his book

Puritan Village, a study of the founding of the seventeenth-century town of Sudbury, Massachusetts. Powell explained how the settlers in Sudbury came from three different traditions in England—the open-field system, the incorporated borough, and the enclosed farm. "As representatives of different local cultures moved from areas of England to become leaders of early town groups," Powell wrote, "they were forced to adjust to each other's different habits as they attempted modifications of basic English institutions and customs."[41] The institutions and landholding pattern in Sudbury consequently were the result of a compromise between these diverse traditions. Similarly, the settlers in New Netherland came from several different agricultural traditions on the European continent. As will be documented in the following chapters, the Dutch-American barn can be traced to the peasant houses in one culture area and the Dutch farmhouses were adapted from the farmhouses in another. Other culture traits, such as the hay barracks, the landholding patterns, tools, equipment, and even the family structure followed the same pattern of selective adaptation.

CHAPTER 2

Farmhouse

A perplexing problem in understanding what has been called the Dutch colonial farmhouse has been determining its defining characteristics. The term "Dutch colonial" itself is a problem. According to Rosalie Fellows Bailey, "the name is really a misnomer for it [the farmhouse] came into existence after the fall of the New Netherland government and reached its greatest height in the half century after the American Revolution."[1] Furthermore, as we have seen, only half the population of New Netherland actually came from the Netherlands; the rest were a heterogeneous mixture of people of German, Flemish, Walloon, French, Scandinavian, and English heritage. Nevertheless, a distinct regional culture, of which these farmhouses were the most visible manifestation, did develop during the colonial period, and the ethnic group that gave the region its identity was the Dutch.

Local historians Rosalie Bailey and Helen Wilkinson Reynolds considered a Dutch house to be one in which a Dutch family lived.[2] This genealogical, as opposed to architectural, definition sounds reasonable, but it fails to account for the possibility that a Dutch family might live in something other than a Dutch house. In fact, during the eighteenth century many wealthy Dutch families in New York and New Jersey lived in English houses. Nor did Bailey and Reynolds look for European prototypes for the "Dutch colonial" house. Bailey just asserted

33

that it is "a distinctive architecture and our only indigenous form until the coming of the modern skyscraper."[3]

Architectural historian Hugh Morrison considered the gambrel roof to be the defining characteristic of the Dutch colonial farmhouse, especially in northeastern New Jersey and southeastern New York. Morrison distinguished between the Dutch gambrel and the New England gambrel. In the Dutch gambrel the upper slope is short with a pitch of about twenty-two degrees, and the lower slope is long with a pitch of about forty-five degrees. In the New England gambrel the upper and lower slopes are about equal in length, and the lower slope has a steep pitch of about sixty degrees. Morrison acknowledged, however, that the Dutch gambrel did not appear in America until the eighteenth century, and it has no prototype in the Netherlands.[4] It did have a prototype in England. As cultural historian Thomas Jefferson Wertenbaker has noted, the gambrel roof occurred in the vicinity of Cambridge, and in America it was introduced to New England, Maryland, and Virginia.[5] Thus the gambrel roof not only was located where Dutch and English settlers lived, but also in regions where only English settlers lived. This suggests that it was an English architectural trait borrowed by the Dutch.

Furthermore, a careful look at framing shows no essential difference between Dutch and English gambrels. In both, the front and rear purlins, which extend the length of the house, rest on vertical posts set on the horizontal second-story girts. A horizontal cross tie runs between the front and rear purlin posts at either gable. On either side of the ridge two sets of rafters form the upper and lower slopes of the gambrel. The lower set rises from the plate to the purlin, and the upper set from the purlin to the peak, where it is joined by the upper set from the other side.[6]

The similarity in framing between Dutch and New England gambrels is demonstrated by comparing the Sickles House in Pearl River, New York, and the Elisha Pitkin House in East Hartford, Connecticut. On the outside the Dutch gambrel of the Sickles House looks very different from the English gambrel of the Pitkin House. However, the cross sections show a similarity in the framing. The overhanging eave of the Sickles House is not part of the basic structure of the gambrel. Although many "Dutch" gambrels were original in some houses, in others they were additions. For example, the framing of the Steuben-Zabriskie House in River Edge, New Jersey, shows a smaller, pitched roof within the gambrel roof. This means that the original garret was enlarged into a full second story by the addition of the gambrel roof. Thus, the "Dutch" gambrel roof was probably a borrowing of an English architectural feature, rather than a defining characteristic of the Dutch farmhouse.

Thomas Jefferson Wertenbaker singled out the overhanging eave as a defining characteristic. He argued that it can be traced to the "flying gutters" on Flemish cottages in Belgium, the place of origin of the early settlers in New York and New Jersey. This explains, Wertenbaker maintained, the similarity between what he called the "American Flemish cottages" in New York and New Jersey and the French colonial farmhouses in Quebec Province, Canada.[7] Architectural historian Alan Gowans disagrees, arguing that Wertenbaker's comparison is based on the assumption that there was an extensive emigration from Flanders to Quebec. Gowans doubts this assumption, because, he states, the *Quebecois* were Catholics and the Flemings were Protestants.[8] However, Gowans confuses nationality with culture areas. The culture area of the Flemish cottage, as we have seen, extended from western Protestant Belgium into northwestern Catholic France.

The real problem is not explaining the occurrence of the overhanging eave on the Quebec farmhouses; they have floorplans similar to the Dutch farmhouses.[9] The problem is explaining the occurrence of the overhanging eave on farmhouses in Connecticut. For example, the Joseph Hotchkiss House in East Haven has an overhanging eave, but its floorplan is that of the New England house type. Gowans suggests that the overhanging eave is not characteristic of any one nationality; it was, he states, a vestige of the overhang on the nearly universal thatch roof.[10]

While Gowans is probably right about the origin of the overhanging eave, he is wrong when he attempts to extend the idea into a general theory about the origin of the Dutch farmhouse in America. He maintains that the wealthy Dutch merchants introduced the urban house type into America, but that the farmhouse of the rural Dutch folk "was too primitive to require such craftsmen. It was also too primitive to survive long."[11] He argues that the Dutch farmhouse that

developed in America was not a recognizable type that can be traced
to Europe. Instead it evolved by the "primitive principle of additive
composition." [12]

So considered, the rural house type of New Netherlands *[sic]* is a distinctive
and significant cultural expression. But it was not, like the urban type, an
expression of Dutch (or Flemish, or any other) national tradition transplanted
to the New World. Materially and culturally destitute to a degree unparalleled
in New England or Virginia or even New France, the lower classes on New
Netherlands *[sic]* developed an architecture based on the universal principles
of primitive art; whatever of national tradition appeared in it was diverse,
vestigial, incidental. That is the truth behind the theory that this was an
indigenous American creation. [13]

Leaving aside the elitist assumption that the urban merchants produce beautiful and lasting architecture, but the rural folk do not, and
the invidious comparison that the Dutch folk were more primitive than
the English folk, Gowans is wrong about the difference between the
urban and rural house types. He calls the Bronck House in West
Coxsackie, New York, an urban house, even though this farmhouse
has a prototype in the rural province of Zeeland in the Netherlands. [14]
Other architectural details considered characteristic of the Dutch
farmhouse in America are the jambless fireplace, Delft tiles, the so-
called "Dutch" door, the closet stairway, the front stoop *(stoep)*, and
Dutch-bond brickwork. There are problems, however, with defining
the Dutch farmhouse as the sum total of these architectural details.
Rarely does one house possess all these features, and some of them
occur in buildings that are not Dutch. For example, Dutch tiles were
found in archeological sites in Jamestown, Virginia. [15] And Dutch and
Flemish bond brickwork were introduced into England in the late
seventeenth century and were used extensively in Maryland and Virginia in the eighteenth century. In fact, it is estimated that about 90
percent of the brick houses in Maryland had Flemish bond masonry. [16]
Also Flemish bond is found in patterned brickwork houses built by
English Quakers in southern New Jersey.
What we need is a theoretical approach to determine the essential
characteristics of house types. Folklorist Henry Glassie provides such
a theory for analyzing material folk culture, including folk architecture. He states that folk objects can be analyzed in terms of their

fundamental components: use, form, and construction. Construction varies in different environments, because of the availability of different building materials. The same house type may be constructed of stone in places where stone is abundant and wood where there is abundant timber. Use may change over time. A room built as a parlor in the nineteenth century might be used as a living room in the twentieth century. Any typology, or system of classification, should be based on form. The form of an object, according to Glassie, can be divided into primary and secondary characteristics. The primary characteristics define the type, but the secondary characteristics may be culturally significant. Glassie states that the floorplan is a primary characteristic; the roof, porches, and architectural details are secondary characteristics.[17]

This seemingly simple distinction between primary and secondary characteristics helps clarify much of the confusion in defining the Dutch-American house type. The gambrel roof and the overhanging eaves are secondary characteristics that are culturally significant. The gambrel roof shows the English influence on Dutch-American architecture; the overhanging eaves show the survival of the overhang on thatch roof houses. But these secondary characteristics do not define the house type. It is the floorplan, excluding the additions and alterations, that defines the house type.

In his later work on folk housing in middle Virginia, Glassie provides a theoretical model for explaining architectural change. He rejects the evolutionary model of architectural historians like J. Frederick Kelly, who saw architectural change in terms of a biological metaphor in which more complex forms evolved out of simpler forms.[18] In its place, Glassie suggests a linguistic metaphor in which architectural change is compared to the transformational grammar of linguist Noam Chomsky. The architectural designer draws upon a repertory of geometric forms and uses a set of rules to generate formal details, just as a native speaker of a language draws upon linguistic phonemes and uses grammar to generate words. Just as sentences are then generated from words, again using grammar, so are house types and subtypes generated from architectural forms using what Glassie terms an "artifactual grammar." In middle Virginia, Glassie found six base structures from which seven house types were generated, which account for nearly two-thirds of the houses in the region. "New structures are always transformed out of old structures, and even if its design is very complex, the new artifact is the result of melding ideas drawn from old artifacts," Glassie writes.[19]

Based on an examination of measured drawings of approximately two hundred farmhouses in New York and New Jersey in the Historic American Building Survey, I found four basic floorplans that can be traced to the Netherlands, thus forming the repertory for what I call the Dutch farmhouse. These Dutch floorplans are the following: (1) two rooms with chimneys on one or more gable ends (e.g., the Samuel DesMarest House in River Edge, New Jersey); (2) two rooms divided by a central hall with one or two chimneys on the gable ends (e.g., the Jan Breese House formerly in Rensselaer, New York); (3) three rooms in a row with one or more chimneys on the gable ends and/or an interior chimney (e.g., the Johannes Hardenberg House formerly in Kerhonkson, New York); and (4) two large rooms in the front with two or more smaller rooms in the rear (e.g., the Peter A. Hopper House in Fair Lawn, New Jersey).

By the middle of the eighteenth century, there developed two new floorplans that were structurally different from these Dutch farmhouses, in the sense that they had no prototypes in the Netherlands. These are what I term the Dutch-American farmhouse, although they have been termed Georgian by architectural historians. These floorplans are: (1) the so-called full-Georgian, consisting of a central hall with two rooms on either side (e.g. the John Hopper House formerly in Hackensack, New Jersey) and (2) the two-thirds Georgian, consisting of a side hall with two rooms along one side of the hall (e.g., the David Baldwin House in Midland Park, New Jersey).

In addition, there is a basic difference between English and continental framing traditions. For example, the Wick House in Morristown, New Jersey, while it might not be a typical English farmhouse, does demonstrate the basic differences. It has a frame like a solid box built around a central chimney. Four horizontal sills rest on the rectangular foundation of stone or brick. Cellar girts extend between the front and rear sills on either side of the central chimney. The first-floor joists are built across the width of each room between the cellar girts and the end sills. Four corner posts are located at the corners formed by the sills, and four chimney posts are located where the cellar girts meet the front and rear sills. Smaller studs frame the exterior wall between the posts. On the second floor the front and rear plates run parallel to the front and rear sills on the first floor, and the second-floor end girts run parallel to the first-floor end sills. The front and rear plates and the end girts rest on top of the corner and chimney posts. Unlike houses in New England, the Wick House has no summer beam —a large beam that extends from the midpoint of the end girts to the midpoint of the chimney girts on the second floor.[20] The second-floor joists run between the front and rear plates. The plates support the rafters, which in the Wick House are "common" rafters—that is, they are all the same size and are evenly spaced. There is no ridgepole; the paired rafters are joined at the peak with mortise and tenon joints. Eight purlin posts, resting on the chimney girts and end girts, support two purlins, which extend across the rafters, the length of the building. Four collar beams increase the support between the paired rafters. The Wick House also has vertical gable supports resting on the end girts and on the gable collar beams. This type of framing can be traced as far back as the Middle Ages in England.[21]

The framing of the Dutch farmhouse is quite different. It is essentially the same as the framing of the Dutch barn.[22] The Jan Martense Schenck House, originally at Flatlands (New Amersfoort), Brooklyn, is a good example.[23] Unlike the boxlike English frame, the continental frame resembles a series of goal posts, known as H-bents, each consisting of two vertical posts connected by a large anchor beam and reinforced by diagonal corner braces. Atop the posts on either side of the H-bents run horizontal plates, which support the widely spaced rafters of the pitched roof.[24] The paired rafters are reinforced by collar beams and joined at the peak by mortise and tenon joints; here too there is no ridgepole. This frame is a survival of a medieval tradition widespread throughout northern Europe.[25]

One needs only to compare the cross section of a Dutch farmhouse, such as the De Wint House in Tappan, New York, to that of a typical farmhouse in Flanders to see the similarity in framing. Some confusion, however, might be caused by New England houses like the Old Trup House in Easton, Connecticut. Its plates are raised several feet above the second-story floor, thereby giving a superficial impression from the cross section of being the H-bent frame. However, when one looks at the entire frame of the house and its floorplan, it is evident that it is English, not Dutch. Glassie showed a similar phenomenon in English barns in Otsego, New York.[26]

The archeologist James Deetz states that there are three types of evidence for documenting domestic architecture in America: (1) surviving buildings, (2) archeological remains, and (3) written descriptions. He cautions against generalizations based soley on surviving buildings, because they may not be typical. In fact, they often are atypical, because the dwellings of common people are more likely to be destroyed than those of the wealthy.[27] Even when we look at present-day buildings, we must disentangle the history of the house. Architecture is not static. Additions are built; rooms are modified. We must not make the mistake of assuming that because a house has a certain floorplan today, that it always had that floorplan.

Using a combination of sources, including written documents, archeological evidence, and existing buildings, it is possible to reconstruct the change from the Dutch farmhouse to the Dutch-American farmhouse. There were three stages to this development. The first stage occurred during the Dutch period from 1624 to 1664, when New Netherland existed as a colony of the Dutch West India Company. During this stage there was a selection of certain architectural traditions from the various culture areas that crosscut the Netherlands and an adaptation of these traditions to a new environment in America. In the second stage, which began after the English conquest of New Netherland in 1664, there was the development of four regional subtypes (the upper Hudson River Valley; the middle Hudson River Valley; northern New Jersey and Rockland County, New York; and western Long Island and Monmouth County, New Jersey) based primarily on the availability of different construction materials. The third stage began about 1750 and continued well into the nineteenth century. During this stage there developed what I term the Dutch-American farmhouse as distinct from the Dutch farmhouse. The following is a documentation of these three stages, citing specific farmhouse as examples. In some cases the change from Dutch to Dutch-American can be seen in modifications to the same house.

The first European dwellings in New Netherland were crude, temporary buildings. In a deposition dated 1688, Catherine Trico, one of the first settlers in the Wallabout section of Brooklyn, described the earliest houses as "hutts of Bark."[28] Her description was confirmed in Nicolaes van Wassenaer's comment that some of the houses in New Amsterdam in 1626 were built "of the bark of trees."[29] In 1650, Cornelius van Tienhoven, the secretary of New Netherland, provided a more detailed description of these buildings.

Those in New Netherland and especially in New England, who have no means to build farm houses at first according to their wishes, dig a square pit in the ground, cellar fashion, six or seven feet deep, as long and as broad as they think proper, case the earth inside with wood all round the wall, and line the wood with the bark of trees or something else to prevent the caving in of the earth; floor this cellar with plank and wainscot it overhead for a ceiling, raise a roof of spars, clear up and cover the spars with bark or green sods, so that they can live dry and warm in these houses with their entire families for two, three, or four years, it being understood that partitions are run through those cellars which are adapted to the size of the family.[30]

Domine Jonas Michaelius, the Dutch Reformed minister, described these dwellings as "hovels and holes in which they [the Dutch] huddled rather than dwelt."[31]

Within a few years, more substantial structures were built in the European architectural tradition. Architectural historian John Fitchen asserts that separate farmhouses and barns were "the established pattern on this side of the Atlantic in the Dutch-inhabited areas from the time of the very first colonial settlers."[32] There is documentary evidence that combined barns and dwellings were built in New Netherland in the early seventeenth century. It wasn't until the second half of that century that the separate barn and dwelling became dominant in New York and New Jersey. This was about the same time this arrangement emerged in Zeeland and Flanders.

Kiliaen van Rensselaer reported that in 1631 the settlers in his patroonship of Rensselaerswyck had established two farms on one of which they built a "brick house, eighty feet long, the threshing floor twenty-five feet wide and the beams twelve feet high, up to the ceiling."[33] The reference to a threshing floor within a farmhouse suggests that it was a combined barn and dwelling.

In 1642 Johannes Winckelman contracted with two carpenters to build a farmhouse at Achter Col (where the Hackensack River empties into the New Jersey Meadows).[34] According to the contract, the carpenters, Pieter Cornelissen and Abraham Clock, were to build a farmhouse ninety feet long and twenty-four feet wide inside the posts. It was to consist of ten bents, set nine feet apart. It was to have "two side aisles *(uytlaten)* as long as the house, one being nine feet wide and the other twenty feet wide" and "at the end of the building a large, wide door, consisting of two upper and two lower doors, and over the door an opening to pitch hay and straw in."[35] A. J. F. Van Laer translated *uytlaten* to mean "doors," but Kenneth Scott and Kenn Stryker-Rhodda maintain that the word, which literally means "outlets," refers to aisles running the full length of the house.[36] The reference to the bents indicate the Continental framing tradition, and the reference to the side aisles suggests that this was probably a combined barn and dwelling similar to those in the Aisled House culture area.

There is also archeological evidence of the existence of the combined barn and dwelling arrangement in New Netherland in the early seventeenth century. From 1971 through 1974 the New York State Office of Parks and Recreation excavated the remains of two farmhouses at Schuyler Flats (present-day Colonie, New York). One was a red brick dwelling built in the late seventeenth or early eighteenth century by the Schuyler family. The other, located just south of the brick farmhouse, was an early seventeenth century structure. It was probably the farmhouse mentioned in a letter dated 1643 from Jacob van Curler, commis of Rensselaerswyck, to Kilaien van Rensselaer. The letter cites a contract with Jan Cornelissen, a carpenter, to build a farmhouse 120 feet long and twenty feet wide. Forty feet of the length were to be the dwelling and the rest would house the farm laborers, the cattle, and the horses.[37]

The archeological excavation uncovered an L-shaped cellar, twenty-six feet long and twelve feet wide, with the ell adding another five feet to the width. The walls of the cellar were constructed of wooden boards nailed horizontally to upright posts. Short sections of the wall were built of soft, red brick, which were evidently the footings for the walls of the house. It is thought that the house was constructed of red brick and red tile. The building apparently collapsed into the cellar in the late seventeenth or early eighteenth century.[38] The similarity of construction of this cellar to van Tienhoven's description above is notable. Paul Huey, the archeologist who supervised this excavation, believes that this site indicates the existence of an Aisled House in seventeenth-century Rensselaerswyck.[39] However, the Aisled Houses in northern Europe did not have excavated cellars. More likely this structure was an example of the Zeeland Barn Group, in which the dwelling part of the combined barn and dwelling was constructed of brick and had an excavated cellar.

Not all the farmhouses in New Netherland in the early seventeenth century were combined barns and dwellings; historical documents also indicate separate barns and farmhouses. A 1638 inventory for the farm named Achtervelt, owned by Adries Hudde and Wolphert Gerritsen, in Flatlands (present-day Brooklyn) mentions "one house surrounded by long, round palisades; the house is 26 feet long, 22 feet wide, 40 feet high with the roof, covered above and all around with boards" consisting of "two garrets, one above the other, and a small chamber on the side with an outlet (*uytlaet*, meaning an aisle running the full length of the house on the side)." Listed separately was "one barn, 40 feet long, 18 feet wide and 24 feet high with the roof."[40] The framing of the farmhouses and barns were similar; both used the H-bents of the Continental framing tradition. In 1646 Thomas Chamber was contracted to build a farmhouse in Rensselaerswyck to be sixty feet long and twenty feet wide "in all its parts and members similar to the barn at Poentje," except that the dwelling was to be "apart and separate."[41]

The Dutch architectural historian Henk Zantkuyl has shown that these seventeenth-century wooden houses with a single side aisle were similar to houses that can be found today in the village of Holysloot in the Waterland region of North Holland.[42] On the basis of building contracts Zantkuyl has reconstructed the plans of several of these single side aisle houses in New Netherland.[43]

The main factor was evidently not the place of origin of the craftsman. They came from several different provinces, and there doesn't seem to be any correlation with the type of farmhouses they built. Of the carpenters in New Amsterdam and Rensselaerswyck in the seventeenth century whose place of origin is known, there were four from Amsterdam in North Holland, two from Leiden in South Holland,

and one each from Gouda in South Holland, Naerden and Hoorn in
North Holland, Houten and Breukelen in Utrecht, Kampen in Overijssel, and Nykerck in Gelderland. Two came from Osnaburgh and
Hamburg in Germany. In Rensselaerswyck there was an English carpenter named Thomas Chambers, who was nicknamed "Clabbordt"
(or clapboard), and in Gravesend there was a black carpenter named
Jacob Hellekers or Jacob Swart, who was known as the "Black Carpenter of Gravesend."[44]

Thus, at least three different farmhouse arrangements were brought
from northern Europe to New Netherland: (1) the Aisled House with
its combination barn and dwelling, (2) the Zeeland Barn Group arrangement with its combination barn and dwelling with an excavated
cellar, and (3) the separate barn and farmhouse, including the single
side aisle house reconstructed by Zantkuyl. While the floorplan of the
Zeeland Farmhouse and the linear arrangement of the barn and farmhouse were brought to America, there is no evidence that the Zeeland
barn itself was ever built here. The only barn type constructed here
seems to have been the aisled type.

There is documentary evidence that some of the dwellings in New
Netherland had no chimneys, like the peasant houses in the eastern
provinces of the Netherlands. Augustus Van Buren, a local historian,
noted that one of the ordinances Stuyvesant promulgated in Wiltwyck
(Kingston) in 1661 banned the construction of any plaster or wooden
chimneys or the kindling of any fire in houses with walls or gables
made of straw or in the center of floors of other houses covered with
thatch unless there was a solid plank ceiling in the house.[45] In 1669
Willem Teller complained to the Court of Albany, Rensselaerswyck,
and Schenectady that several people at Schenectady residing near his
farm "have no chimneys in their houses, from which great accidents
may result."[46] And an archeological excavation at the original site of
the Demarest House, though to have been built circa 1679 in New
Milford, New Jersey, uncovered the remains of a structure attached to
the rear of the farmhouse. These consisted of post holes forming a
rectangle with an area of stone and carbon remains in the center.[47] In
1749 Peter Kalm commented upon the jambless fireplaces common in
Dutch farmhouses in America. "The fireplaces among the Dutch were

always built in, so that nothing projected out, and it looked as though they made a fire against the wall itself."[48]

Building materials varied from place to place, depending on availability. Walls were constructed of either wood, stone, or brick. In 1646 Father Isaac Joques wrote that "there are some houses built of stone; lime they make of oyster shells, great heaps of which are found here."[49] The lime was used to make mortar and plaster.[50] However, Father Joques noted, the early houses in Rensselaerswyck had no masonry, except for their chimneys. "All their houses are merely of boards and thatched, with no masonry except the chimneys. The forest furnishing many large pines, they make boards by means of their mills, which they have here for the purpose."[51]

There has been much debate about whether brick was brought from the Netherlands as ballast. In some places this was the case. For example, in 1642 Govert Loockmans and Cornelis Leendersen of New Amsterdam issued a bond to the master of the ship Coninck David for, among other things, "seventy-five guilder for freight of brick and tiles."[52] In March 1644, the ship *Fama* arrived at the Dutch settlement in the Lower Delaware Valley bringing saws, grindstones, millstones, flour, tools, salt, clothing, food, shoes, wine, kettles, and 6,000 bricks.[53] In 1749 Peter Kalm noted about the houses in Albany that "some are slated with tiles from Holland, because the clay of this neighborhood is not reckoned fit for tiles."[54] But brick and tile were made in certain places in New Netherland from an early date. In 1628 Reverend Jonas Michaelius noted that "they bake brick here [in New Netherland], but it is very poor."[55] During 1641 and 1642 Kiliaen van Rensselaer searched for a brick and tile maker to send to his patroonship.[56] By the end of the seventeenth century, brickmaking was a thriving industry both in New York and New Jersey. In 1683 the General Assembly of New Jersey regulated the size of brick at 9½ inches × 4½ inches × 2¾ inches. This English common brick contrasted to the Dutch brick which was 1½ inches × 3 inches × 7 inches and light yellow in color.[57]

Tile was used for the roofs of houses. A 1639 deposition concerning the buildings erected on Manhattan Island during the administration of Director Wouter van Twiller mentions "an excellant barn, dwelling house, boat house and a brewery covered with tiles, on farm No. 1."[58] Thatch was also used for roofs, but it was a fire hazard. In 1636 Cornelis van Voorst, agent for Michael Pauw at the patroonship of Pavonia (present-day Jersey City, New Jersey), fired a cannonade salute to some departing visitors and accidentally set fire to his house, "which was thatched with rushes, and in half an hour it was entirely consumed."[59] In a deposition dated 1644, concerning the destruction by Indians of a farm owned by Jochem Pietersen Kuyter along the Harlem River, a soldier testified that he saw a burning arrow land "on the thatched roof of the house, and owing to the strong wind the house soon got on fire and burned to the ground."[60] And, according to a 1650 lease, in which Jan Dircksen rented farmland at Katskill from Brant van Slichtenhorst, Dircksen agreed to build a dwelling, hay-barrack, and barn, and "to cut and draw all timber, cut the reed and bring it to the spot, dig out and haul the stone, excavate the cellar, and furthermore bear the cost of board of all the workmen, such as carpenters, mason, thatcher, and others."[61] In fact, thatch was used for roofing well into the eighteenth century. In 1744 Dr. Alexander Hamilton, a Scotsman traveling on Staten Island, noted that "in this island are a great many poor, thatched cottages."[62]

By the eighteenth century, distinct regional differences in Dutch farmhouses in New York and New Jersey developed. These regional differences were the result of a different building materials, different degrees of isolation, and different exposures to English influences. There were four regional subtypes within the Dutch culture area: (1) the red sandstone houses in Bergen, Morris, and Passaic counties, New Jersey, and Rockland County, New York; (2) the wood frame houses in Brooklyn, New York, and Monmouth County, New Jersey; (3) the gray fieldstone houses in the middle Hudson and upper Delaware valleys; and (4) the brick houses in the upper Hudson Valley. Staten Island and the Raritan Valley are border areas, in which both stone and frame houses are found. These regional subtypes roughly correspond to geographic regions that cut across political boundaries. Both Brooklyn, New York, and Monmouth County, New Jersey, lie within the coastal plain, where the soil is sandy and there is little available stone. Thus frame houses were built there. Northeastern New Jersey and Rockland County, New York, lie within the piedmont, where sandstone is readily available. The middle Hudson Valley and the upper Delaware Valley are in the mountain and valley region, which provides gray fieldstone. Thus, the materials of construction in these cases are adaptations to the environment.

The brick houses of the Upper Hudson Valley, however, are not such adaptations. At one time brick houses were common throughout the Dutch culture area in America. The De Wint House in Tappan, New York, is an example of a brick house in what is predominantly the red sandstone region. Old prints provide visual evidence of the existence of brick houses in Brooklyn. That brick houses are found today primarily in the upper Hudson Valley can be explained by the fact that this region was an isolated backwater until the construction of the Erie Canal in the early nineteenth century. As a result, older culture traits survived there. These brick houses are a reminder that materials of construction are not necessarily determined by geography.

To complicate the matter further, some of the houses in the middle Hudson Valley and the upper Delaware Valley are bank houses. That is, they are built into an embankment so that the cellar, which contains the kitchen, is an exposed, lower story on one side of the house (e.g., Van Cortlandt Manor in Westchester County, New York). Some architectural historians think that such houses, which had cellar kitchens on the lower level, were introduced into the Hudson Valley by the Palatinate Germans.[63] However, bank houses are not associated with the Palatinate section of Germany. Another theory is that these houses are transformations of the basic Dutch house type to fit a new environment. Glassie has shown how in Otsego County, New York, a one-level English barn was transformed into a bank barn by the addition of a lower level.[64] There is at least one Dutch barn in upstate New York that has also been transformed into a bank barn (see Chapter 3). It is possible that a similar process was at work in such bank houses.

In 1744 Peter Kalm described the farmhouses north of Albany as follows:

The houses hereabouts are generally built of beams of unburnt bricks dried by the sun and the air. The beams are first erected, and upon them a gable with two walls, and the spars. The wall on the gable is made of nothing but boards. The roof is covered with shingles or fir. They make the walls of unburnt bricks, between the beams, to keep the rooms warmer; and that they might not easily be destroyed by rain and air they are covered with boards on the outside. There is generally a cellar beneath the houses.[65]

The house of Pieter Bronck west of Coxsackie, New York, is an example of the Upper Hudson Valley type. Bronck is thought to be the son of Jonas Bronck, the Dane after whom the Bronx is named. The house consists of two sections. The stone section is thought to have been built by Pieter Bronck in 1663. The brick section, similar to the houses described by Kalm, was built in 1738 by Leendert Bronck. The stone section of the house consisted of one room with a garret above and a steep pitched roof. Similar houses can be found in North Holland, Zeeland, and Flanders, but the prototypes in the Netherlands were normally constructed of brick. While it is not a frame house, the garret floor joists are located several feet below the plate creating the effect of a H-bent. There is evidence in the framing along the west wall and in the attic that the house originally had a jambless fireplace. There are two oval holes in the gable, probably to ventilate grain stored in the garret.

The brick section built by Leendert Bronck is at right angles to the stone house and connected by a covered passageway now known as "the hyphen." It is reminiscent of the head-neck-torso arrangement in Friesland, except the torso is not a barn. Beneath the brick exterior walls was a wooden frame consisting of H-bents. The brick facade is attached to the wooden frame by means of iron anchors. The gable parapets have a decorative mouthtoothing, which is also an architectural detail that can be traced to the Netherlands. The house has two rooms on the ground floor and a central chimney. Contrary to what some researchers have asserted, this type is not an urban house type nor a mixture of urban and rural architectural features; it can be traced directly to farmhouses in the Netherlands.[66]

The Schuyler family house at the Flatts was built by Philip Pieterse Schuyler, who purchased the property in 1672. The roof and interior of the house were burned shortly after his death in 1758, but it was rebuilt by his widow, Margareta. The house was rebuilt in the Georgian style with a gambrel roof. The house was described in 1808 by Mrs. Anne Grant, a Scottish visitor. The house faced the Hudson River along the road to Saratoga. It was a two-story brick house with an attic and cellar. The cellar floor had two spacious rooms. The first

floor had three rooms and a large central hallway. One room was for
the reception of company, and the other two were bedrooms. The
hallway as furnished with chairs and pictures. The family would use
the hallway as a sitting room for informal visits in the summer. The
front of the house had a large portico. In the rear there was an addition
similar to the front portico. The kitchen was on the cellar level, and
the eating parlor was on the main floor. The second-floor rooms were
used by the family during the winter, when the "summer room" on
the first floor was too cold. The floorplan and gambrel roof indicate
that this house was essentially the Georgian style superimposed on a
Dutch house.[67]

Roger G. Kennedy of the Smithsonian Institution has suggested
that these verandas on Dutch-American farmhouses were examples of
Caribbean influences resulting from trade between New Netherlands
and the islands.[68] Zantkuyl, on the other hand, argues that the veranda
was a survival of the side aisle in the seventeenth-century houses from
North Holland.[69] The fact that they don't show up on Dutch-American houses until the late eighteenth and early nineteenth centuries
suggests that they are neither seventeenth-century survivals from the
Caribbean nor from North Holland, but simply the extension of the
overhanging eaves to form the precursor of the nineteenth-century
porch.

The houses in the Middle Hudson Valley generally were built of
gray fieldstone. The Jonathan Hasbrouck House in Newburgh, New
York, was named after its owner at the time of the Revolutionary War,
because it served as George Washington's headquarters from 1782–
1783. Jonathan Hasbrouck was the grandson of Abraham Hasbrouck,
a native of Calais who came to America in 1675 by way of the Palatinate and settled in Esopus (Kingston) and then New Paltz. The oldest
section of the house was the northeast corner, consisting of three
rooms. The architect who studied the house for the historic structure
report to the New York State Historic Trust felt that this section of
the house was built in 1750, as indicated by a stone marked "HB AD
1750," but it is possible that portions of the house were built by the
prior owner of the land, Burger Mynderse. Some time between 1750
and 1770 a room was added to the south, and a second addition of four
rooms was evidently constructed by Jonathan Hasbrouk in 1770. There

is a datestone near the doorway with the inscription "HB AD 1770." This second addition reoriented the house. Previously it faced east toward the Hudson River; now it faced west toward the King's Highway.[70] In 1782 the Marquis de Chastellux described the house as follows:

> The headquarters at Newburgh consists of a single house, neither spacious nor convenient, which is built in the Dutch fashion. The largest room in it, which had served as the owner's family parlor . . . is in truth fairly spacious, but it has seven doors and only one window. The fireplace, or rather the fireback, is against the walls, so that there is in fact but one vent for the smoke, and the fire is in the room itself.[71]

The last comment is evidently a reference to a jambless fireplace.

The Jean Hasbrouck House in New Paltz is said to have been erected in 1692. Jean was the brother of Abraham Hasbrouck, the grandfather of Jonathan Hasbrouck mentioned above. It is thought that the house originally consisted of one room, a cellar kitchen, and a garret. A stone in the east wall contains the date 1712, at which time Jean's son Jacob Hasbrouck was living in the house. This was possibly the date of an expansion of the house. Possibly at this time or more probably toward the middle of the eighteenth century the present floorplan of the house was designed. This consists of a central hallway with two rooms on either side. The right front room as you enter the house probably was the store of Jacob Hasbrouck. Across the hall from the store was the parlor. The two rear rooms, one of which was the kitchen, contained jambless fireplaces. Upstairs was a large garret covered by a very steeply pitched roof. Again, we see here an English Georgian floorplan in a house that was originally Dutch.[72] The only feature that differs from the classical English Georgian floorplan is the location of two interior chimneys between the two rooms on either side of the central hallway, whereas the typical Georgian floorplan had end chimneys. Folklorist Robert St. George has shown that this floorplan was the result of the transformation of a lowland English house form in New England. He cites as an example the Clapp House in Scituate, built in the mid-1720s.[73]

Some of the houses built on western Long Island (present-day Brooklyn) in the seventeenth century were similar to those that became characteristic of the Upper Hudson River Valley. In 1679 Jasper

Danckaerts noted that the village of New Utrecht had "many good stone houses."[74] He specifically mentioned the house of Jacques Cortelyou. Another stone house Danckaerts described was the De Hart Bergen House in Gowanus. None of these houses are still standing. The Nicasius de Sille House in New Utrecht was one and a half stories with stone walls and a terra cotta tile roof. We know about it from a nineteenth-century lithograph. The Vechte-Cortelyou House in Gowanus was especially interesting, because the gable ends were brick but the walls were stone.

Notwithstanding these stone houses, the houses that became characteristic of the Dutch houses in Brooklyn were of wooden frame construction. The Pieter Claesen Wyckoff House is an example. Pieter Claesen was born in Norden in East Friesland, and came to New Netherland in 1657. He lived at Rensselaerswyck, where he married the daughter of Hendrick Van Ness, a wealthy brewer at Fort Orange in 1645. Some time prior to 1652 he moved to New Amersfoort, where he bought land. In 1655 he became the superintendent of Pieter Stuyvesant's tobacco plantation there, and served in the office of *schepen* (magistrate) three times between 1653 and 1663. In 1667 he became a patentee of Flatlands. Tradition has it that Pieter Claesen Wyckoff built the house on order of Wouter Van Twiller, but this cannot be proven. The chain of title to the property can only be traced back to 1737, when it was owned by his grandson Pieter Wyckoff Jr.[75]

The house was known to have existed as early as 1718. At that time it consisted of two main rooms with smaller backrooms. The house was constructed with heavy timber framing consisting of H-bents. Major alterations were made in the house about 1750 and again about 1820. The 1750 alterations consisted of a major addition to the east. In 1820 a center hallway was installed and the ceilings of the small rear rooms were raised. These changes were dated by a study of the framing and from nail samples from the floors. The house still stands today. In its present form it has one and a half stories and a kitchen wing with a lean-to shed. The main house has six rooms on the first floor, five rooms on the garret floor. There is a full cellar under the front rooms and a crawl space under the rear rooms. The kitchen wing has 2 rooms on the first floor and 2 rooms in the garret. There is a crawl space below the kitchen wing.[76]

The Jan Martense Schenck House built circa 1675 on an island in
Jamaica Bay in what was called New Amersfoort, later known as
Flatlands, represents an interesting problem of restoration. In 1952 the
house was dismantled and donated to the Brooklyn Museum by the
Atlantic, Gulf and Pacific Company, the owners. The house was
stored for twelve years and then reconstructed inside the Brooklyn
Museum in 1964. The original floorplan of the house was a central hall
with one room on either side. An L-shaped kitchen wing was added
on the rear at a later date. However, when the house was reconstructed
in the Brooklyn Museum, they changed the floorplan adding a central
chimney and eliminating the central hallway.[77] Correspondence between Marvin D. Schwartz, the curator of decorative arts at the Brooklyn Museum, and the Dutch architectural historian H. J. Zantkuyl
indicates that the reason for the alteration was the existence of mortise
holes in the beams of the central hall. Zantkuyl hypothesized that they
must have held trimmer beams that framed a chimney. The fact that
the rafters did not join in the central part of the roof suggested to him
that they possibly rested on a chimney.[78] But it seems highly unlikely
that a busy Dutch-American farmer and miller would dismantle a
central chimney simply to keep up with the latest style. Furthermore,
there did exist in the Netherlands houses with one room on either side
of a central hallway. Zantkuyl used the restored Schenck House as
evidence to argue that Dutch farmhouses in America were based on
prototypes in the town of Holysloot in the Waterland region north of
Amsterdam.[79] Evidence for the existence of these single-aisled, frame
houses in New Netherland can be found in seventeenth-century building contracts. But this is not sufficient reason to radically alter the
floorplan of a house that already conforms to a traditional Dutch house
type.

Monmouth County, New Jersey, was settled in part by Dutchmen
from Brooklyn, and there is a definite similarity in the architecture.
Both areas were characterized by wood frame construction. The Holmes-
Hendrickson House in Holmdel, New Jersey, is thought to have been
built by William Holmes between 1752 and 1756. In 1756 Holmes
sold the house to his first cousin, Garret Hendrickson, who was the
grandson of Daniel Hendrickson, who migrated to Monmouth County
from Flatbush circa 1693. The house consists of two large rooms in the

front with two smaller rooms in the rear. There is a kitchen wing.[80] While the facade appears similar to the wooden Dutch houses in Brooklyn, the measured drawings of the Holmes-Hendrickson House in the Historic American Buildings Survey reveal both the continental H-bent framing and English framing. The fact that the plate is raised several feet above the garret floor makes the Holmes-Hendrickson House appear similar to certain houses in Connecticut that also have overhanging eaves. Yet unlike the houses in New England that have a New England floorplan around a central chimney, the Holmes-Hendrickson House has one of the floorplans of the Dutch farmhouse type. Thus, the house represents a mixture of English and Dutch framing with a Dutch floorplan.

The Holmes-Hendrickson House might be compared to the Minnie Schenck House, originally located at Manhasset on Long Island, but moved in 1967 to the museum village at Old Bethpage. Both Monmouth County, New Jersey, and Nassau County, New York, were areas of secondary settlement for the Dutch; both were settled by branches of families that first settled in Brooklyn. Minnie Schenck (1700–1767) was the grandson of Roelof Martense Schenck, who emigrated from the Netherlands in 1660 and settled in Flatlands. When the Minnie Schenck House was constructed circa 1730, it consisted of two large front rooms and three smaller rear rooms. The house was modified circa 1765 giving it an English Georgian floorplan with two rooms on either side of a central hallway.[81] Like the Holmes-Hendrickson House, the Minnie Schenck House represents the emergence of the Dutch-American house type.

The farmhouse in Bergen, Passaic, and Morris counties, New Jersey, and Rockland County, New York, were built of red sandstone. In 1778 James Thacher described the Dutch towns, churches, and farmhouses in the vicinity of Paramus and Aquackanonk (present-day Passaic, New Jersey). "These towns," he wrote, "are inhabited chiefly by Dutch people; their churches and dwelling houses are built of rough stone, one story high. There is a peculiar neatness in the appearance of their dwellings, having an airy piazza, supported by pillars in front, and their kitchens connected at the ends in the form of wings."[82] The John Hopper House that once stood in Hackensack was a good example. It had an English Georgian floorplan consisting of a central hallway with two rooms on either side. One wing was the kitchen, and the other wing was the slave quarters.

The Ackerman-Zabriskie-Steuben House in River Edge, New Jersey, shows the transition from a Dutch farmhouse to a Dutch-American farmhouse. It is believed that the house was built by David Ackerman who came to New Amsterdam from Blaricum as a boy in 1664. In 1686 he moved with his own family and settled on the west bank of the Hackensack River. His will, dated 1710, mentions a house as well as mills. It is thought that the house originally consisted of a central hall with one room on either side, which is in the Flemish tradition. Evidence in rafters of the garret suggest that the house may have originally had a hipped roof. Upon the death of David Ackerman, the house was inherited by his son Johannis, who circa 1720 expanded it by building an extension to the north. One architect believes that Johannis removed a fireplace that once existed along the north wall. A second addition was made about 1740 with the construction of small rooms to the rear of the original building and a root cellar. When Johannis Ackerman died in 1744, the house was inherited by his son, Nicholas, who sold it in 1745 to Jan Zabriskie, who was the grandson of Albrecht Zaborowski, who imigrated in 1662 from Poland to New Amsterdam and became culturally Dutch. John Zabriskie made the final addition to the rear of the first addition circa 1755, which must have included the expansion of the second story under a gambrel roof in the Dutch-American style. John sided with the British during the Revolutionary War, and his property was confiscated by the State of New Jersey and awarded to Baron Friedrich von Steuben, who never lived in the house.[83]

An interesting phenomenon that occurred in the Hackensack Valley, including both Bergen County, New Jersey, and Rockland County, New York, was the twin-door house. These houses had either a two-room or a four-room floorplan. They are not found in the Netherlands and do not appear in America until the eighteenth century. Historian Firth Haring Fabend suggests that they may have been designed to accommodate two generations of the same family. However, as we shall see, the Dutch-American family tended to be nuclear, rather than extended. Fabend notes that several such twin-door houses were built in the Upper Pascack Valley from 1783 to 1810. She attributes this resurgence of the twin-door house to a nostalgia on the part of the Dutch for the traditions of their forefathers in the face of the eighteenth-century upheavals involved in the coetus-conferentie schism in the Dutch Reformed Church and the American Revolution, which also split the Dutch into two factions.[84] However, there is some doubt whether the twin-door house can be considered traditionally Dutch. It cannot be traced to the Netherlands; on the other hand, there are twin-door houses in the German sections of Pennsylvania.

Henry Glassie explains these twin-door houses in Pennsylvania as an alteration of the continental central chimney house to fit the Georgian esthetic. That is, the facade gives the impression of symmetry associated with Georgian architecture, but the floorplan behind the facade is not symmetrical. "This synthetic type," writes Glassie,

is the result of the same kind of mental activity that generated the common New England house type, which packaged the old English saltbox house in a symmetrical container. In both houses, the Old World interiors were externally disguised to be acceptable. Both house forms teach us that the skins of houses are shallow things that people are willing to change, but people are most conservative about the spaces they must utilize and in which they must exist.[85]

Thus, while Fabend may be right about these houses being an expression of a traditional mentality, it is because of the floorplan, not necessarily the twin door.

Although regional differences were evident in the architecture, each region underwent a similar transition from Dutch to Dutch-American house types. The Dutch-American house type was Dutch and English in framing with a Georgian floorplan. One distinctive feature in northern New Jersey and on western Long Island was the gambrel roof, which was itself English in origin. But Dutch-American architecture was distinctly different from English architecture in either New England or the South. In some houses the transition can be seen in the modifications and additions made by subsequent owners; other houses were built originally in the Dutch-American style.

A rare, detailed description of the construction of a late eighteenth-century farmhouse in the Upper Hudson Valley is contained in the unpublished diary of Dr. Alexander Coventry, a Scottish physician who settled among the Dutch farmers in the town of Hudson, New

York. "[I] intend to build a house one story and a half high, forty feet by twenty, with a lintel—a hall through the center twelve feet wide. [I] do not expect to build anything remarkable," he wrote.[86] The house was probably typical of many of the Dutch-American farmhouses constructed in that region.

Coventry hired craftsmen to work on the house, and he had as many as twenty neighbors at the house raising. Several craftsmen were Dutch, but their ethnicity was probably not as important as the regional tradition that was fully developed by then. Despite the communal effort at the house raising, most of the work on a day-by-day basis was done by hired carpenters and masons. Coventry paid them mostly in barter. He needed to borrow equipment and draft animals from his neighbors.

The house took nine months to complete. He began work in late August 1786, and it was completed in early June 1787. He began with cutting timber for the house. He noted that he needed sills 40 feet long and how difficult it was to find perfect ones that long. Half the length of the sills they cut turned out to be rotten. By the end of August, with the help of four men, he was able to cut "2 sills 56 by seven, 22 plates 5 by 6, 40 ft. long; the beams 2 and 14 in number."[87] As many as twelve men helped with the cutting and hewing at various times. He even bought some of the timber from neighbors. He purchased some beams for $2.00 from one neighbor; he bought 2,000 feet of boards from Mrs. McMakin of Kinderhook for $5.00 per thousand. He described the communal effort of cutting timber as follows:

18 Sept. Went this morning to get timber with the following people. Caleb and John Lobdell, Titus Finch, Thos. Whitlock, Thomas Crossman, Matthew Ghoes, Andrew Martin, William Wallace, and Mr. Howard. We wrought about two hours when the rain stopt us. Went out again in the P.M. and with the aforesaid men, except the two Lobdells and Mr. Finch. It rained some, however, we have got all the beams cut, eight of which are hewn, and sixteen of the rafters cut down.[88]

On September 19 Coventry went with Titus Finch and John and Caleb Lobdell to the proposed site of the house. They tested the ground to find a suitable location for the cellar foundation, but discovered slate rock all over no deeper than nine inches below the ground. Finally, they located a suitable site, staked it out on the ground, and cleared the brush and trees. The next day Finch and one of the Lobdells began to frame the house, while three other men went over to the creek to hew timber. On September 21 four men continued to hew timber, while one man drew the beams and another man drew the rafters. They brought the beams across the creek to the site of the house. The next day they finished hewing all the rafters and the cellar beams and transported them across the creek. They had to hew another plate, because the one they had done previously was not suitable. Coventry noted in his diary: "Have got 13 trees for beams, having two out of one tree; 14 for rafters, and 6 for cellar beams, in all 14 good, and 20 small trees."[89]

On Saturday, September 23, while still working on the frame, they began excavating the cellar. They continued through the beginning of the following week. On Monday, they brought five cartloads of stone for the foundation, and on Tuesday seven more cartloads. They also transported the remainder of the rafters to the construction site. On September 27, three men worked on the cellar, while the carpenters continued with the framing. The next day they had the house raising.

28 Sept. At work to-day at the frame. Finch, 2 Lobdells, and little John Lobdell, Ghoes, and Maize. Building the wall at the cellar. There were Caleb and Daniel Lobdell, Howard Whitlock, and the negro Harry, and they got 4 corners up by noon. After dinner they began to raise. There were about 20 hands, viz., Finch, 3 Lobdells, Whitlock, Cardogan, Wallace, Baker, Samuel, Benjamin, Martin, Isaac Decker, Thos. Ghoes, Timothy Allen, and Maize. They wrought very briskly and got it finished a little after sundown. A number of women, old and young, were present. They all went a frolicing to David Williams, and being all hearty, having finished 2½ gallons of rum, their mirth ended in a quarrel between A.M. and G. who fought.[90]

The following day the carpenters came for their pay. They charged 6 pounds, 6 shillings per day for 8 days work. Alexander Coventry's brother, William, paid them in goods. In addition, Caleb Lobdell was given a pair of stocking valued at 10 shillings, a piece of cloth valued at 4 shillings, and another piece of cloth in advance for working 1 day at "stoning" the cellar.

Worked commenced again on November 14, when a carpenter named Ezekiel Butler constructed a scaffold and began to nail roof boards on the rafters. At the same time, the mason resumed work on the cellar wall. The next day it rained, and the masons went home early. Two carpenters planed the clapboards, but they were not able to shingle because of the wind. On November 16, the masons finished the south end of the cellar, and four days later, the carpenters began to board up the north end of the house. On some days the masons went home early because of bad weather; on other days they worked only half a day because they were also constructing another house in the neighborhood. Finally, on November 25, the carpenters finished the two gable ends of the house. Coventry noted that there were two windows and a chimney on each gable end. It had taken them six days to board up the gable and finish the windows.

The next week the carpenters began to board up the west side of the house. By November 30 they had closed the back side and put some roof boards on the front side. Then on December 2 the carpenters erected a "stage" and began to shingle the back side of the house. Coventry noted on January 1, 1787, that four masons were working on the chimney. On January 13, Elias Butler, one of the carpenters, cased the door and nailed on some clapboards that he had been planing for the previous two days.

The transportation of building materials to the site continued to be a problem. On February 2 Coventry had to send two sleighs to the sawmill across the river to get two loads of boards. On February 26 he had to get three sleigh-loads. By March 1 he reported that the sashes for the windows were finished. Then on March 3 he received 700 bricks, 3 pounds of putty, and 300 panes of glass. Carting the bricks to the house was a major job. He had to borrow a team of oxen from a neighbor.

On March 28 a new mason offered to work for him in exchange for payment in grain after the harvest. The mason began to work on the front cellar, but work was again interrupted, first by rain and then freezing weather. On April 2 the men laid the foundation for chimneys. There were three chimneys in the house—one at the north end, one at the south end, and a kitchen chimney at the west end. By April 15 the masons had built up the brick above the chamber fireplace, and by April 16 had the south chimney built up to five rows above the roof ridge. On April 17 they finished both front chimneys and pencilled them. In all they had taken four days on each chimney.

The carpenter finished the window sashes on April 20, and by May 1 they were "ploughing" the plank for the chamber floors. On May 28 the mason and a helper began to construct the oven. In addition, work commenced on lathing the walls. Coventry described the method of lathing as follows:

Maize split the laths, and lathed the posts, the method we used. Ezekiel Butler plowed the pieces of boards, which were nailed on the posts, and the ends of the lath being adapted to the furrow, we slipped them in by that means, saved a quantity of nails. The thicker the lath, the better it answers the purpose.[91]

On June 7, 1787, Coventry's tenants, Mr. John Butler and his family, moved into the new house.

What is notable about this description of the construction of a late eighteenth-century farmhouse in the Upper Hudson Valley is that much of the labor was done by skilled craftsmen working under contract. While they were paid in barter, this actual work was not so different from the way houses are constructed today. Contrary to generalizations about division of labor and specialization not developing until after the Industrial Revolution, this description is evidence to the contrary. The actual house raising, however, was done as a communal effort with the help of Coventry's neighbors. This was followed by the traditional "frolic" or work party. The word was most likely derived from the Dutch *vrolijk*, meaning "merry, jolly, gay, cheerful."

Estate inventories provide information about how artifacts were distributed within the farmhouse and how the use of interior space changed over three centuries. For example, the inventory of Jan Jansen Damen, dated July 6, 1651, offers a rare view of what could be found inside a combined farmhouse and barn in the seventeenth century. In "the large front room" among other things were a single bed and bolster (a long underpillow for a bed); a double bed and bolster; blankets, pillows, sheets; a chamber pot; a warming pan; several Bibles; an inkstand; a firelock; a rapier; a powder horn; and several chests containing sheets, linen, clothing, buttons, and money. Apparently, this room was used in part as a bedroom, probably for more than one member of the family, as indicated by more than one bed and bolster. In "the entrance hall" were among other things pewter measures, plates, bowls, dishes, spoons; a pewter flagon, basin, mug, and funnel;

brass candlesticks; copper potlids; earthen dishes, wooden dinner plates; jugs; a sieve; a pothanger; a pothook; andirons; a simmer; a salt cellar (a dish for salt); milk tubs; water pails; an ash shovel; and a chest containing beaver skins, linen, and a pair of shoes. This room probably was used for food preparation and eating. In the "pantry" there were among other things butter molds; copper griddles for pancakes; wooden pint measures for milk; a bellows, pewter platters; earthen dishes; a pair of scales; a cutting blade; a saw; and a gridiron. The "cellar" contained beer barrels, butter tubs, a tap auger, and some earthern pots.[92] Damen was a brewer and a farmer. The number of artifacts in his estate suggests that he was wealthier than the average Dutch farmer in New Netherland. Nor was his inventory typical of seventeenth-century inventories, which usually did not show room-by-room itemizations.

The inventory of Jacques Cortelyou of New Utrecht, dated January 20, 1694, was more typical. The items were not listed room by room, nor does it show which items were inside the farmhouse. However, the household items do appear in proximity to each other on the list. His worldly possessions included three beds, pillows, blankets, sheets; a cupboard; two tables; twelve chairs; a churn; milk and washing tubs; milk and beef casks; pails; a bake trough; wooden dishes; pewter plates, pots, spoons, porringers; a brass mortar, a candlestick; a warming pan, stewpan, and skillet; brass and iron kettles; an iron frying pan; a roast pan; a roasting spit; two pairs of tongs; earthen plates and dishes; a Bible; and "three score old books."[93] This inventory supports the view that for the average Dutch farmer in seventeenth-century America there was a scarcity of material possessions, which, if historian Simon Schama is correct, was the opposite of the "embarrassment of riches" common in the Netherlands at the same time.[94]

It is not until the late eighteenth and early nineteenth centuries that we find many room-by-room inventories. This was a reflection of the trend away from undifferentiated living space and toward more specialized and private uses of space inside the farmhouses and the trend away from a poverty of artifacts toward a plethora of material possessions.[95] Such generalizations must be modified by class differences; the more wealthy the farmer, the more the material possessions. From these inventories and other documents we can piece together the uses of such areas within the farmhouse as the garret, the cellar, and the different rooms.[96]

The garret, for example, often was used for crop storage. The record book of Rensselaerswyck shows that in the spring of 1667 there was a great ice flow that "carried and destroyed the large colony's dwelling house, barn, brewery and all that was in them, the garrets being full of wheat and the rear chamber (*'t achterhuys*) full of oats."[97] In a letter dated April 1667 to his father-in-law, Oloff Stevensz Cortlandt, Jeremias van Rensselaer mentioned how during the spring thaw forty houses and barns were swept away, including his own house. He explained that "my garret and also the rear chamber were filled with oats, but that is gone now."[98]

The garret continued to be used for crop storage in the eighteenth and nineteenth centuries in New Jersey. The 1757 inventory of Simon Van Wickle of Somerset County mentions "Wheat in the House and Barn." The 1815 inventory of Cornelius Lozier of Franklin Township in Bergen County notes some casks of rye, a barrel of flour, sugar, and meal in the garret. In 1821 Jacob Van Ness, who lived along the Passaic River in New Jersey, had in his garret rye, wheat, and buckwheat. In 1821 Abraham Staats of Franklin Township in Somerset County had some bushels of wheat and a cask of smoked meat in his garret. And in 1880 Martin J. Cook of Montville in Morris County had two sacks of dried apples in his garret.

Spinning wheels for flax and wool were also found in the garret. Cornelius Lozier had two spinning wheels in his garret, and Abraham Staats had two woolen wheels and coarse and fine hatchels for cleaning flax. In Martin J. Cook's garret there were some woolen and cotton yarn and a quilting frame. It is not clear from these inventories alone whether the garret was used as a work area or whether this textile equipment was just being stored there. According to Frederick Banfield Hanson, "the number of spinning wheels and the amount of wool and flax in garrets indicates the importance of that area as a work room. . . . Since the garret was dry, that area was the usual place to produce thread and yarn."[99] According to architectural historian Abbott Lowell Cummings, spinning and weaving were sometimes done in the attic of farmhouses in New England.[100]

The garret was also used as sleeping quarters for some members of the family. The 1800 inventory of Joseph Sigler of Essex County, New Jersey, mentions a "south bed room in [the] kitchen garret" containing "one Bed, Bedding Carpet" and a "north bed room in [the] kitchen garret" containing "one Bed, Bedding &c." A bed, bedding, and several bedsteads are listed in the garret in the 1815 inventory of Cornelius Lozier. George Doremus' garret in 1830 contained two beds and bedding, and Martin J. Cook in 1880 had a bedstead, some straw beds, some feather beds, sheets, a bolster, a pillow, blankets, a trundle bedstead, and bed quilts in his garret. In New England the attics also contained bed and bedding, indicating that here too they were occupied by family members.[101]

The inventories that specifically mention articles in the cellar suggest that it had multiple uses as a dairy, summer kitchen, and root cellar for storing fruits and vegetables. The inventory of Joseph Sigler lists in his cellar apples, potatoes, turnips, and pumpkins, as well as pork and beef barrels, some casks, an old harness, a buffalo robe, and several beehives. Cornelius Lozier's inventory shows that he had two cellars, one of which was a kitchen cellar. In the kitchen cellar were such things as an arm chair, a table, a bed and bedding, chests, baskets, tumblers, spoons, knives and forks, earthenware, a pewter tankard, a steelyard (a balance device for weighing things), a pair of andirons, a canteen, a trammel (a contrivance hung in a fireplace to support pots, kettles, etc. over the fire), a hammer, and tongs. In the regular cellar were a cask with salt fish, a gridiron, a jug, a table, a churn, earthen pots, some candles, two small churns, an ax, some jugs and an iron pot. It is possible, although purely conjecture, that the bed and bedding in the cellars of George Doremus and Cornelius Lozier might have been sleeping quarters for the slaves.

Martin Cook's cellar also shows multiple uses as dairy, kitchen, and root cellar. In it he had two lots of potatoes, a lot of smaller potatoes, a barrel of salt pork, a barrel of smoked hams, a churn, a butter bowl, a ladle, stoneware and earthenware pots, a bench, chairs, a table, pie dishes, plates, a lot of tubs, and numerous tin milk pails. The 1796 inventory of Hezekiah Van Orden of Catskill, New York, indicates two cellars. In his "fore cellar" were several churns, tubs of different sizes, a barrel with tar, a dyeing tub, a beef tub, a soap trough, an iron ladle, and some benches. In his "black cellar" were a cider hogshead, a fish tub with fish, earthen pots and jugs, and a cask.

In those nineteenth-century inventories in which there is a room-by-room breakdown the name of the room often indicates its use. For example, the 1821 inventory of Abraham Staats was divided into the following rooms: dwelling room, bedroom adjoining, parlor, entry, room in back of parlor, "bedroom back entry," and upstairs. The major pieces of furniture in each room confirm the use of the room. The dwelling room had a desk, a stand, a table, and chairs; the bedroom adjoining had a bed, bedstead, and bedding, a chest, a desk, and a tea table; the parlor had a tea table and several "waiters" (waiting tables); the entry had a table; the room in back of the parlor had a bed, bedstead, and bedding and a dining table; the "bedroom back entry" had a Dutch cupboard; and upstairs there was an old table, two barrels of whiskey, a bedstead, a table, some Windsor chairs, and trunks and chests. The occurrence of a bed, bedstead, and bedding as well as a dining room table in the room in back of the parlor indicates a survival into the nineteenth century of the multiple uses for room common during the colonial period.

Often the names of the room were not descriptive of their uses, with the exception of the kitchen. For example, the 1798 inventory of Hezekiah Van Orden indicates a long room, a little room or chamber, a back room, a back kitchen, a fore kitchen, a pantry, and a storeroom. The furniture in each room, however, reveals its use. The long room had an old bedstead; the little room or chamber had six tables, a small stand and sixteen chairs; and the back room had six Windsor chairs, two cupboards, a chest, a writing desk with drawers, and two beds. This inventory also suggests the survival of undifferentiated living space.

By the late nineteenth century the bed and bedstead disappeared from the front room, which by then was used solely as a parlor. This is seen in the 1880 inventory of Martin J. Cook. The rooms listed in his inventory were a front room, the kitchen, and the bedroom over the kitchen. The front room had a bureau, a walnut table, a lounge, a Boston rocker, six cane-bottomed chairs, and a stand. Thus, the multiple uses of rooms that characterized the seventeenth and eighteenth centuries persisted into the early part of the nineteenth century. The parlor had emerged as a room exclusively used for entertaining visitors.[102]

In conclusion, the cultural processes that shaped the Dutch-American culture region can be seen in the transition from the Dutch farmhouse to the Dutch-American farmhouse. After a brief period of living in temporary dwellings, the Dutch in New Netherland built permanent farmhouses that were replicas, with some modifications to fit a new environment, of certain house types that were used in Europe. By the late seventeenth century, regional differences could be seen between the brick houses of the Upper Hudson Valley, the fieldstone houses of the Middle Hudson Valley, the red sandstone houses of northern New Jersey and southeastern New York, and the frame houses in Brooklyn, New York. Despite these adaptations to the environment, these houses could be described as Dutch farmhouses, because their framing and floorplans could be traced back to prototypes in Europe. By the middle of the eighteenth century, a new type of hybrid architecture emerged under the dominant English influence. These farmhouses were unlike anything in the Netherlands or on the European continent. They had Georgian floorplans, English and Dutch framing, and many had gambrel roofs in the English tradition. But they differed from farmhouses in England, New England, and the South, and they were associated with the Dutch in New York and New Jersey. In other words, they were a distinct farmhouse type that we may term Dutch-American.

CHAPTER 3

Landscape

According to John R. Stilgoe, the word "landscape" entered the English language from the Dutch *landschap*. However, because the English imported the word in reference to Dutch scenery painting, the English meaning was somewhat different from the original Dutch. To the English it meant large-scale, rural vistas. But the Dutch meaning was similar to the German term *landschaft*, which, according to Stilgoe, was the antithesis of "wilderness." In the folk imagination of the Middle Ages, the wilderness was "the objectification of chaotic evil." Landschaft, on the other hand, meant "the land shaped by men."

A landschaft was not a town exactly, or a manor or a village, but a collection of dwellings and other structures crowded together within a circle of pasture, meadow, and planting fields and surrounded by unimproved forest or marsh. Like the Anglo-Saxon *tithing* and the old French *vill*, the word meant more than an organization of space; it connoted too the inhabitants of the place and their obligations to one another and to the land.

Landscape, according to Stilgoe, represented a tenuous balance between artifice and husbandry, which in nineteenth-century America became industry and farming.[1]

Adriaen van der Donck described the landscape of New Netherland at the time of the first effective settlement by the Dutch. Van der Donck had been the *schout* for the Rensselaer family at Rensselaerswyck and later the owner of Colendonck (present-day Yonkers). His book, *A Description of the New Netherlands*, was originally published in 1656, to encourage settlement in New Netherland. Although some of his descriptions were colored by that purpose, for the most part it is a reliable source for the Dutch perception of the New World environment.

Van der Donck noted that the countryside had hills and mountains in some places and was level in others. He described the highlands as "a place of high, connected mountain lands, about three miles broad, extending in curved forms throughout the country; separated in some places, and then again connected." Some places in the mountains were tillable with a fertile soil of clay mixed with stone, but other mountainous regions had rocks and ravines and were overgrown with timber. Near the coast the soil was light and sandy and mixed with clay. Along the rivers and near the coast there was much level land drained by brooks. This level land contained fresh and salt meadows, good for pasturage and hay, except during the spring when they were often flooded. Van der Donck noted the similarity of this land to the lowlands and outlands in the Netherlands, and he suggested that it could be diked and cultivated. Much of the lowlands were covered with timber and brush—what the Dutch called *kreuple bosch*. But, van der Donck noted, where such land was cleared and cultivated, it was "wonderfully fertile."[2] Stilgoe comments that the Dutch found sandy and gravelly soils and marshes acceptable because of their similarity to land in the Netherlands, whereas the English avoided such land.[3]

The first step in settlement was to clear the land. Cornelius van Tienhoven, secretary of the province, advised new settlers to arrive in the spring, so they could spend the summer clearing the land and building houses. "All those who arrive in New Netherland," he wrote, "must immediately set about preparing the soil to be able, if possible, to plant some winter grain and to proceed the next winter to cut and clear the timber. The trees are usually felled from the stump, cut up and burnt in the field, unless such as are suitable, for building, for palisades, posts, and rails."[4] Stilgoe notes that clearing land was a new experience for both the English and the Dutch, since the forests had long been cleared from their native countries by the seventeenth century. He suggests that they would have been better advised to use the Indian gird-and-burn method of land clearing.[5] Besides clearing the field, the Dutch also drained the marshes, as suggested by van der Donck.

A provisional order in 1624 granted all colonists in New Netherland free land, but they had to settle at places assigned to them, and they were told what crops to plant.[6] In January 1625, Director Willem Verhulst was instructed to give each family "as much land as they can properly cultivate," each person drawing his share by lot. "Where there was no tide," his instructions noted, "the dwellings shall be erected as far as possible down-stream, so that the produce may be more easily brought down to the barns in barges." Furthermore, the instructions advised "that all hilly lands upon which the sun, at noon, being in the south, shines perpendicularly are the best; that the hills lying on the east side of the rivers are the least suitable for being planted with vines and grains, but those on the west side are the best, especially those extending in a southerly direction."[7] Additional instructions, dated April 22, 1625, ordered that once they had secured a suitable location, the settlers should "make a plan and stake off the boundaries of the plot where they wish to locate their houses and lots, taking care that on one side thereof there runs a river."[8] These instructions explain the settlement pattern along river valleys, a tradition that continued into the nineteenth century.

During the Dutch period, three distinct settlement patterns emerged in New Netherland—the isolated farm, the patroonship, and the agricultural village. Each of these settlement patterns had a prototype in different regions of the Netherlands.

Although the Dutch West India Company was primarily concerned with the fur trade, they also had an interest in agricultural exports, including timber, grain, wine, and timber extracts.[9] The company sent colonists to establish their own farms as well as hired farmers to work for a set number of years on the company's farms. The 1629 Charter of Freedoms and Exemptions provided that private freemen "may with the approbation of the director and council there choose and take possession of as much land as they can properly cultivate and hold the same in full ownership either for themselves or for their masters." In addition, "they shall also have rights of hunting . . . in common with others in public woods and rivers."[10] Following a tradition in the Netherlands, the farms were given names.[11]

A map titled *Manatus Gelegan op de Noort Rivier* (Manhattan Situated on the North River), dated 1639, shows both farms *(bouweries)* and plantations. The difference, according to Isaac Newton Phelps Stokes, is that the former were fully developed farms with cattle and other livestock, while plantations were probably devoted exclusively to raising tobacco or other crops. On Manhattan Island there were thirteen plantations, including those of Thomas Sanderson, "Old Jan," Jan Pietersen van Housem, Wouter van Twiller, Barent Dircksen Swart, Francis Lesley, Thomas Betts, Jan Cornelissen von Rotterdam, Hendrick Pietersen van Wesel, Barent Dircksen van Noorden, Jacob van Corlaer, David de Provoost, Hendrick de Provoost, Hendrick Jansen, and an unidentified person named "Snyder." Across the Hudson River, in what had been the patroonship of Pavonia, were the plantations of Hendrick Cornelissen van Vorst at Hoboken, Maryn Adriaensen at present-day Weehawken, and three plantations at Paulus Hook. On Staten Island was the plantation of David Pietersen de Vries, and on Nut Island (now Governor's Island) was the plantation of Wouter van Twiller. Long Island, in what is now Brooklyn, had two commenced and three completed plantations of tile makers and the plantations of Joris Rapelje at Wallabout and Claes Carstensen at present-day Williamsburg. The *bouweries* listed on Manhattan Island included those of Barent Dircksen van Noorden, Johannes de la Montagne, Cornelis van Tienhoven, Domine Everadus Bogardus, Antony Jansen of Salee, Jan Claesen, Cosyn Gerritsen van Putten, Jochem Pietersen Kuyter, and six *bouweries* owned by the Dutch West India Company, one of which was leased to Willem van Twiller. Van Twiller also had *bouweries* on Ward's and Randall's Islands in the East River, and Jan Claessen Alteras leased a *bouwery* from the company on Hog Island. In what is today New Jersey were the *bouweries* of Cornelis van Vorst and Jan Evertsen Bout. And in what is today Brooklyn were the *bouweries* of Wolphert Gerritsz and Andries Hudde at New Amersfoort (now Flatlands) and that of Dirck Volchertsen at Norman's Kill (Bushwick Creek). In the Bronx was the house named "Emaus" of Jonas Bronck at Morrisania.[12]

The tradition of small, isolated farms can be traced back to *kampen*, or scattered farms in which individual reclaimers settled in the wastelands of Salland, Twente, and the Achterhoek.[13] That the Dutch drew upon a settlement pattern associated with wastelands indicates that they approached the wilderness of America in a traditional way. In additional to the small farms or plantations on and near Manhattan Island, large patroonships or manors appeared along the Hudson River Valley. The Charter of Freedoms and Exemptions of 1629 also established the patroonship system. It provided that anyone who agreed to bring to the colony fifty people over the age of fifteen within four years would receive "four leagues along the coast or one side of a navigable river, or two leagues along both sides of river, and as far inland as the situation of the occupants will permit."[14] The Dutch league *(mijl)* equals 4.611 English miles. The charter specified that the patroon would "forever own and possess from the Company as a perpetual fief of inheritance, all of the land lying within the aforesaid limits, together with the fruits, plants, minerals, rivers and springs thereof."[15]

The most successful of these patroonships was Rensselaerswyck, registered on November 19, 1629, by Kiliaen van Rensselaer, a wealthy Amsterdam merchant and one of the directors of the Dutch West India Company. The boundaries of his patroonship were described as "beginning above and below Fort Orange, on both sides of the [Hudson] river with the islands therein, as many leagues downwards as the Assembly of XIX has determined."[16] By July 1634, van Rensselaer reported, the patroonship consisted of three farms named Rensselaersburch, Weelysburch, and Godijnsburch on West Island, a farm called Blommaertsburch on the west side of the Hudson River, a farm named Laetsburch on the east side of the Hudson River, and a dwelling house outside Fort Orange (present-day Albany).[17]

A 1651 census of Rensselaerswyck listed the farms of Thomas Chambers on the east side of the North (Hudson) River, Evert Pels, Cornelis Van Nes, Theunis Dirckse behind Papscanee Island, Juriaen Westvael and Claes Segerts on Papscanee Island, Cornelis van Bruckelen, Jan Helms on Betelhems Island, Aret Jacobsz on the mainland, Johan Barentse and Cornelis Segers on Castle Island, Thomas Jansen on the Bevers Kill, Cornelis Teunesse van Bruckelen, a farm named Blommendael of Arion Huijberts, and one called de Vlackte (the Flatts) of Arent Corlaer. It also mentions a tobacco plantation used by Jacob Havick.[18] A map of the Manor of Rensselaerswyck, drawn by

J. R. Bleeker in 1767, shows that the settlement pattern of farms arranged along both sides of the Hudson River was still evident over a century later.

The patroonships might be thought to be based on the feudal *hoofdhof* (chief farmstead of the lord's bailiff) and *hoeven* (peasant holdings) in the Netherlands. However, this arrangement in the Netherlands was associated with the *kransesdorpen* (ring villages), which were not brought to America. More likely they were based on the *geestdorp* settlement pattern of the western coastlands of the Netherlands. Specifically, the similarity is striking to the *opstrekkende landerijen* (elongated holdings) associated with the reclamation lands, which were relatively narrow strips of land extending back from the dike. The pattern dating back to the twelfth century was for the Bishops of Utrecht to grant reclamation rights to knights, chapters, and religious orders as a way to colonize these previously uninhabited areas.[19] Thus, the reclamation lands of the western Netherlands were for the Dutch what Scotland and northern Ireland were for the English—the frontier on which colonization forms were developed that were used in America.[20]

The third type of settlement pattern in New Netherland developed later than the dispersed farms and the patroonships. This was the agricultural town, which wasn't established in New Netherland until the 1640s. In 1900 Albert E. McKinley argued that "the town was by no means a spontaneous, natural growth among the Dutch."[21] Donna Merwick has argued the opposite, that the Dutch had a strong town tradition in contrast to the English.[22] Neither is completely right. The English in New England initially settled in agricultural towns, whereas the Dutch did not. But this was not because the Dutch had no tradition of agricultural towns. The Charter of Freedoms and Exemptions of 1640 provided for a town form of government "should it happen that the dwelling-places of private colonists become so numerous as to be accounted towns, villages, or cities."[23] But the fact remains that the Dutch had to be ordered by the Dutch West India Company to settle in towns as a defensive measure during the Indian wars of the 1640s. In 1645 the company sent an instruction to the Director and Council in New Amsterdam "that the colonists settle themselves with a certain number of families in some of the most suitable places, in the manner of villages, towns and hamlets, as the English are in the habit of doing, who thereby live more securely."[24] During the 1640s the Dutch allowed New Englanders to settle in towns on Long Island, and they even gave these towns charters. Three English towns were chartered by the Dutch before any Dutch towns were chartered: Hempstead in 1644, Vlissingen (Flushing) in 1645, and Gravesend in 1645. Two more English towns were chartered in 1656: Rustdorp (present-day Jamaica) and Vreedland (present-day Westchester). After the 1645 instruction from the company, the Dutch began to charter Dutch towns as well. Five were established on Long Island: Breukelen (Brooklyn) in 1646, Midwout (present-day Flatbush) and New Amersfoort (present-day Flatlands) both in 1654, and New Utrecht and Bushwick both in 1661.[25]

Flatbush provides a good example of the land division in a typical Dutch-American agricultural town. Forty-eight farms, all of uniform width, were laid out along the Flatbush Road. Twenty-four were on the west side of the road with the land extending to the town border of New Utrecht or the hills, whichever came first. The other twenty-four were on the east side of the road with land extending east to Twiller's Flat. A dispute between Flatbush and Flatlands over the ownership of these flats delayed the distribution of the woodlands. When it was settled in 1666 by arbitration, the property owners of Flatbush divided their woodlands in the northern part of Twiller's Flat by allotment into forty-eight strips. Each farmer received one strip of woodland.[26] A similar pattern of land division was followed by the other Dutch towns on Long Island.

In 1679, Jasper Danckaerts describes his travels through these agricultural towns. After crossing the East River, he and his companion, Gerrit Evertsen van Dyn, "went up the hill, along open roads and a little wood, through the first village, called Breukelen, which has a small and ugly little church standing in the middle of the road." The location of the church in the middle of the road was a Dutch tradition; the church in Beverwyck (Albany) was similarly situated. Danckaerts and his companion proceeded through the town of Breukelen and turned right toward Gouanes, passing "several plantations where Gerrit was acquainted with almost all the people." Toward evening they arrived at the village of New Utrecht, named by Jacques Cortelyou, who came from the province of Utrecht. Cortelyou's farm was located a half-hour's ride outside town. Danckaerts noted that the village had burnt down some time ago, but was rebuilt with "many good stone houses." He also described the flats, which the Dutch found desirable for settlement. "There is towards the sea a large piece of low flat land which is overflowed at every tide, like the *schorr* with us, miry and muddy at the bottom, and which produces a species of hard salt grass or reed grass. Such a place they call *valey* and mow it for hay, which cattle would rather eat than fresh hay or grass." The adjoining corn lands, he noted, were "dry and barren for the most part." "Behind the village, inland, are their meadows, but they also were now arid. All the land from the bay to the Vlacke Bos [Flatbush] is low and level, without the least elevation." He noted a heath, on which sheep could graze, which was drained by navigable creeks that were "very service-able for fisheries." Here he saw a grist-mill driven by water from the creek. They then rode to Vlacke Bos, which he described as "a village situated about an hour and a half's distance from there, upon the same plain, which is very large." He noted that "this village seems to have better farms than the bay, and yields full as much revenue. Riding through it, we came to the woods and the hills, which are very stoney." They passed through the village of Breukelen again on their way back to the ferry.[27]

A map titled "Plan of the Town of Brooklyn and Part of Long Island," based on a survey done in 1766 and 1767 by B. Ratzer, shows that the basic landscape characteristics described by Danckaerts some ninety years earlier still were evident, especially in the layout of the town of Brooklyn and its surrounding fields.

The village of Harlem on Manhattan Island was laid out similarly to the Dutch towns on Long Island, except that it had two parallel streets, between which were arranged the house lots *(erven)*. Every four lots formed a block, separated by cross streets. Garden plots *(tuynen)* were located on one of the two streets. Each house lot was assigned one garden plot, measuring five by twenty Dutch rods. Each house lot was also assigned four morgens of farm land *(bouwland)* in long strips upon Jochem Pieters Flat, thus giving each farmer access either to the *Groote Kill* (Harlem River) or to the creeks. A small parcel of marsh or meadow was also allotted to each farmer to provide salt hay for his cattle. These lots were located in such places as Little Barent's Island or on the opposite side of the Harlem River. The meadows in the Bay of Hell Gate were reserved for the benefit of the church, as was some of the *bouwland* in the village. In a later division, the large plain, known as Van Keulen's Hook, south of the village was divided in the same way as Jochem Pieter's Flat. An upland area to the southwest was reserved as a commons.[28]

It is not necessary to look to New England for models for the Dutch agricultural towns, even though they were substantially similar to those in New England. The *brinkdorpen*, common on the Drenthe plateau in the eastern Netherlands, were the same kind of towns.[29]

The village of Bergen (now part of Jersey City, New Jersey) was surveyed in 1660 by Jacques Cortelyou. It was intended to be a stockaded village, because Indians raids had previously destroyed the nearby patroonship of Pavonia. The village was laid out as a square crossed by two streets at right angles with a rectangular public square in the center. Each settler was allocated a home lot within and farm lots outside the stockaded village. The larger farm lots, following the pattern set by the patroonship of Pavonia, were located along the Hudson River and were irregular in shape. The smaller farm lots were laid out along either a road or a navigable stream and were long strips in shape.[30] Thus, Bergen resembled a combination of the *geestdorpen* and the *brinkdorpen* of the Netherlands.

When the English conquered New Netherland in 1664, there were changes in the landholding patterns. The colony was transformed from a corporate colony under the Dutch West India Company to a proprietary colony of the Duke of York, who became King James II of England. He kept the northern part of the colony, which he renamed New York, and he subdivided the southern part into the proprietary colony of New Jersey, which he granted to Sir George Carteret, and John, Lord Berkeley. They in turn sold their holdings to other proprietors, who in 1676 divided the colony into East and West Jersey. In 1673 the Dutch reconquered the colony, but the English regained control after a few months. In 1702 East New Jersey and West Jersey were united into a single royal colony of New Jersey. Despite the English conquest, the Dutch settlers retained their cultural identity, although their culture was significantly altered by English influence. In fact, there was a greater expansion of Dutch settlement in New York and New Jersey under English rule than under Dutch rule. The English replaced the Dutch patroonships with manors. The only patroonship that successfully made the transition was Rensselaer-swyck, which was regranted to the van Rensselaer family in 1685. Other manors granted under English rule included Fordham Manor in 1671, Livingston Manor in 1686, Pelham Manor in 1687, Philipsburgh Manor in 1693, Van Cortlandt Manor and Morrisania both in 1697, and Scarsdale in 1701. A number of these manors were granted to wealthy Dutch landowners, and many of the tenants on them were also Dutch.

In addition to the manors, the English also granted to groups of people large tracts of land, known as patents. The difference between the manors and the patents, according to historian Sung Bok Kim, was that a patent was granted to a group of unrelated individuals and there was no lordship title conferred. Also, patents tended to involve fee simple ownership of land, rather than tenancy. There were some exceptions, as in the case of a few patents that had tenants on them.[31]

In New Jersey the patents included the Navesink Patent in 1665, the Piscataway Tract in 1666, the Aquackanonk Patent in 1679, the Ramapo Patent in 1709. The New York patents included the Saratoga Patent in 1684, the Rombout Patent in 1685, the Great Nine Partners' Patent in 1699, and the Beekman Patent in 1703. The Tappan Patent in 1687 was on the disputed boundary between New York and New Jersey. The land in the Tappan Patent was divided in such a way that there would be an equal division of good and bad land. Lots of fifty morgen (approximately 100 acres) were laid out along the east bank of the Hackensack River. Meadows in two locations were distributed so that each shareholder received six morgen (approximately twelve acres). One lot was set aside for the Dutch Reformed Church and another lot for the courthouse. The farmhouses were dispersed in three neighborhoods.[32]

The chartering of towns also continued under English rule. Shrewsbury was chartered in 1665, New Paltz in 1677, Aquackanonk in 1679, Hackensack in 1693, Richmond in 1690, and New Brunswick in 1731. Aquackanonk (present-day Passaic, New Jersey) provides a good example of the land division in a Dutch town founded under English rule. In the first division, the area fronting the Passaic River was divided into fourteen house lots, consisting of 100 acres each. Every lot had 650 feet of river frontage. The second division added fifty acres to the rear of each lot. The individual parcels were numbered and assigned by lot. A triangular church lot of fourteen acres was also surveyed.[33]

On Staten Island, Richmond was subdivided in 1688 into four towns: Castletown, Northfield, Southfield, and Westfield. The older Dutch towns of Old Dorp and New Dorp were included in Southfield.[34] In 1679 Jasper Danckaerts described the island as being thirty-two miles long and four miles wide "with projecting points and indented bays, and creeks running deep into the country." The eastern part of the island was "high and steep" and sparsely inhabited. The south side was "a large plain, with much salt meadow or marsh, and several creeks." The western part was flat and marshy in the vicinity of a large creek, "high and hilly" north of the creek, and level and well-populated in the northwest. The central part of the island was hilly and mostly uninhabited. The woods were used for pasturage for horses and cattle. "There are now about a hundred families on the island," Danckaerts wrote, "of which the English constitute the least portion, and the Dutch and French divide between them about equally the greater portion. They have neither church nor minister, and live rather far from each other, and inconveniently meet together." Only three of the seven houses in the Dutch town of Old Dorp were occupied. "The others," according to Danckaerts, "were abandoned, and their owners have gone to live in better places on the island, because the ground around this village was worn out and barren, and also too limited for their use."[35]

In the eighteenth and nineteenth centuries the manors of New York were disrupted by tenant rebellions. There were revolts in 1755, 1766, and in the 1790s and the 1840s. Historians disagree about whether these revolts were fundamentally class conflicts or the result of a boundary dispute between Massachusetts and New York, pitting Yankees against Yorkers.[36] Beginning in the 1730s, the heirs of Van Cortlandt Manor began to subdivide their land, until by 1776 it is estimated that 37 percent of the manor had been sold to outsiders.[37] Frederick

Philipse sided with England during the Revolutionary War, and in 1779 Philipsburgh Manor was confiscated and broken up. In 1787 the New York legislature abolished all feudal obligations and tenure within the state. But, Sung Bok Kim argues, the manors had always been more capitalistic than feudal, and the "lords" of the manors were really nothing more than justices of the peace. "The governance of the manors," Kim writes, "an integral part of the provincial system, thus took on the same character as the governance of the large nonmanorial land patents, and the manorial lords' behavior patterns approximated those of any ordinary landlords in the province."[38] The anti-rent riots of the 1840s led to a clause in the New York constitution of 1846 prohibiting feudal tenures and the lease of agricultural land for periods of more than twelve years. However, this clause did not apply to leases already in effect. During the 1850s the courts gradually whittled away at the tenancy arrangements on Livingston Manor and Rensselaer-swyck, until by 1860 all the manors in the Hudson River Valley had been broken up.[39]

Perhaps the reason that the transition from Dutch to English land-holding patterns was relatively smooth is that the Dutch and English patterns of agricultural towns, isolated farms, and large manors were essentially the same.

"Fences are a conspicuous feature of the cultural landscape whereby men have claimed parcels of land for their own occupation or cultivation," writes H. F. Raup. "It is in itself physical evidence that lands are no longer owned communally, but have been distributed for individual use."[40] While fences were not unknown in Europe, they were a more conspicuous part of the American landscape. The open-field system was characteristic of much of northern Europe in the seventeenth century, and its landuse pattern of nucleated villages surrounded by land allotments in strips of land at various locations so as to equally divide good and bad land made undesirable the enclosure of land by fences. Also Europe didn't have the extensive forests that were to be found in the northeastern part of the North American continent. Enclosures that did exist consisted of post and rail fences, board fences, wattle fences, hedges (usually of hawthorn), and some stone walls. A German book published in 1702 in Nurenberg depicts the construction of these European fence types.[41] In the polder districts of the Netherlands, ditches or dikes took the place of the fence.[42]

Adriaen van der Donck remarked that fences were one of the main differences between the Netherlands and New Netherland. In 1655 he wrote that "the fencing and enclosing of the land does not cost much; for instead of the Netherlands dykes and ditches, they set up post and rail, or palisado fences, and when new clearings are made, they commonly have fencing timber enough on the land to remove, which cost nothing but the labour."[43] The palisado fence or palisades was probably a reference to upright logs as in the forts on the frontier. As early as 1638, the farmhouse of Andries Hudde and Wolphert Gerritsen at Flatlands was described as being "surrounded by long round palisades."[44]

That fencing land was not part of the agricultural backgrounds of many of the settlers of New Netherland might explain the fact that the authorities of the colony repeatedly had to order the settlers to build and maintain fences in order to protect their crops from livestock. On July 1, 1647, Director Willem Kieft and his Council ordered all inhabitants of New Netherlands "well to fence their lands, that the cattle may not do any damage."[45] The fiscal was ordered to build a pound to keep horses, cows, pigs, or goats that caused damage, and fines were levied against their owners. On July 26, 1647, the Director and Council appointed three surveyors "to condemn all improper and disorderly buildings, fences, palisades, posts, rails, etc. and to prevent their erection in the future." In addition, anyone who intended "to build or put palisades around their gardens or lots in or near the City of New Amsterdam" had to obtain inspection and permission from these surveyors."[46]

Disputes over fences and the failure to fence arose. In 1668 the magistrates of Albany, Rensselaerswyck, and Schenectady noted that "many questions, disputes, and accidents arise among the patentees at Schaenhechtede on account of their failure to fence in their land, so that the horses and cattle go upon it and cause great damage to one another." Therefore, they ordered all the patentees of Schenectady "to provide their land with proper fences, according to the contract made with one another."[47] On the other hand, in 1662 the people of New

Amersfoort (Flatlands) complained to the Director General and Council of New Netherlands about the fences built by the people of the neighboring village of Midwout (Flatbush). They argued that the Director and Council

have granted to the people of Midwout as pasture for their cattle two flats, called Wouter van Twiller's and Curlaer's flats, across which several public roads run to the flats belonging to Amersfoort. The people of Midwout have fenced in not only their said flats, but also the woods and thereby obstruct your petitioner's cattle drift and passage, which will finally cause the ruin and destruction of the village of Amersfoort.[48]

Therefore, the people of New Amersfoort petitioned the Director and Council to order the people of Midwout to stop fencing their land in the flats and woods.

Detailed descriptions of the post and rail fences of New Netherland can be seen in seventeenth-century building contracts. For example, in 1642 Wauter Davel contracted to fence the plantation of Tonis Cray on Manhattan Island. The contract specified that "the above named Wauter Davel shall (cut the posts) as heavy as a man can carry, seven feet (long, the) posts to be set twelve feet apart, and to have holes through them through which five rails, (one above the) other shall be stuck in such (a way) that no hogs, cows or horses shall be able to come into the aforesaid plantation."[49] In 1644 Thomas Hall and Thomas Goodman "contracted to set up for Jan Damen two hundred and fifty rods of posts and rails, the posts to be placed from eleven to twelve feet apart, five rails one above the other, so close and tight that hogs, goats and other cattle cannot pass through."[50]

In 1643 Cornelis Jacobsen Stille rented the farm of Cornelis van Tienhoven at Smits Valley on Manhattan Island. According to the lease, van Tienhoven delivered with the farm "the land properly set off with posts and rails," which Stille was bound "to deliver back at the end of three or six years properly fenced for cattle." Furthermore, Stille agreed to "inclose within his palisades the land which at present lies (unfenced) between the *Smits valey* and the height, and cultivate the same, and should any more land be added to farm it shall in like manner be fenced and tilled by him."[51] In the 1790s William Strickland noted the post and rail fences in Bergen County, New Jersey, which he contrasted unfavorably to the hedgerows of England.

"Throughout all the country, which I have passed, the property is divided by five or six rowed post and rails which greatly disfigure the look of the country; but the evil will soon work its own cure, by rapidly increasing the scarcity of timber; I have not yet seen one yard of planted hedge in America."[52]

Post and rail fences continued to be built into the nineteenth century. The farm journal of Adriances Van Brunt mentions the construction of post and rail fences on his farm near Brooklyn in the early nineteenth century.

[April] 30 [1829] . . . Cooper fixed up all the board fences round about A.M. Sharpened rails P.M. . . .

[May] 19 . . . Old Mr. Doxy setting Fence around the Hog orchard, old George Brown setting Fence next to the woods began [May] 18 and finished [May] 22nd . . .

[February] 4 [1830] . . . Went to the Woods. Cut post and rail timber in Jane and S. Marie's woods for Mr. Shepherd their tenant.[53]

Besides the post and rail fence, by the mid-eighteenth century other fence types were seen on the landscape. In 1744, while traveling on western Long Island, Dr. Alexander Hamilton noted: "The road here for several miles is thick upon each side with rows of cherry trees, like hedges, and the lots of land are mostly enclosed with stone fences."[54] In 1790 Dr. Alexander Coventry described a stone fence in the Upper Hudson River Valley, including the cost and time involved in constructing it.

There is a considerable stone fence here: some walls 3½ (feet) high with one rail, and a cap, some places post with 2 rails, and under part stone, and some places 4 feet high. They lay up this for between 8d and a shilling a yard and a man's day's work is completed at 4 rods. The wall is laid up loose of middle sized stone and generally laid along the top.[55]

As we have seen, the stone fence had prototypes in Europe and on the British Isles, but in America it was primarily associated with New England. Its occurrence in upstate New York was probably another example of English influence.[56]

Another fence typed noted in the Dutch-American culture area in the eighteenth century was the worm fence. It was also known as the

rail fence, zigzag fence, Virginia fence, or timber fence. In 1749 Peter
Kalm described one of these fences near Cohoes Falls.

I here saw a kind of fence which we had not seen before, but which was used
all along the Hudson where there was a quantity of woods. It can be called a
timber fence, for it consisted of long, thick logs, and was about for feet high.
It was made by placing the long logs at right angles to and upon short ones
and fitting them together by having suitable crescent-shaped hollows in the
short logs (in the manner of building log cabins). Such a fence is possible only
where there is plenty of trees.[57]

According to William Strickland, this kind of fence was unlike anything he had seen in England nor did he find them very appealing.

The country [on the east bank of the Hudson River at Tappan Zee] resembles
the best parts of Hertfordshire, and would be still more like it, were the fields
only divided by well planted hedges instead of the vile railings which everywhere so greatly disfigures it, and here wood being still plentiful, the railing is
of the worst description, what they call worm fencing, which is not easy to
describe either by words or the pencil.[58]

Perhaps it was because the worm fence required much wood that it
was unknown in Europe. It appears to have been an indigenous American fence type. It also had the advantage of being quickly assembled,
and it was portable. The worm fence was generally associated with the
frontier phase of settlement, and the post and rail fence with a more
advanced stage of agricultural development.[59] However, among the
Dutch in New York and New Jersey it was just the reverse; the worm
fence was the successor to the post and rail fence. The reason seems to
be that that post and rail fence tradition was brought from northern
Europe, while the worm fence represented a later Americanization of
the Dutch-American culture.

The hay barrack (hooiberg), a covered barn or stack for storing
unthreshed grain or hay, was also a common feature on the Dutch-
American landscape. In America it consisted of four or five poles and
a moveable roof. Sometimes it had a moveable base to keep the hay off
the ground. The poles had holes in which pegs were inserted; this
allowed the roof and/or base to be raised or lowered. In the Netherlands there were two methods for raising the roof. The first was by
means of a mechanism on the ground consisting of an upright rod
resting on a horizontal beam, which was attached by ropes and pulleys

to a cross-bar. The hand-powered circular motion of the cross-bar was transformed to an upward thrust on the vertical rod which moved each corner of the roof. The other method was by means of a simple screw, which rested on a peg inserted in one of the holes on each pole just below the roof frame. The screw was turned by a bar inserted in its base. This second method required climbing a ladder to get to the base of the roof.[60] A mechanism documented to have existed in America to raise the roof of the barrack consisted of a "sweep" (lever), a "temple" (spacer), and a "bolt" (pivot). One corner was raised or lowered at a time, usually requiring two people to complete the operation.[61]

The hay barrack was a common feature in Europe among Germanic people. It can be traced back as far as the Middle Ages in Germany, the Netherlands, France, and Italy. The Dutch architectural historian R. C. Hekker described regional differences in hay barracks in the Netherlands. In the Frisian culture area, hay was normally stored inside the barn, except in North Holland between Haarlem and Amsterdam, where it was stored in a separate wooden barn with a tile roof, known as a *kaakberg*. In the Compartmented House, Zeeland Barn, and Flemish Barn culture areas, hay and grain also were stored inside the barn. The Aisled-House culture area was the main region for the hay barrack. In the eastern part of the region, near the German border, hay was stored in the loft above the central aisle, and the unthreshed grain was stored in a separate roofed stack or barn. In the western part of the culture area, grain was stored in the loft, and hay was kept in the barrack outside. In Betuwe, the *schuurberg* consisted of four poles, side walls, and a moveable thatched roof. In West Twente, the *steltenberg* consisted of four poles, side walls, and a moveable tile roof. In Veluwe, the hay barrack had one or two poles, no sides, and a moveable thatched roof, while in South Holland and Utrecht, the hay barrack had four or five poles, and the roof was raised by means of a screw mechanism.[62]

In America, hay barracks were found not only among the Holland Dutch, but also among the Pennsylvania Dutch (actually Germans) among whom it was called a *shutt-sheier*.[63] The barrack was also used for storing grain crops as well as hay. In 1732 a black named Jack was arrested in Ulster County for burning down a barrack filled with wheat.[64] The estate inventory of Nicholas de Meyer mentions wheat, rye, and hay in the barrack.[65] In the Netherlands it was the tradition when the barrack was filled to place a flag or green linden branches on top and to have a harvest meal to which the neighbors were invited.[66]

As early as 1631 there were "two hay barracks, each of five poles fifty feet high" on the two farms named Rensselaersburch and a hay barrack of "4 poles, 50 feet above the ground" at another farm named Laetsburch, both at Rensselaerwyck.[67] A 1638 inventory of the farm at Flatlands named Achtervelt, belonging to Andries Hudde and Wolphert Gerritsen, mentions "1 hay rick, with five posts, 40 feet tall."[68] A 1643 inventory of the farm known as Vredendael noted the following farm structures: "The farmhouse, barn, a barrack of four posts, cook house and hog pen." Among the tools listed in the same inventory was "1 jackscrew for the hay barrack."[69] A lease of a farm near the Smith's valley on Manhattan Island by Cornelis Jacobsen Stille from Cornelis van Tienhoven specifies that "the secretary shall be bound to have a [hay] barrack of five posts erected on condition that the lessee shall bring the timber to the building."[70] The Van Bergen Overmantel, a folk painting depicting the farm of Marten van Bergen in Leeds, New York, as it appeared in 1733, shows two hay barracks, each with six poles. One is completely full with hay, and the other is partially full with the base raised.[71]

In 1748, the Swedish naturalist Peter Kalm noted hay barracks in southeastern Pennsylvania and southwestern New Jersey. He wrote that

many people, especially in the environs of Philadelphia, had haystacks with roofs which moved up and down. Near the surface of the ground were some poles laid, on which the hay was put, that the air might pass freely through it. I have mentioned before that the cattle had no stables in winter or summer and were obliged to graze in the open air during the whole year. However, in Philadelphia, and in a few other places, I saw that those people who made use of the latter kind of hay-stacks, viz., that with the moveable roofs, commonly had built them so that the hay was put a fathom or two above the ground, on a floor of boards, under which the cattle could stand in winter when the weather was bad. Under this floor were partitions of boards on all sides, which however stood far enough from each other to afford the air a free passage.[72]

When Kalm reached the Hudson River Valley south of Albany, he wrote: "The land on both sides of the river was chiefly low, and more carefully cultivated as we came nearer to Albany. Here we could see everywhere the type of haystacks with moveable roofs which I have described before."[73]

A full description of a hay barrack in Hunterdon County, New Jersey, is contained in a letter written on November 13, 1787, by Mrs. Mary Capner.

Barracks are a building I have not described to you, tho I noticed them at the first coming into the country. Tommy has made one for his Bro. (It has) four poles fixed in the ground at the distance of fifteen feet in a square. The poles are squared fifteen feet or more at top and five feet at bottom unsquared. This is all above ground. In the square part of the poles there are holes bored thro at the distance of twelve inches big enough for a strong iron pin to put thro to support four wall plates which are tennanted at the ends, then some light spars are put upon the wall plates and thatch upon them. When it was only five feet from the ground, the roof can be raised at pleasure 21 feet or any distance from the ground between that and five feet. These are to put hay or any kind of grain under and the roof is always ready to shelter it from hasty rains which is common here in summer. Those that have only two cows have the bottom part boarded at the sides and a floor laid over and the hay at top and the cow stable under.[74]

The thatched roof was used on hay barracks well into the nineteenth century. An 1854 article in *Harper's Magazine* makes reference to a thatched-roof barrack. "We crept slyly around a 'barrack,' as it is called, of standing hay, and the pegs at a corner-post. We climbed up to the top of the hay-mow, under the straw-thatched roof, and lay down."[75]

In 1788, Dr. Alexander Coventry described the construction of a barrack on his farm near Hudson, New York. On Friday, June 6, he went out in the morning with Finch and they cut down six trees for the barrack. On Tuesday, June 17, he and Jonathan transported all the timber, except two pieces, to the spot where they wanted to construct the barrack. On July 2 he went over to Major Hellenbeck's and with his permission cut down twenty-eight pine trees for the spars for the barrack. On July 30 while Preston and Coleman were mowing and Jonathan was raking hay, he cut some hoops for the top of the barrack. Then on July 31 he had Barnet Follock begin work on the barrack with the assistance of Coleman and Preston. Coventry obtained some straw from W. C. and a small load from Whitlock. They succeeded in tying

on the laths and laying about two "rounds of thach." On August 1
Follock finished the barrack with the help of Preston and Coleman.
But they encountered difficulties in raising the roof for want of the
proper equipment.

> Saturday, 2 Aug. Warm and clear in A.M. Cloudy, with a shower in the
> west in P.M. but which did not reach us. Preston and Coleman tried to raise
> the top of the Barrack, but could not for want of iron pins, therefore they
> stacked hay, and Preston built a nice, well-shaped stack. There were about
> 100 cocks . . .
> 7 . . . Jonathan B. and Preston mowing and making hay. Went over the
> neck to see Salisbury, from thence to Thomas Follock's where I borrowed a
> barrack lever.[76]

The Verplanck family papers from Westchester County from about
1800 contain a description of how to thatch a barrack. They note that
barley or rye straw is best for thatching, although some people think
that wheat straw is better because it is more wooly and spongy, and
thus more likely that rain will soak through it. It warns that the grain
should not be removed from the straw by flailing, because that would
bruise it. Instead a coarse flax or hemp hatchet should be used.[77] A
Treatise on Agriculture and Practical Husbandry in the Verplanck
papers makes the following recommendation: "I would advise all Farmers
to have a mowstead or scaffle frame of timber, or a Dutch barn or
barrack with four or five posts and a moveable roof, which is excellent
for the preservation of corn."[78]

The technique of stacking a barrack was the following. The hay
must not be stacked wet nor should it be packed too tightly, because
the hay secretes a watery liquid as a result of its natural fermentation,
which might result in spontaneous combustion. A long, iron pole with
a cross and hook at the end was thrust into the center of the stack to
test it. If the end of the pole was cool enough to hold in the hand, the
stack was safe; but if it was sizzling hot, the hay must be removed.
After the hay has settled, the roof of the barrack was lowered, and a
section was cut away from the bottom for ventilation.[79] The Verplanck
treatise recommends that in making a wheat or barley stack, the ears
of the sheaves should be laid uppermost to keep the middle of the stack
full, or else the rain will run into the ears and damage them.[80]

Hay barracks continued to be used into the nineteenth century, as indicated by references to barracks and related equipment in estate inventories. The 1805 inventory of John Parleman of Pequanock Township, New Jersey, mentions a "quantity of Rye in barrick unthreshed."[81] The 1816 inventory of John Day of English Neighborhood, New Jersey, mentions "a lot of hay in the barrack."[82] The 1838 inventory of William Colfax of Pompton, New Jersey, mentions "one Barrick Rye" and "Three Barrick Poles."[83] And the 1878 inventory of John H. Van Dien of Bergen County, New Jersey, mentions "Hay in Barrack (in Dunker Hook Meadow)" and "Rye in Barrack not thrashed."[84]

Cultural geographer Peter O. Wacker notes that newspaper advertisements indicate that as early as 1730 barracks were adopted by non-Dutch ethnic groups. He indicates that barracks show up on farms of non-Dutch families in New Jersey, Pennsylvania, New York, Maryland, Massachusetts, Virginia, Ohio, and on Prince Edward Island. He hypothesizes that in pioneer areas, the barrack, which could be erected quickly, preceded the erection of a barn, thus making it "an ideal structure for the pioneer agriculturist." "The rapid acceptance and wide diffusion of the barrack," Wacker writes, "partially refutes the idea that Dutch culture traits were generally rejected by other culture groups."[85]

Wacker also states that the barrack has virtually disappeared from the state of New Jersey.[86] Don McTernan, however, found seven hay barracks in 1978 in Bergen, Morris, Warren, and Hunterdon counties, but knows of no surviving barracks in New York and Pennsylvania.[87] Perhaps the reason for the longer survival of the hay barrack in New Jersey was that New Jersey continued to raise grain crops throughout the nineteenth century, while in New York the grain belt shifted to the Genessee Valley and was replaced by dairying and orchard crops.

Occasionally, the term "Dutch barn" was used to mean a barrack. In 1793, Patrick Campbell, a Scottish traveler through the Niagara region of New York State, commented on a large farm consisting of a "good house, but still larger barn of two stories, several office houses, [and] barracks, or Dutch barns." He added that "the barracks or Dutch barns were foreign to any Scotchman whatever."[88] The Treatise on Agriculture in the Verplanck family papers refers to "a Dutch barn or barrack with 4 or 5 posts and a moveable roof."[89] However, most

references to the Dutch-American barn refer to a large, wooden structure for sheltering crops, livestock, or farm equipment as well as for
providing an indoor work space.

As previously noted, some combined dwellings and barns were
built in New Netherland in the early seventeenth century. The estate
inventory of Jan Jansen Damen, dated July 6, 1651, provides a rare
look at what kinds of things would be found inside such a structure. It
mentions an "entrance hall," a "large front room," a "pantry," a "cellar
under the house," and "the rear part of the house or the barn." In the
barn section were listed sacks of hops, barley "in the rick," a bed with
a pillow, several old chairs, a keg of nails, an old grain sieve, and
various tools, including an iron spade, whips, pitch forks, and plow
shares, a dung fork, a wooden rake, an ax, a flail, some reaping hooks,
and several Flemish scythes. In the loft of the barn were barley, malt,
wheat, rye, oats, and peas, also some barrels "with a little wheat and
corn feed for poultry," various kinds of rope, some bags of flour for
bread, a beam and scales, winnowing baskets, and various tools, including sickles, a hatchet, and an adze. Also mentioned in the inventory were horses, cows, a bull, an ox, pigs, as well as wagons, plows,
harrows, and sleighs. But it is not clear whether these were in the barn
or outside it.[90] Because the house section had a cellar, this structure
was not of the aisled-house type. It does show that the barn was used
for storing equipment and crops.

Separate barns were also constructed in the early seventeenth century in New Netherland. The inventory of the farm of Andries Hudde
and Wolphert Gerritsen at Flatlands, dated July 29, 1638, mentions a
house and a separate "barn, 40 feet long, 18 feet wide and 24 feet high
with the roof."[91] These Dutch-American barns had the same framing
as the aisled house combination dwelling and barn, that is, consisting
of a series of H-bents.[92] The building contract, by which Harmen
Bastiaensen agreed on February 8, 1675, to build a barn at Kinderhook, New York, for Jan Maertensen, specified that the barn should
be "fifty feet long and twenty-six feet wide, with an extension [*uytlaet*,
meaning a space for bays and stalls] on each side, ten feet deep and
running the full length of the barn," and that there should be "at each
end a gable with a sloping peak." Furthermore, the barn should be
constructed with "five bents with five loft beams, of which five bents

three are to have brackets, a double door at the front end of the barn, and one door in each of the extensions." Finally, the barn should have "a horse manger forty feet long."[93]

Some of these early barns had thatched roofs. In 1642, David Pietersen de Vries wrote: "I was not long home, when there came some chiefs from Ackinsack [Hackensack], and from Reckawanck, which was close by men, and informed me that one of their Indians, who was drunk, had shot a Dutchman dead, who was sitting on a barn thatching it."[94] There were still some barns with thatched roofs in New York State in the 1790s, although most of them by this time had shingle roofs. According to the account book of Joseph Depuy, whose farm was located near Kingston, he credited Simon Krom on July 7, 1792, with 7 shillings 6 pence for "1½ Day Labour Taching [Thatching] my Barn." On July 10 Depuy sold "20 Bunches of Tach Straw" to Dirick Wesbruek, and on July 11 he sold "25 Bunches of Tach Straw" to John Schonmaker.[95] Probably it was thatch left over from his barn. In 1797, Juljan U. Niemcewicz, traveling in the vicinity of Albany, noted: "The houses in this section are poorer than elsewhere, almost every one of them is a tavern. It was here, for the first time, that I saw a barn roofed with straw. The inhabitants for the most part are Dutch."[96]

In 1679, when Jasper Danckaerts and his traveling companion visited the farm of Jacques Cortelyou at New Utrecht, they slept in the barn. His vivid description tell us what it was like inside one of these Dutch-American barns.

After supper, we went to sleep in the barn, upon some straw spread with sheep-skins, in the midst of the continual grunting of hogs, squealing of pigs bleating and coughing of sheep, barking of dogs, crowing of cocks, cackling of hens, and, especially, a good quantity of fleas and vermin, of no small portion of which we were participants; and all with an open barn door, through which a northwest wind was blowing. Though we could not sleep, we could not complain, inasmuch as we had the same quarters and kind of bed that their own son usually had, who had now on our arrival crept in the straw behind us.[97]

The fact that Cortelyou's son usually slept in the barn is revealing not only of the use of space in the Dutch-American barns, but also of the status of sons in the Dutch-American families.

In 1748, Peter Kalm described the Dutch barns he saw in New Jersey between Trenton and New Brunswick.

The barns had a peculiar kind of construction in this locality, of which I shall give a concise description. The main building was very large, almost the size of a small church; the roof was high, covered with wooden shingles, sloping on both sides, but not steep. The walls which supported it were not much higher than a full grown man; but on the other hand the breadth of the building was all the greater. In the middle was the threshing floor and above it, or in the loft or garret, they put the unthrashed grain, the straw, or anything else, according to the season. On one side were stables for the horses, and on the other for the cows. The young stock has also their particular stables or stalls, and in both ends of the building were large doors, so that one could drive in with a cart and horses through one of them, and go out at the other. Here under one roof, therefore, were the thrashing floor, the barn, the stables, the hay loft, the coach house, etc.[98]

When Kalm arrived at the region north of Albany, he noted: "The barns are generally built in the Dutch way, as I have before described them; for in the middle was the threshing floor, above it a place for hay and straw; and on each side stables for horse, cows, and other animals. The barn itself was very large."[99]

The use of the center aisle of the Dutch-American barn as a threshing floor is confirmed by Dr. Alexander Coventry. In February 1788 he asked his neighbor Van Alstine "for his barn to thresh my wheat in."[100] He explained how he threshed the wheat using a block, which was a conical shaped stick of wood, the small end of which revolves around a post in the middle of the barn floor, while two horses at the large end draw it in a circular direction over the wheat.[101] Coventry also confirmed the practice of driving the farm wagon right into the barn in order to unload the hay. "[April] 17 [1790] . . . Went up to Old Mr. van Rensselaer's barn, and there saw some strange (Dutch) husbandry. Standing on the barn floor, was a waggon loaded with coarse, swamp hay, which was very musty."[102] In November 1808, Coventry described a barn raising. "Had a number of men to raise the old barn; got the frame up in A.M. and ¾ of roof, which we slid upon long poles with the rafters on it. The roof was taken down in quarter sections, by sliding on long poles. Would have finished the raising had not the rain stopt us."[103]

In 1809, Mrs. Anne Grant described the Schuyler family barn at the Flatts in great detail, including the uses to which the barn was put. She described it as "the most spacious barn" she ever saw, being one hundred feet long and sixty feet wide. The roof sloped from "a very great height in the midst" to about ten feet where it met the side walls. The entire structure was built of wood, resting on a stone foundation that raised it three feet above the ground. On this foundation rested beams, and on them was laid "a very massive oak floor." A large sill sloped downwards in front of the barn door on the gable end. There were large, folding doors in the front and rear of the barn. Twelve-foot aisles ran the length of the structure on either side, one of which was divided off for cattle, the other used as a manger. On either side of the large doors were smaller ones for the cattle and horses. The cattle and horses stood with their heads facing the center threshing floor. The floor of the aisles was constructed of thick planks, which were turned to allow dung and litter to drop into receptables below. In the spring the dung was carted down to the river. On one side there was an extremely large chest for holding thrashed grain. The roof was supported by large crossbeams, on which were stretched long poles, thus forming a loft, in which crops were stored. When the grain or hay was cut or reaped, it was loaded on a wagon and brought right into the barn. Often a large number of grasshoppers, butterflies, and cicadas were brought in along with the hay. From on top of the wagon, the hay was then forked into the loft, whose center portion was reserved for this purpose. When the wagon was unloaded, it was driven out the rear door of the barn. Thus, Mrs. Grant noted, "the whole crop and cattle were . . . compendiously lodged under one roof."[104]

Nineteenth-century inventories indicate that the uses of the Dutch-American barn were much the same as in the eighteenth century. When Joseph Sigler of Essex County, New Jersey, died in 1800, the assessors listed the following items in his barn: 300 sheaves of rye, 60 bundles of straw, a fanning mill, forks, rakes, flails, casks, baskets, cart ropes, 2 "shoats in the stye," 60 "fowles," 1 mare and colt, 1 "iron grey" horse, 1 grey horse, 3 milch cows, 1 heifer, and 1 "steer for beef."[105] The 1815 inventory of Cornelius Lozier of Franklin Township, New Jersey, listed the following articles "in and about the Barn": a lye cask, a grind stone, 2 tar buckets, 1 set of harness, 1 wagon, a plough, 3 bee hives with bees, 2 tubs, a pail, 1 chamber pot, 2 black mares, 3 hogs, a harrow, an old sled and tacking, an ox chain, a wood sled, a pleasure sleigh, a wheelbarrow, a cross-cut saw, a scythe, a dung fork, barrels, baskets, a windmill, a yoke of oxen, 5 milch cows, 2 heifers, 7 sheep, rye meal, and 900 sheaves of rye.[106] And when George Doremus died in 1830, he had in his barn 1 fanning mill, forks, shovels, 3 cows, 1 yoke of cattle, 11 sheep, 8 lambs, poultry, hogs, and pigs.[107] Thus, the barn continued to be used for storage of crops, tools, and equipment and sheltering livestock.

The degree to which the form of the Dutch-American barn was in part related to its function can be seen in the transformation of the barn on the Wemple farm in Dunnsville, Albany County, New York, documented by the Historic American Building Survey in the 1930s. The Dutch barn was ideally suited for either grain production or a mixed agriculture in which both grain and livestock were raised. The large door was well suited for farm wagons to be driven into the barn, and the garret for grain storage. However, with the transformation of agriculture in upstate New York to dairy farming in the early part of the twentieth century (see Chapter 4), the form of this particular barn was modified into the bank barn more typical of New York dairy farms. This transformation was similar to the transformations that the Dutch-American farmhouse underwent (see Chapter 2).

In summary, the landholding patterns, barracks, and barns of the Dutch-American culture area reveal the process of selective adaptation. At least three settlement patterns—the isolated farm, the large estate, and the agricultural village—were adapted from the eastern provinces and the reclaimed land in the western provinces. The five-pole hay barrack that became dominant in New York and New Jersey was closest to those found in the provinces of Holland and Utrecht, and the Dutch-American barn was an adaptation of the aisled peasant houses and barns of the eastern provinces of the Netherlands. After a brief period in the early seventeenth century when combination dwellings and barns were built, these structures were modified in the late seventeenth century into the separate barns more typical of America.

A Frisian farmhouse from Midlum, demonstrating the head-neck-torso arrangement. Nederlands Openluchtmuseum, Arnhem. Photograph by David S. Cohen.

A *loshoes* from the Twente region of Overijssel, illustrating the aisled house type. Nederlands Openluchtmuseum, Arnhem. Photograph by David S. Cohen.

A compartmented farmhouse from Elsig and Wallenthal, Germany. Rhein-ische Freilichtmuseum. Photograph by David S. Cohen.

Flemish farmhouse in Wulpen, near Veurne, Belgium. Photograph by David S. Cohen.

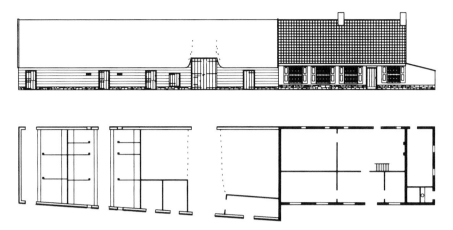

Connected farmhouse and barn in Biezenstraat, Zeeland. From R. C. Hekker, *De Zeeuwse Hofstede*, redrawn by Peter Felperin.

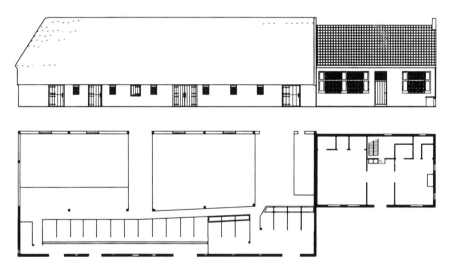

Connected farmhouse and barn in Biggekerke, Zeeland. From R. C. Hekker, *De Zeeuwse Hofstede*, redrawn by Peter Felperin.

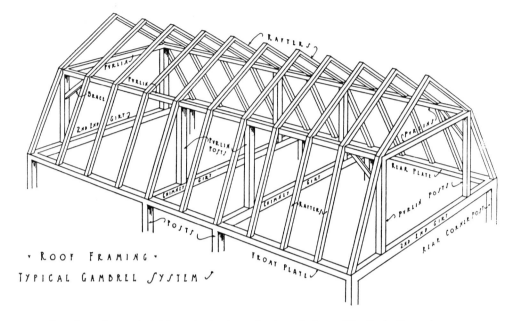

· ROOF FRAMING ·
TYPICAL GAMBREL SYSTEM ✓

Framing of a typical New England gambrel roof. From *The Early Domestic Architecture of Connecticut* by Frederick Kelly. By permission of Yale University Press.

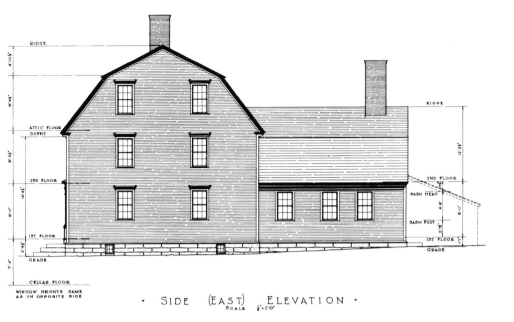

• SIDE (EAST) ELEVATION •
SCALE ¼"-1'-0"

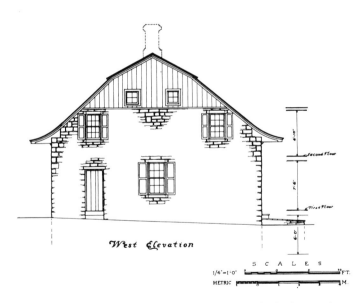

West Elevation

SCALES
1/4"-1'-0"   FT.
METRIC   M.

Elevations of the Elisha Pitkin House, East Hartford, Connecticut, and the
Sickles House, Pearl River, New York, showing the apparent difference in the
exterior appearance of the New England and the Dutch gambrel roofs. Historic American Building Survey, Library of Congress.

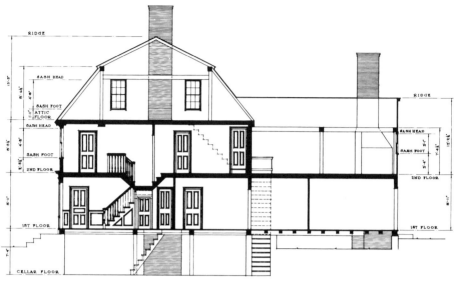

· CROSS SECTION ·
SCALE ¼"-1'-0"

FRED C. WALZ - DEL

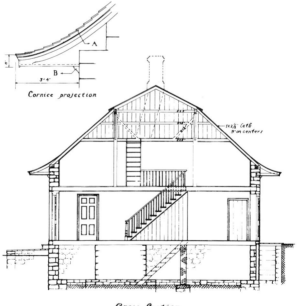

Cornice projection

Cross section

Cross sections of the Elisha Pitkin House and the Sickles House, showing the structural similarity of the New England and the Dutch gambrel roofs. Historic American Building Survey, Library of Congress.

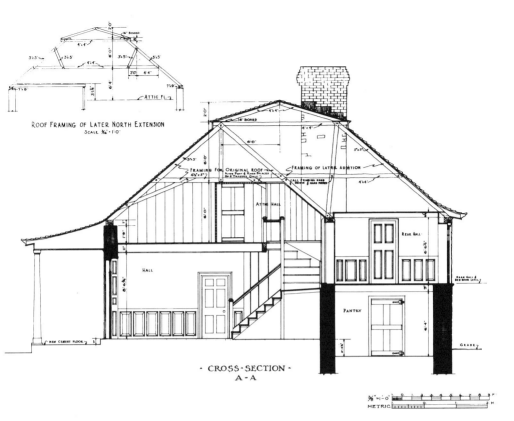

ROOF FRAMING OF LATER NORTH EXTENSION
SCALE ⅜"=1'-0"

- CROSS-SECTION -
A - A

Cross section of the Steuben-Zabriskie House, showing a pitched roof within the gambrel roof. Historic American Building Survey, Library of Congress.

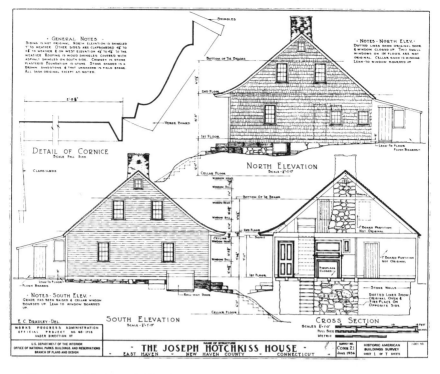

Elevation of the Joseph Hotchkiss House, East Haven, Connecticut, showing an apparent similarity to the overhanging eaves of the Flemish cottage. Historic American Building Survey, Library of Congress.

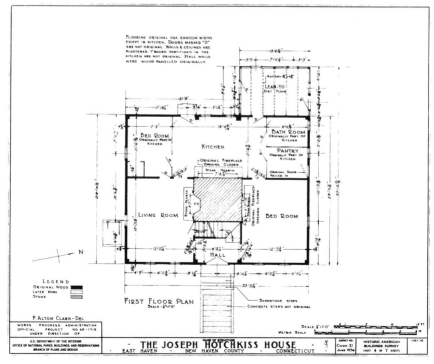

Floorplan of the Joseph Hotchkiss House, showing it to be a typical New England farmhouse. Historic American Building Survey, Library of Congress.

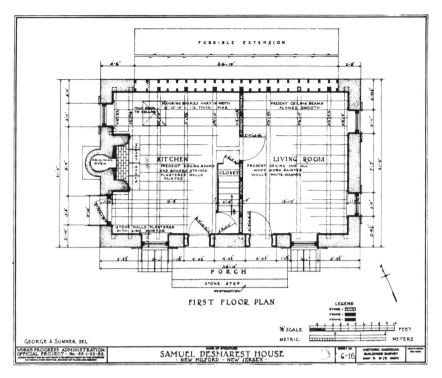

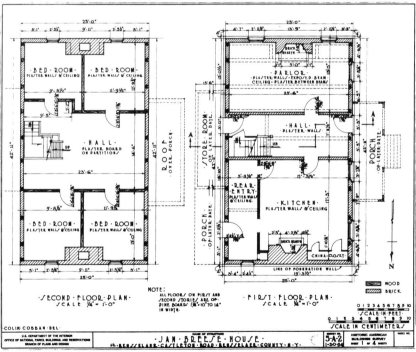

Four Dutch farmhouse floorplans: (a) the Samuel DesMarest House, River Edge, New Jersey; (b) the Jan Breese House, formerly in East Greenbush, New York; (c) the Johannes Hardenbergh House, formerly in Kerhonkson, New York; and (d) the Peter A. Hopper House, Fair Lawn, New Jersey. Historic American Building Survey, Library of Congress.

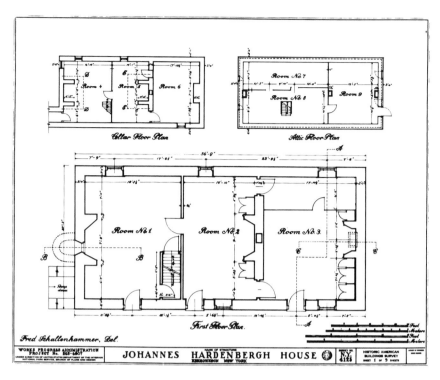

Cellar Floor Plan

Attic Floor Plan

First Floor Plan.

Fred Schallenhammer, Del.

WORKS PROGRESS ADMINISTRATION
PROJECT No. 265-6807
UNDER DIRECTION OF UNITED STATES DEPARTMENT OF THE INTERIOR
NATIONAL PARK SERVICE, BRANCH OF PLANS AND DESIGN

JOHANNES HARDENBERGH HOUSE

KERHONKSON NEW YORK

SURVEY No.
N.Y.
4126
HISTORIC AMERICAN
BUILDINGS SURVEY
SHEET 1 OF 5 SHEETS

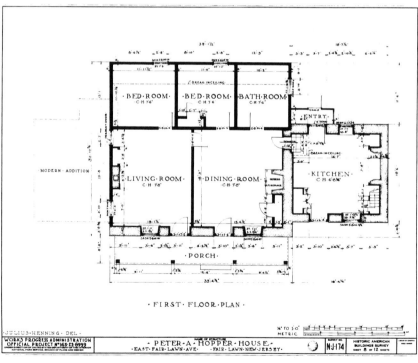

· FIRST · FLOOR · PLAN ·

· JULIUS · HENNING · DEL ·

WORKS PROGRESS ADMINISTRATION
OFFICIAL PROJECT N° 165-FX-6999
UNDER DIRECTION OF UNITED STATES DEPARTMENT OF THE INTERIOR
NATIONAL PARK SERVICE, BRANCH OF PLANS AND DESIGN

· PETER · A · HOPPER · HOUSE ·
· EAST · FAIR · LAWN · AVE · · FAIR · LAWN · NEW · JERSEY ·

SURVEY No.
N·J·174
HISTORIC AMERICAN
BUILDINGS SURVEY
SHEET 8 OF 12 SHEETS

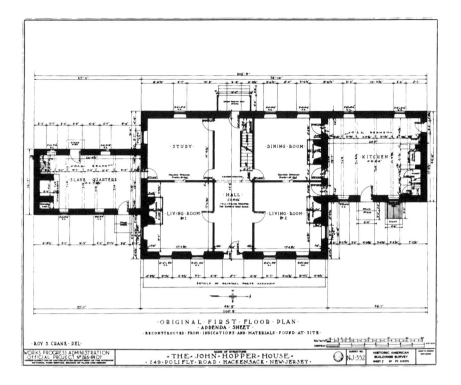

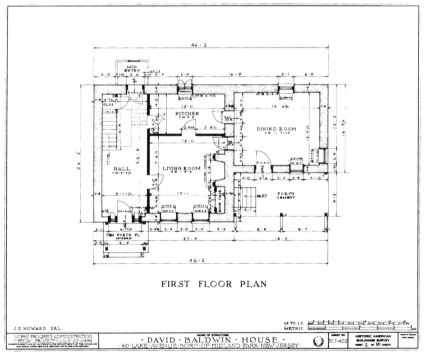

Two Dutch-American farmhouse floorplans: (a) the John Hopper House, formerly in Hackensack, New Jersey; and (b) the David Baldwin House, Midland Park, New Jersey. Historic American Building Survey, Library of Congress.

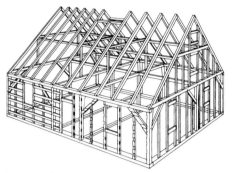

BIRDSEYE· PERSPECTIVE· OF· RESTORED· FRAME· OF· HOUSE·
FLOOR· JOISTS· OF· FIRST· AND· ATTIC· FLOORS· AND· FRAMING· OF· NORTH· AND· WEST· WALLS
OMITTED· IN· THIS· DRAWING· TO· PREVENT· CONFUSION· SEE· SHEETS· #· 3· &· 4· FOR· LAYOUT· OF· SAME·
THE· FRAME· IS· OF· OAK· THE· SILLS· PLATES· & · GIRTS· BEING· MORTISED· TENONED· AND· PEGGED· TO·
EACH· OTHER· OR· TO· THE· POSTS· AND· BRACES· THE· WINDOW· JAMB· STUDS· ARE· MORTISED· AND· TENONED
BUT· NOT· PEGGED· THE· HEAD· & · SILL· PIECES· OF· THE· WINDOWS· ARE· GAINED· INTO· THE· STUDS· AND· TOE·
NAILED· WITH· WROUGHT· IRON· NAILS· AS· ARE· THE· SHINGLES· LATH· ON· THE· SOUTH· FRONT· THE· SHINGLE
LATH· ON· THE· ROOF· ARE· SURFACE· NAILED· TO· THE· RAFTERS· AT· THE· RIDGE· THE· RAFTERS· ARE· HALVED· PINNED

The framing of the Wick House, Morristown, New Jersey, showing a modified version of the English framing tradition. Historic American Building
Survey, Library of Congress.

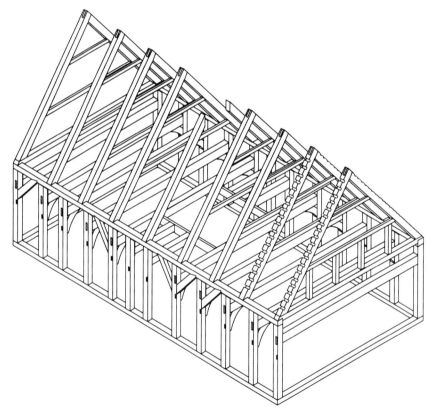

The framing of the Jan Martense Schenck House, formerly in Flatlands,
Brooklyn. From *The Jan Martense Schenck House* by Marvin D. Schwartz,
redrawn by Peter Felperin. By permission of the Brooklyn Museum.

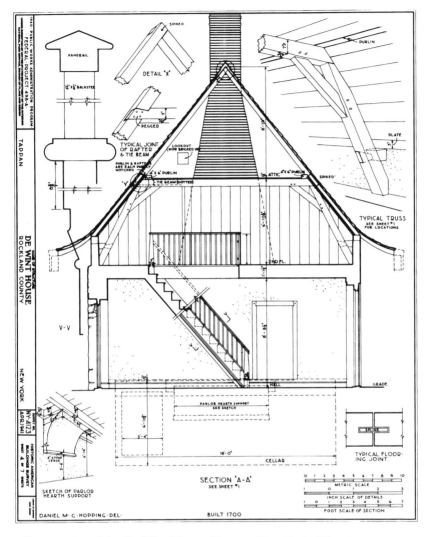

Cross section of the De Wint House, Tappan, New York. Historic American Building Survey, Library of Congress.

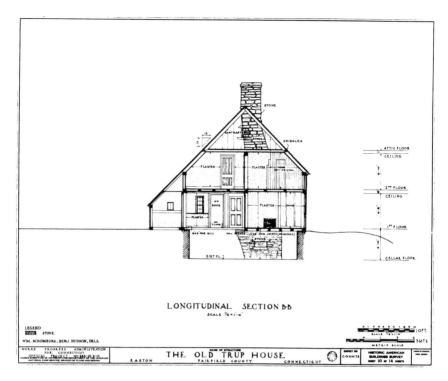

Cross section of the Old Trup House, Easton, Connecticut, showing an apparent similarity with the Dutch H-bent. Historic American Building Survey, Library of Congress.

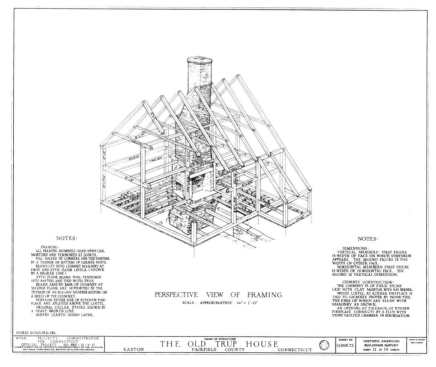

A perspective view of the framing of the Old Trup House, demonstrating the structural difference between the Dutch and English farmhouse types. Historic American Building Survey, Library of Congress.

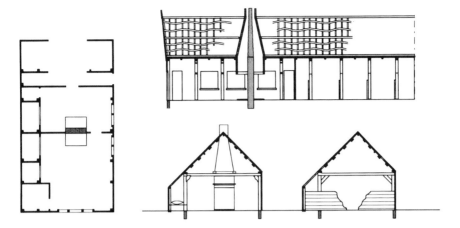

Reconstructed floorplan of a middle seventeenth-century house in Holysloot, Waterland, North Holland. From "De Houten Huizen van Holysloot," by H. J. Zantkuyl. Redrawn by Peter Felperin.

Van Cortlandt Manor, Westchester County, New York, an example of a banked Dutch-American farmhouse. Photograph by David S. Cohen.

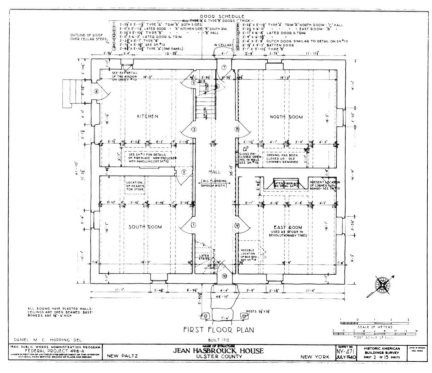

Floorplan of the Jean Hasbrouck House, a variant of the Dutch-American farmhouse type. Historic American Building Survey, Library of Congress.

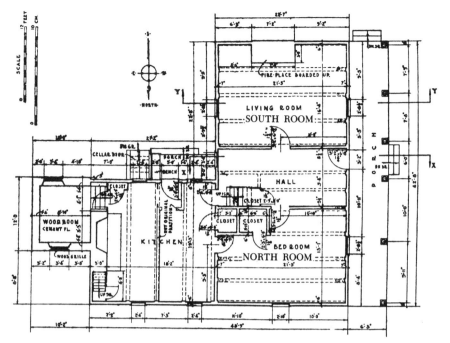

Plan of the house in 1934.

Plan of the house as reconstructed.

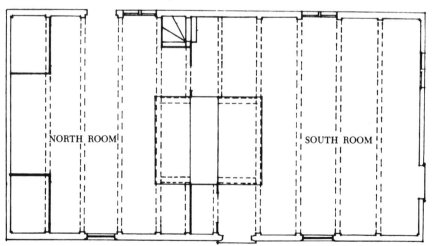

Floorplans of the Jan Martense Schenck House, before and after restoration. From *The Jan Martense Schenck House* by Marvin D. Schwartz. Permission of The Brooklyn Museum.

A Dutch Barn: The Haring Barn, Rockleigh, New Jersey. Photograph by R. Merritt Lacey. Historic American Building Survey, Library of Congress.

A bi-level Dutch barn on the Wemple Farm, Dunnsville, New York. Photograph by Nelson E. Baldwin. Historic American Building Survey, Library of Congress.

A Dutch plow, Mohawk Valley, New York, circa 1750. New York State
Historical Association, Cooperstown.

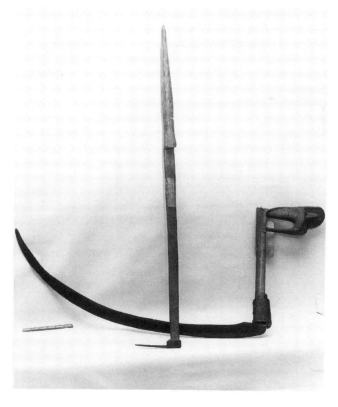

A sith and mathook, Schoharie Valley, circa 1775–1850. Schoharie County
Historical Society.

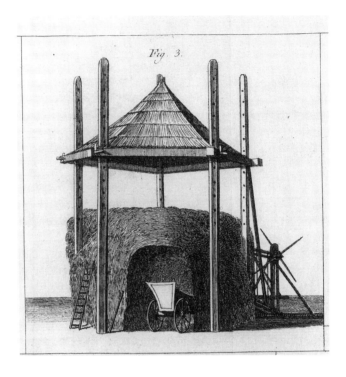

A Dutch wagon and hay barrack, circa 1810. From *Natuurlyke Historie van Holland* by J. Le Francq van Berkhey. Library of Congress.

Van Bergen Overmantel, Leeds, New York, 1732–33, showing a Dutch farmhouse, a Dutch barn, a hay barrack, and a Dutch wagon. New York State Historical Association, Cooperstown.

CHAPTER 4

Farming

"The fundamental difference between agriculture in the Netherlands and that of the Hudson Valley," wrote historian Alice Kenney, "was that the latter concentrated on the growing of grain, first for subsistence and then for market." Dutch farmers in the Netherlands, on the other hand, specialized in market gardening (vegetables), orchard crops (fruits), and fodder for livestock (clover).[1] Actually, this is a bit of an oversimplification. Grain was raised in the eastern provinces of the Netherlands, as we have already seen, and the notion that agriculture in seventeenth-century America was subsistence at first is not totally accurate either. While grain didn't become a major export until the latter part of the seventeenth century, farmers were bringing their crops to market locally in New Amsterdam by mid-century. In 1656 the Director General and Council established Saturday as market day in New Amsterdam because "the people from the country bring various wares, such as meat, bacon, butter, cheese, turnips, roots, straw, and other products of the farm to this City for sale."[2] By 1680 cash crops were being shipped by Hudson River sloop to New York City. In that year Jasper Danckaerts commented upon the existence of commercial agriculture in the vicinity of Esopus. "At the mouth of the creek, on the shore of the river, there are some houses and a redoubt, together with a general storehouse, where the farmers bring in their grain, in order that it may be conveniently shipped when the boats come up here."[3] As scholars are discovering in reference to other

regions of colonial America, it probably more useful to think in terms
of relative percentages of subsistence and commercial agriculture, rather
than subsistence versus commercial agriculture.[4]

As early as the seventeenth century, Dutch farming in America
included grain, fruit, and garden produce. In 1655 Adriaen van der
Donck noted that the cleared land was grubbed (that is, the roots were
removed) and plowed twice, once for summer grain and a second time
if a winter grain, such as rye or wheat, was planted. Manure was
seldom used. If the land became "foul and weedy," some Dutch
farmers would sow peas, which were probably the large gray peas
known as Old Wives. But most of the land was too rich for cultivating
peas, and some of the land had to be sown with wheat and barley
before it would yield a crop of peas. Two crops of peas could be raised
on the same land in one season. The first crop was sown near the end
of March or in early April and was harvested in early July. Then the
land was plowed, and the second crop of peas was sown, which was
harvested in late September or early October. The same system, van
der Donck noted, could be used with buckwheat. But since wheat and
rye were abundant, little buckwheat was sown.[5]

Another major crop was maize (Indian corn), which the Dutch
called "turkey wheat." After the timber had been removed and the
brush burned, the Dutch used a broad hoe to form rows of hills about
six feet apart. Five or six grains of maize were planted in each hill.
Some farmers also planted the stalks of corn as poles for the plants to
climb. The new crop was weeded and cleaned with a broad adze, and
the weeds were placed in a row between the hills. This was followed
by a second weeding, after which the weeds from the first and second
weedings were piled around the corn hills to prevent additional weeds
from growing. Van der Donck noted that the Dutch grew pumpkins
around the maize.[6] While he did not mention it, maize and pumpkins
were originally American Indian crops, not known in Europe. The
techniques of maize cultivation were adaptations of those used by the
Indians; the English colonists in America used similar methods.

Tobacco was another crop borrowed from the Indians. Van der
Donck wrote that tobacco was "well adapted to prepare the land for
other agricultural purposes."[7] In addition, barley grew well in New
Netherland, but it was not cultivated as much as in Europe, where it

was a staple grain. Van der Donck also noted that "flax and hemp will grow fine, but as the women do not spin much, and the Indians have hemp in abundance in the woods from which they make strong ropes and nets, for these reasons very little flax is raised."[8]

"The Netherland settlers, who are lovers of fruit, on observing that the climate was suitable to the production of fruit trees, have brought over and planted various kinds of apple and pear trees which thrive well," wrote van der Donck.[9] While the English introduced the first quinces to America, he noted, the Dutch brought over their own stock and seeds. They also grew Spanish cherries and morellos (a type of sour cherry). Peaches did especially well, and they also grew morecotoons (a kind of peach), apricots, several varieties of plums, almonds, persimmons, cornelian cherries, figs, several kinds of currants, gooseberries, and thorn apples. He noted that olives would thrive, but they were not cultivated; and while many kinds of grapes grew wild, the Dutch did not introduce the best German grapes for winemaking. "In short," he summarized, "every kind of fruit which grows in the Netherlands is plenty already in New Netherlands, which have been introduced by lovers of agriculture, and the fruits thrive better here, particularly such kinds as require a warmer climate."[10]

Finally, van der Donck described the garden produce, some of which were native to America and others that were introduced from the Netherlands. They consisted of various cabbages, parsnips, carrots, beets, endive, succory (or chicory), finckel, sorrel, dill, spinach, radishes, Spanish radishes, parsley, chervil, cresses, onions, and leeks. The Dutch had herb gardens consisting of rosemary, lavender, hyssop, thyme, sage, marjoram, balm, onions, wormwood, belury, chives, pimpernel, dragon's blood, five-finger, tarragon, laurel, artichokes, and asparagus. Also, pumpkins grew with little or no cultivation. In Europe, van der Donck wrote, they were "generally despised as a mean and unsubstantial article of food," but in America as they were "of so good a quality that our countrymen hold [them] in high esteem."[11] Another vegetable native to America was squash, about which van der Donck wrote: "The natives have another species of this vegetable peculiar to themselves, called by our people *quaasiens* (squash), a name derived from the aborigines, as the plant was not known to us before our intercourse with them."[12] Van der Donck also noted that melons thrived in New Netherland, even on newly cleared woodland, provided it was weeded. One variety of melon that grew especially well was the citrull or water-citron, or watermelon. It was not grown in the Netherlands, but it was known there as a result of being occasionally imported from Portugal. In addition, cucumbers and calabashes or gourds were abundant. They also raised turnips, peas, and various kinds of beans, including horse beans, Turkish beans, and large Windsor beans, called by the Dutch farmers *tessen* or house beans.

Many of the same crops continued to be grown in the eighteenth century. Although corn or maize is generally considered a frontier crop, it was cultivated by Dutch-American farmers throughout the eighteenth century. In 1749, Peter Kalm wrote:

They sow corn in great abundance; a loose soil is reckoned the best for this purposes, for it will not thrive in clay. From half a bushel they reap a hundred bushels. They reckon corn a very suitable kind of crop, because the young plant recovers after being hurt by frost. They have had instances here of the plants freezing off twice in the spring, close to the ground, and yet surviving and yielding an excellent crop. Corn has likewise the advantage of standing much longer against a drought than wheat. The larger sort of corn which is commonly sown here ripens in September.[13]

According to a contemporary treatise on agriculture, corn was cultivated in eighteenth-century New York in the following manner. The land was broken up in November so that the turf would be "rolled by the frost" during the winter. In the spring, as soon as the ground thawed, the land was plowed and harrowed. Then furrows were made with a plow or drag at five-foot intervals. A second set of furrows was plowed across the first set of right angles, thus dividing the field into squares. Where the furrows intersected, a broad Dutch hoe was used to make holes, which were filled with a compost consisting of pasture ground, rotten dung, lime and ashes, and five grains of seed. When the corn sprouted about two or three inches above the ground, a small triangular harrow was run between the plants, and the weeds were horse-hoed. The same was done crosswise. In the middle of September, the tops of the stalks, known as the spindles, were cut off, dried, and used as fodder for the milch cows. In mid-October the corn was harvested. It was put into baskets and spread in piles for the huskers.

"The husking time is generally a frolick among the country people," the treatise notes, referring to the work parties that accompanied this phase of the harvest. After the corn had dried, it was stored in a corn crib, which kept it good for several years. The husks were stacked or put in the stable and used as fodder for the cattle.[14]

Wheat became one of the main crops in New York and New Jersey during the eighteenth century. Peter Kalm described its cultivation in the Hudson River Valley.

Wheat is sown in the neighborhood of Albany to great advantage. From one bushel they get twelve sometimes; if the soil is good, they get twenty bushels. If their crop amounts only to a ten-fold yield, they think it a very mediocre one. The inhabitants of the country round Albany are Dutch and Germans. The Germans live in several great villages, and sow great quantities of wheat which is brought to Albany, whence they send many boats laden with flour to New York. The wheat flour from Albany is reckoned the best in North America, except that from Sopus [Esopus] or King's Town [Kingston], a place between Albany and New York. All the bread in Albany is made of wheat. . . . Wheat is so plentiful that they make a malt of that.[15]

In 1786 Alexander Coventry noted that the Dutch in upstate New York raised large crops of wheat, sometimes plowing 200 acres, but they used no manure.[16] The Duke de la Rochefoucault-Liancourt, who traveled through New York State in 1795, observed that the farms near Schenectady yielded twenty-five to thirty bushels of wheat per acre and that "the grain suffers but very seldom, and in a trifling degree, from the Hessian fly, and from blights; the climate is healthy: the usual mart for the production of the country is Albany."[17]

Wheat and peas were sown in alternate years. According to Peter Kalm, "the Dutch and Germans who live hereabouts sow peas in great abundance; they grow very well, and are annually carried to New York in great quantities." However, he noted, lately the peas in upstate New York were destroyed by a worm that previously infested Pennsylvania, New Jersey, and southern New York State. "It is a real loss to this town [Albany], and to the other parts of North America, which used to get so many peas from here for their own consumption and that of their sailors."[18]

Rye, oats, and barley were also cultivated, but not in the same quantity as wheat. It was thought that barley did not yield as great a profit as wheat. Oats were sown primarily as feed for horses.[19] Wheat or rye, maize, and white clover were rotated. In the 1790s William Strickland wrote about agricultural practices in northern New Jersey:

The fields for a mile or two on this side of Paterson bear the aspect of a new country, being full of stumps of trees cut off about a yard above the ground, as is the custom in clearing woods, much labour being thereby saved. . . . When the wood is thus tolerably cleared away, the usual practice is to sow wheat or rye among the stumps, after breaking up the ground as well as it can be done, however imperfectly that may be; the next year Mays [maize] is planted among them, which by its thick shade, greatly promotes their destruction; after this they rapidly disappear, when the ground is better plowed, and the same crops alternately sowed; as long as it will produce anything. It is then laid bye as they call it, and nature immediately covers it with a thick mat of White Clover, and all manner of weeds; and a fresh piece of land is sought out, is cleared, and treated in the same manner.[20]

Red clover and other "cultivated grasses" increased in importance in the late eighteenth and early nineteenth centuries as forage crops for livestock.[21]

A new crop in eighteenth-century New York and New Jersey was potatoes. Peter Kalm mentioned that in New York "potatoes are planted by almost everyone. Some people preferred ashes to sand for keeping them during winter. . . . The Bermuda potatoes have likewise been planted here, and succeed pretty well. The greatest difficulty is to keep them during the winter for they generally rot in that season."[22]

Eighteenth-century travelers often commented upon the fact that each farm had an orchard. Alexander Coventry wrote that the farmhouses in the Upper Hudson River Valley "are surrounded by fine orchards and neat gardens which embellish the banks of this noble river, affording a beautiful prospect to the stranger while he sails past."[23] William Strickland described the farms in Bergen County, New Jersey, as "neat farm houses, with a little garden to each, and an ample orchard loaded with fruit."[24] And Peter Kalm noted about Staten Island that "near every farm house was an orchard with apple trees."[25] Kalm described the fruit trees in the vicinity of Albany:

The several sorts of apple trees were said to grow very well here, and bear as fine fruit as in any other part of North America. Each farm has a large orchard. They have some apples here which are very large, and very palatable; they are sent to New York and other places as a rarity. People make excellent cider in the autumn in the country round Albany.[26]

While Adriaen van der Donck commented upon the absence of flax and hemp cultivation in seventeenth-century New Netherland, Peter Kalm noted in 1749 that "they sow as much hemp and flax as they want for home consumption."[27] In 1774, while traveling through the Mohawk Valley, Abraham Lott noted that "the wheat, Indian Corn, Peas, Flax, Grass and in short every thing the Earth Produces, grew here in the most luxuriant manner."[28] And the farm account book of Joseph Depuy from uptstate New York has entries during the 1780s and 1790s concerning sowing flax seed, braking flax, spinning flax, and weaving linen.[29]

In nineteenth-century New Jersey, according to historian Hubert Schmidt, changes in crops were mainly a matter of emphasis. Some minor crops disappeared and some new ones were added, but the major field crops remained the same. One major difference was that the farmers began to use various fertilizers, such as manure, potash, lime, and plaster of Paris. Corn continued to be an important crop. However, the Hessian fly plague in the late eighteenth century destroyed many strains of wheat, except the hardiest. Farmers in New Jersey turned to rye as a substitute. Oats, which had been an important crop both for grain and hay, continued to be grown, although after 1870 oat production began to decline. Most farms also had a patch of buckwheat for use as feed for swine and poultry. Because it was not sown until summer, farmers planted buckwheat on lands they were unable to plant with oats or corn, which were sown earlier in the year. Timothy became an important cultivated grass used for feed for horses. Also, red clover was grown in abundance, in addition to other hay crops such as redtop, orchard grass, burnet, and sainfoin. Potatoes became a commercial crop in the nineteenth century; however, in 1875 the "Notorious Colorado Bug" attacked the New Jersey potato crop. Schmidt describes the pumpkin as "a colorful field crop of some interest, but of no great importance." The old practice of growing pumpkins in the cornfields continued, although some farmers had separate pumpkin patches. Field pumpkins were used as supplemental feed for cattle in the fall, and garden pumpkins were for human consumption. Apples had always been an important fruit in New Jersey, but the demand for applejack and brandy in the late eighteenth and early nineteenth centuries led to an expansion of orchards. But growing apples was usually a subsidiary activity. Proximity to New York City and improved transportation made for a variety of other truck crops, including tomatoes, sweet corn, squash, peppers, kohlrabi, peas, beans, potatoes, watermelons, and pumpkins. Flax continued to be grown through the mid-nineteenth century, but was discontinued as ready-made clothing began to replace homespun.[30]

In nineteenth-century New York, the completion of the Erie Canal had a major impact on the Hudson and Mohawk valleys. The wheat belt shifted westward to the Genesee Valley. Rye continued as the grain for locally made bread, and barley, used mainly for brewing beer, became the main cash crop of the Mohawk Valley. Farmers in the Hudson Valley began to specialize in orchard crops, such as apples, peaches, and pears. On Long Island market gardening expanded to meet the demand for fresh fruit and vegetables in nearby New York City. By mid-century, the Hudson Valley specialized in orchard crops, Washington and Rensselaer counties in flax, and Schoharie and Montgomery counties in broomcorn.[31]

The journal of Adriances Van Brunt for his farm near Brooklyn in 1828 provides a picture of commercial agriculture in close proximity to the rapidly growing metropolis of New York City. The grain crops he grew were wheat, rye, oats, and corn. The vegetables were peas, potatoes, turnips, kidney beans, and cabbages. And the fruits were cherries, raspberries, Bell pears, and apples. He referred to these crops as "market truck," and there are periodic references to taking the truck to Washington Market. He used salt grass as fodder and manure as a fertilizer.[32]

Local historian Benjamin Myer Brink described nineteenth-century Dutch-American agriculture in the vicinity of Saugerties, New York. He noted that hay was an important crop on every farm. It was used only as fodder for the animals, since there was no market for it. Potatoes were a profitable market crop. Potash and pearl ash from the forests were used as fertilizers. Every farm had a tobacco patch, primarily for self-consumption, because everyone smoked, chewed, or used snuff. In addition, apple orchards were common, although there were not as many varieties as today. Some of the old varieties, such as the Straat and Esopus Spitzenbergh, did not survive. The vegetables grown were turnips, cabbages, and onions. Every farm had a flax field, as long as linen was used for homespun clothing. "One of the pleasantest recollections of the boyhood days of the writer," Brink wrote, "is a scene in which half a dozen or more men were cradling grain together, each man one step behind the one leading him, and each clad in a suit of homemade white linen."[33]

In addition to arable farming, livestock raising was also important in New Netherland from the outset. In April 1625, the Directors of the Dutch West India Company dispatched to the newly established settlements in New Netherland two ships containing "one hundred and three head of livestock—stallions, mares, bulls and cows—for breeding and multiplying, besides all the hogs and sheep that they thought expedient to send thither."[34] Upon their arrival, the livestock was kept on Nutten Island (present day Governor's Island) for several days and then transfered to Manhattan Island, where they were put out to pasture. In 1655, Adriaen van der Donck noted that "the tame stock, which at the settlement of the country were brought over from the Netherlands . . . differ little from the original stock."[35]

The horses, according to van der Donck, were brought from Utrecht, but were supplemented by the English breed, which, he noted, were lighter and not as well-suited for agricultural work, although better for riding. There were also horses of the Arabian breed as well as some imported from the Dutch West Indian island of Curacao, but van der Donck noted that these did not do well in the colder climate of New Netherland.[36] The breed remained distinct through the end of the eighteenth century, when Alexander Coventry noted that "the horses are of a middling size; not so round as those in Scotland; more sharpt boned, thin-shouldered,and sharp rumped; long tailed and most of them brown color."[37] The horses were used as draft animals, either to plow or pull wagons. This tradition was noted in Bergen County in the 1790s by William Strickland.

No man is seen here on horse back, all people travelling in waggons drawn by two horses abreast, and as they generally go a sharp trot, they kick up a surprising dust. . . . A Dutchman never walks or rides; if he has but to go a mile or visit his neighbor, he puts his horse to his waggon to convey him thither.[38]

Unlike Pennsylvania, where horses were the main draft animals for plowing and hauling wagons in the eighteenth century, in the Dutch-American culture area both horses and oxen were used.[39] Adraien van der Donck noted in seventeenth-century New Netherland that "oxen do good service there, and are not only used by the English, but by some of the Netherlanders also, to the wagon and plough."[40] In the eighteenth century William Strickland wrote that "most of the carriage work and plowing of the country are performed by able, large oxen, which are trained to peculiar degree of docility; two working in a plough or several pair in a carriage require nothing to guide them, but the voice, or the small switch of perhaps a boy who drives them."[41] In New England oxen were used extensively. Thus, New York and New Jersey were culturally as well as geographically between Pennsylvania and New England.

The cattle in New Netherland in the seventeenth century were mostly of the Holland breed. Van der Donck noted that they did not grow as large as in Holland, because the hay in America was not as good and because they began mating them in their second year, rather than waiting until they were fully grown as was the tradition in the Netherlands. At first the Holland cattle were subject to disease, when they were fed only fresh hay. But this was prevented by feeding them salt hay and giving them salt and brackish water. There were also cattle from the province of Utrecht. While they thrived and gave good milk and much tallow, they were also not as large as those in the Netherlands. The Dutch also purchased English cattle from New Englanders. Van der Donck noted that the English breed did as well as the Holland cattle and did not require as much care, being able to exist unsheltered all winter. The English cattle did not grow as large as the Dutch cattle, did not give as much milk, and were cheaper, but they provided fat and tallow equal to the Dutch breed. He noted that "they who desire to cross the breeds, and raise the best kind of stock, put a Holland bull to their English cows, by which they produce a good mixed breed of cattle without much cost."[42]

In the eighteenth century Alexander Coventry described the cattle in upstate New York: "The cows are of small size and different colors, such as light brown, red, and spotted, with big short horns, of the Dutch or Aldernay breed."[43] William Strickland noted that the cattle "are in general very good, much resembling our [British] short-horns; some are very handsome. All cattle are driven occasionally to the river, which here is salt, and of which they drink plentifully, otherwise salt is regularly given to them."[44] About the cattle in Bergen County, he wrote:

Good cattle are generally to be met with here, and teams of stout, but clean oxen. They greatly resemble in figure, size and color, the short horned breed of the North of England, both probably being descended from the same stock, this country having been originally colonized by the Dutch, and our cattle being said to have been originally brought from Holland.[45]

Thus, the cattle were a mixed breed of Dutch and English.

Hogs were "numerous and plenty" in New Netherland, according to van der Donck. "Some of the citizens," he wrote, "prefer the English breed of hogs, because they are hardy, and subsist better in winter without shelter; but the Holland hogs grow much larger and heavier and have thicker pork."[46] They were allowed to forage for acorns in the woods and lowlands. When acorns were scarce, the hogs were fattened on "Turkey wheat" or maize.

In addition, there were sheep and goats. Van der Donck commented that the Dutch in New Netherland did not keep as many sheep as the English in New England, but they did thrive nevertheless. The sheep were raised primarily for their wool, rather than for mutton. However, the sheep had to be protected against wolves. Also, he observed that "New Netherlands throughout is a woody country, being almost everywhere beset with trees, stumps and brushwood," and as a result the sheep lost most of the wool.[47] In the eighteenth century William Strickland noted that the sheep resembled the Cheviot breed. Some had horns, and most had gray faces and legs and long necks and legs. They weigh about sixteen pounds and produce about three pounds of wool each, but the wool was generally "coarse and harsh."[48]

Van der Donck noted that the inhabitants of New Netherland kept more goats than sheep, but unlike sheep, goats were in no danger when they became lean. Also goats gave good milk and did not cost much, yet were very prolific. Thus, they were ideal for new settlers and farmers of lesser means. "The New Netherlanders also have every kind of domestic fowls, as we have in Holland," he wrote, "such as

capons, turkeys, geese, and ducks." They also kept pigeons and domestic animals, including cats and dogs. The dogs were trained for
hunting.[49]

Inventories provide some insight into the relative numbers of each
kind of livestock. In 1638 the farm known as Achtervelt at Flatlands
had 3 milch cows, 1 two-year-old heifer, 1 yearling heifer, 2 old oxen,
1 young ox, 1 young calf, 2 old mares, 1 yearling mare, 1 three-year-
old stallion, and a four-year-old gelding.[50] Emmaus, the farm of Jonas
Bronck, at the time of his death in 1643 had 2 five-year-old mares, 1
six-year-old stallion, 1 two-year-old stallion, 1 yearling stallion, 2 one-
year-old mares, 5 milch cows. 1 two-year-old cows, 2 yoke of oxen, 1
bull, 3 yearling heifers, and hogs "number unknown, running in the
woods."[51] The 1651 inventory of Jan Jansen Damen indicated that his
stock consisted of 1 seven-year-old gelding, 1 four-year-old mare, 1
twelve-year-old mare with a young filly, 1 yearling mare, 6 milch
cows, 3 two-year-old heifers, 1 one-year-old heifer, 1 two-year-old
bull, 1 three-year-old ox, 3 bull calves, 1 heifer calf, 2 one-and-a-half-
year-old barrow (castrated male) pigs, 2 one-and-a-half-year-old sows,
1 half-year-old barrow, 1 half-year-old boar, and 7 two-month-old
pigs.[52] And the inventory of Jacques Cortelyou of New Utrecht in
1694 listed 1 horse, 3 mares, 1 colt, 5 three-year-old cows, 5 two-year-
old cows, 4 one-year-old cows, 6 calves, and 6 sheep.[53] The fact that
the livestock was meticulously listed by age reflects the importance
placed on it.

A list of the livestock at the patroonship of Rensselaerswyck was
included in a 1634 report to the Dutch West India Company. As of
April 1633, there were on the farm named Rensselaersburch 6 horses,
including 2 mares with foal, 5 head of cattle, including 2 cows with
calf, 6 hogs, and 16 sheep, and at the farm named de Laetsburch 6
horses, including 2 yearlings, 4 head of cattle, including 1 ox and 1
bull, 5 hogs, and 22 sheep.[54] According to an inventory of animals at
Rensselaerswyck in 1651, the stock had grown considerably. It listed a
total of 128 horses and 158 cattle on 18 different farms. Some livestock
were given names. For example, the cows and horses on the farm
called The Flatts, used by Arent van Corlaer, included 1 gray mare
named *de patroon* (the patroon), 1 gray mare named *poest* (possibly
belonging to Jan Barentsz Wemp, nicknamed *Poest*), 1 black mare, 1

bay mare called *snuijt* (Snout), 1 bay mare with a blaze named *rosbeier*,
1 black mare with a star, 1 black gelding named *hanes* (Hans), 1 bay
gelding named *spiering* (Smelt), 1 brown stallion without a mark, 1
sorrel colt with a blaze, 6 red, full-grown cows, 2 black full-grown
cows, 1 black ox, 4 oxen, 2 bulls, and 3 heifers. And on the farm of
Evert Pels there were 1 bay gelding named *pingsterblom* (Pinkster Flower),
1 stallion named *konning* (King), 1 black stallion named *dick* (Dick), 1
old mare named *de valck* (Thick Head), 1 black filly, 1 old cow with a
blaze, 1 old cow named *kronhoorn* (Crooked Horn), 1 red cow with a
star, 1 red heifer, 1 bull, and 3 heifer calves.[55]

Typically, the patroon supplied the livestock for his tenants, and
the increase in the number of livestock was split by the landlord and
tenant. For example, the lease dated July 20, 1654, of a farm to Jean
Labatie specified that "the lessee shall receive two mares, two stallions
or geldings, one filly, three cows and one full-grown heifer, one half
the increase of which shall belong to the lessee."[56] The division of the
increase was to occur every three or four years, but the initial number
of livestock had to be returned before any division.

In the Dutch towns, cattle grazed on the commons from April until
November, usually under the care of a herder. Young horses, cattle,
and swine would be branded or marked and turned out in the common
woods in the spring and summer. During the fall and winter, they
were sheltered in barns.[57] Jasper Danckaerts noted in 1679 that on
Staten Island "the woods are used for pasturing horses and cattle, for
being an island, none of them can get off. Each person has marks upon
his own by which he can find them when he wants them."[58] In 1748–
49 Peter Kalm wrote about the farms in the Upper Hudson Valley
that "the people are forced to keep their cattle in stables from the
middle of November till March or April, and must find them hay
during that time."[59] And in 1786 Alexander Coventry noted about
Dutch farming practices that "the colts run out the whole winter,
through ever so severe, and live chiefly on the roots of the grass which
they paw up, though under two feet of show. This cold and famine
stunt their growth so that when spring comes, their ribs are as bare of
fat as the fields they fed off are of verdue, there being no root of good
grass left."[60]

Using the 1675 tax lists for the Dutch and English towns on Long

Island, historians Percy Wells Bidwell and John I. Falconer contrasted
the livestock on 153 Dutch farms and 271 English farms. Ninety-seven
percent of the Dutch farms had "neat" cattle (i.e., working oxen, beef
cattle, and dairy cattle), as compared to 89 percent of the English
farms. The average number of cattle per farm was 8.1 for the Dutch
and 9.8 for the English. Twenty-one percent of the Dutch farms had
sheep compared to 43 percent of the English farms. The average
number per farm was 5.9 for the Dutch and 12.7 for the English.
Eighty-four percent of the Dutch farms had horses over one year old
as opposed to 85 percent of the English. The average number of horses
per farm was 3 for the Dutch and 2.4 for the English. And 50 percent
of the Dutch farms had swine compared to 64 percent of the English
farms. The average number per farm was 2.4 for the Dutch and the
same for the English. The biggest difference, however, was in oxen.
Only 24 percent of the English farms had oxen four years old or over,
whereas 72 percent of the Dutch farms had oxen. The average number
of oxen per farm was 2.2 for the Dutch and 3.1 for the English.[61]

The kinds of livestock did not change much in the nineteenth
century, even though the breeds probably became less distinct. The
1838 inventory of William Colfax of Pompton, New Jersey, listed 9
hogs, 1 yoke of red oxen, 1 yoke of brown oxen, 1 yoke of Sussex
steers, 1 old bay horse, 1 young bay horse, 1 bay horse, poultry, 6
pigs, 6 small pigs and sow, 1 sow, 1 yoke of oxen, 1 white-faced ox, 7
cows, and 1 dog.[62] And the 1855 inventory of Adrian Van Houten of
Passaic County, New Jersey, includes 7 shoats (young weaned pigs), 1
large hog, 1 sow, a lot of turkeys and geese, a lot of chickens, 5 yews
and lambs, 5 heifers, 6 cows, 1 yoke of oxen, 2 brown mares, 2 bay
horses, and 4 hives of bees.[63] Thus, the livestock had become a bit
more diversified with a greater emphasis on poultry than in the colonial
period. But the tradition of raising cattle and hogs and using horses
and some oxen as draft animals remained remarkably the same, reflecting the strong sense of tradition among Dutch-American farmers.

In the Hudson and Mohawk valleys of New York State in the
second quarter of the nineteenth century, many farmers began to
specialize in dairying. Orange County became famous for butter and
Herkimer County for cheese. By mid-century, dairying became the

predominant source of income, and most arable farming was in fodder crops.[64]

Most of the tools and equipment found on Dutch-American farms were similar to those on neighboring Anglo-American farms. But three farm implements were distinctively Dutch—the Dutch plow, the Flemish scythe or *sith*, and the Dutch wagon. These were common through the early nineteenth century in the Dutch culture area of New York and New Jersey. The mechanization of agriculture in the middle nineteenth century resulted in standardized farm equipment and the demise of these distinctive features of the Dutch-American farm.

The Dutch plow or hog plow, as it was sometimes called, differed from the English plow or bull plow. These terms were not used consistently; some people used the term bull plow to refer simply to the wooden, as opposed to the cast iron, plow. The Dutch plow had a pyramidal shaped plowshare (the cutting part of the plow), a wooden mold board (which receives the furrow slice from the share, turns it, and pulverizes it), and often only one handle. It seldom had a coulter (a knife-like projection located in the front of the plowshare that initially slices the soil), and sometimes it was mounted on wooden wheels. Its origins can be traced to the province of Zeeland in the Netherlands and the Campine region of northern and eastern Belgium.[65]

The English plow more typically was a swing plow; that is, it was balanced so that it required neither a wheeled forecarriage nor a wooden foot on the end of the beam. It had two handles; the left handle was called the "land handle" and the right the "furrow handle." The English plow had a relatively flat, horizontal share that was either triangular or V-shaped, and it usually had a coulter. Like the Dutch plow it originally had a wooden moldboard. The English plow is thought to have originally come from the Low Countries. The flat, triangular share was used in Groningen, Friesland, North Holland, and the northern part of South Holland. It was brought to England in the sixteenth and seventeenth centuries and was common in Lincolnshire, Norfolk, Suffolk, and Essex, where there was considerable Dutch, Flemish, and Walloon influence.[66]

Writing in the 1770s about plows on New York farms, Hector St. John de Crevecoeur noted that the two-handled plow with a coulter

(the English plow) was best for "rooty, stony land" and was drawn by
four or six oxen or sometimes two oxen and three horses. The one-
handled plow (Dutch plow) was best on level land and was drawn by
either two or three horses abreast.[67] Peter Cousins, in his book *Hog
Plow and Sith*, states that the wheel plow was drawn by three horses.[68]

The Dutch plow shows up in inventories as early as 1638, when the
inventory of the farm named Achtervelt, belonging to Andries Hudde
and Wolphert Gerritsen, mentioned "1 wheel plow and appurtenances."[69] In 1769 Richard Smith stated about the farmers in Albany
County, New York, that "they use wheeled Plows mostly with 3
horses abreast & plow and harrow sometimes on a full Trot, a Boy
sitting on one Horse."[70] J. Dutcher, a manufacturer of cast iron plows
from Durham, New York, recalled the use of the hog plow in the early
nineteenth century:

> As early as the year 1806, when I was a lad, I began to observe the difference
> in the constructions of the plow. At that time there were two kinds in use: one
> was called the Hog plow, which was said to be of Dutch origin, and another
> was called the Bull plow, a Yankee invention. About this time I was learning
> the blacksmith trade, and had considerable to do with the plow, in construct-
> ing and making that part of it called the share. The Bull plow was the most
> esteemed; the other went out of use about the year 1809 or '10.[71]

Dutch plows seemed to have survived slightly longer in New Jersey.
In 1821 "1 Dutch plow" was listed in the estate inventory of Jacob
Van Ness of Caldwell, New Jersey, and in 1833 "three dutch plows"
were listed in the inventory of Henry Berry, a Dutch farmer from
Pequannock Township in Morris County, New Jersey.[72]

Before it died out, the pyramidal share plow spread from the Hudson and Mohawk valleys into Connecticut and Canada. The wheeled
version and single-handled version, however, were not adopted outside
eastern New York. By the middle of the nineteenth century, factory
manufactured plows replaced handcrafted ones, but a light, pyramidal-
shared plow known as the Dagon, Carey, or Connecticut plow, was
manufactured primarily in Enfield, Connecticut, and distributed na-
tionwide.[73] Thus, the Dutch plow is a Dutch culture trait adopted by
other groups in other regions.

The sith, also known as the Hainaut or Flemish scythe, was indigenous to the Low Countries. By the mid-nineteenth century it was used

throughout most of northwestern Germany, western Schleswig-Holstein, along the coast of Friesland, in the Ems Valley of western Oldenburg, and throughout the northern Rhine River Valley.

The sith, or *sicht* in German, was a type of scythe with an L-shaped, wooden handle about sixteen inches long and eight and a half inches wide and a blade about thirty inches long. It was used with a mathook, which consisted of a wooden handle about forty inches long and a small iron hook about four and a half inches long. The sith was used differently than the sickle or the reaping hook. With a sickle, the person stooped low, grasped the crop with the left hand, and cut it with the sickle hook held in the right hand. With a sith and mathook, the person stood nearly upright, held the mathook in the left hand, and cut the crop with the sith held in the right hand. The sith and mathook were more efficient than the sickle or reaping hook. It has been estimated that a person could harvest one-quarter to one-third of an acre per day with a sickle or reaping hook as opposed to one acre per day with a sith and mathook. Despite the greater efficiency of the sith and mathook, there is no evidence that the Yankees who migrated into eastern New York State in the eighteenth century adopted the sith. Cousins suggest that it was perhaps because the use of the sith required special skill.[74]

The Dutch in America used the sith and mathook through the eighteenth century. A memorandum from Kiliaen van Rensselaer to Wouter van Twiller, dated July 20, 1632, mentions that van Rensselaer was sending, among other things, "19 Hainaut scythes for grain."[75] An invoice for goods sent to the colony of Rensselaerswyck mentions "4 long grain scythes" and "4 Hainaut scythes for grain."[76] In 1643 the inventory for the farm named Vredendael mentions three good scythes, three Flemish scythes, four "ferrules" (rings) of scythe blades, four ditto for Flemish scythes, and four "mattocks" (mathooks).[77] The 1651 inventory of Jan Jansen lists "in the rear part of the house or the barn": 2 scythe "snaths (handles)," 3 Flemish scythes, 2 scythe handles, and 2 reaping hooks; in the loft there were 10 new Flemish scythes, 12 old Flemish scythes, 3 new scythe blades, 3 sickles, and 12 Flemish scythe handles.[78] In 1769, New Jerseyan Richard Smith noted the use of the sith and mathook on Beekman Manor. "Here was . . . a Scyth with a Short crooked Handle and a Kind of Hook both used to cut down

Grain for the Sickle is not much known in Albany County or in this Part of Dutchess."[79]

As late as 1796, the estate inventory of Hezekiah Van Orden of the town of Catskill, New York, listed "4 old Sythes, 3 new Ditto, and Appurtenances, 2 Scithes & Mathock."[80] But already then the large scythe with a cradle was replacing the sith and mathook in the Dutch-American culture area. In 1786 Alexander Coventry wrote about the scythe and cradle:

This is a method of reaping, much more speedy than with sickles. They have a scythe fixed in the common way, accompanied with five or six fingers of the same length as the scythe, curved in the same manner, and about as large around as your middle finger, and terminating in a sharp point; this gathers the wheat as it is cut, and helps them to throw it very evenly in a row, with the heads all one way. A raker, with very little trouble, may gather it into sheaves, which the binder makes fast or ties; after which, they put it into little stacks, where it remains until they carry it into the barn, which is done immediately after, if convenient. . . . Some men will cut three or four acres a day with this cradle; however, 2 acres a day is considered a good day's work, with good wheat.[81]

While the Dutch-American farmers were more traditional than innovative, by the late nineteenth century mechanical reapers and mowers began to replace the scythe and cradle. Historian Hubert Schmidt noted that John Ten Eyck, a farmer from Somerset County, New Jersey, continued to cut his grass with a scythe and his wheat with a scythe and cradle until 1854, even though his father, James Ten Eyck, Jr., had been one of the inventors of a harvesting machine thirty years earlier.[82] And in 1860 Ralph Voorhees also of Somerset cut part of his wheat "with a machine," but he also had men working with scythes and cradles.[83]

The Dutch wagon in the late sixteenth century, according to folklorist J. Geraint Jenkins, had two pairs of narrow tired, eight-spoke wheels; the rear wheels were usually larger than the front wheels. The body had a deep front board, a somewhat less deep tailboard, and vertical wooden spindles on the sides. Its curved toprail gave it a distinctive profile. It was drawn by two draft horses. Similar wagons were found in England during the sixteenth and seventeenth centuries, but Jenkins believes that the English farm wagon was a cultural borrowing, if not from the Dutch, from the continental wagons. However, the continental wagon normally had four small wheels of equal size, a V-shaped body, and unboarded sides of long spindles.[84]

J. Geraint Jenkins states that the earliest wheeled vehicles were probably two-wheeled ox carts with a center draft pole, known to have existed circa 3,000 B.C. in the Middle and Near East. Four-wheeled wagons with two side shafts for horses appear to have developed in central Germany during the Late Bronze Age. The earliest wagons seemed to have been made by joining together two triangular-framed carts end to end. Jenkins theorizes that the coupling pole that joins the forecarriage and the rear carriage of all European wagons may be a survival of the central draft pole of the rear ox cart. An ox pushed against a yoke over its shoulders, whereas a horse pushed against a collar against its neck. Two curved wooden projections, called hames, were attached to the collar; and two straps of harness, called traces, extended from the collar to chains attached to pivoting swinging bars, known as whiffletrees or whippletrees in western New England, upstate New York, and northwestern Pennsylvania; swingletrees or singletrees in the South and Midlands; and swiveltrees in central New Jersey. These were attached to the doubletree on the tongue of the wagon. Later wagons had draft poles instead of a tongue.[85]

According to Jenkins, the culture area of the cart was restricted to the fringes of Europe, including most of France, the Mediterranean countries, and Scandinavia. The wagon spread from Central Europe to the North European Plain and replaced the cart along the northern part of Mediterranean Europe and the southern part of Scandinavia. The wagon culture area included the mid-continent, including Flanders, the Netherlands, Germany, Poland, and Russia. In some areas both carts and wagons were used. For example, in part of France carts were used to transport dung and root crops and wagons were used for hay and corn. In Picardy wagons carried root crops and large carts hauled hay and grain. The wagon was used exclusively in Poland, Czechoslovakia, Hungary, Austria, and Germany, except for a small region in the Lower Rhine Basin, where the northern European cart was used. In the Netherlands, the wagon was used extensively, except for a narrow strip running from the Frisian Islands, through Gelderland, North Utrecht, and Limburg into eastern Belgium, where the

European cart replaced the wagon in the eighteenth and nineteenth centuries. Carts were used throughout France, except for some isolated regions. Jenkins thinks that the wagon was introduced to Britain by way of the Netherlands. The cart was used for all farm transport in the northern and western parts of Britain. The wagon was limited to southeastern Britain, where it was used to transport hay and corn sheaves, while the cart continued to be used for dung, gravel, and sand. Jenkins thinks that the large road wagon was not suited for farm work in England until the mid-eighteenth century and the enclosure of open fields.[86]

Wagons appear in seventeenth-century New Netherland. While they were not described in any detail, we can only assume that they were Dutch wagons. The inventory of equipment belonging to Andries Hudde and Wolphert Gerritsen at their farm named Achtervelt in 1638 included "one new wagon and appurtenance."[87] The 1643 inventory for the farm named Vredendael mentions "1 wagon, nearly new," while the 1651 inventory of the estate of Jan Jansen Damen mentions "one wagon and its appurtenances, nearly worn out."[88] A 1679 lease for a farm at Schenectady included among the farm equipment to be furnished by the landlord "four wagons in good repair, of which two are to have ironwork complete, one is to have iron axles without bushings, and one is to be a wooden wagon."[89]

There is also pictorial evidence for the existence of the Dutch farm wagon in America. Stokes *Iconography of Manhattan Island* contains a picture dated 1679–80 depicting such a wagon with the notation: "The wagon seen between these two mills is the first representation that we know of a horse drawn vehicle on Manhattan."[90] The portrait of Abraham Wendell painted about 1737 in the collection of the Albany Institute of History and Art also shows a Dutch wagon. And the Van Bergen Overmantel, a folk painting of the Marten Gerritsen van Bergen farm near Leeds, New York, painted about 1735, shows a Dutch wagon loaded with four bags of grain.[91]

A 1750 newspaper advertisement for the auction of the farm of Jacob Van Winckle of Aquackanonk (Passaic), New Jersey, mentions that "also at the said Time and Place, will be sold at publick Vendue, Horses, Cows, Sheep, and Hogs, and all sorts of Utensils for farming, a Dutch Waggon, and Turner's Tools, and several sorts of Household

Goods, &c."[92] Hector St. John de Crevecoeur described the Dutch wagons of Orange County, New York, in the 1760s.

You have often admired our two-horse wagons. They are extremely well-contrived and executed with a great deal of skill; and they answer with ease and dispatch all the purposes of a farm. A well-built wagon, when loaded, will turn in a very few feet more than its length, which is 16 feet, including the length of the tongue. We have room in what is called their bodies to carry five barrels of flour. We commonly put in them a ton of hay, and often more. . . . We can carry 25 green oak rails, two-thirds of a cord of wood, 3,000 pounds of dung. In short, there is no operation that ought to be performed on a farm but what is easily accomplished with one of these. We can lengthen them as we please, and bring home the body of a tree 20 or 30 feet long. We commonly carry with them thirty bushels of wheat and at 60 pound to the bushel this makes a weight of 1,800 pounds, with which we can go 40 miles a day with two horses. . . .

On a Sunday it becomes the family coach. We then take off the common, plain sides and fix on it others which are handsomely painted. The after-part, on which either our names or ciphers are delineated, hangs back suspended by neat chains. If it rains, flat hoops made on purpose are placed in mortises, and painted cloth is spread and tied over the whole. Thus equipped, the master of the family can carry six persons either to church or to meetings. When the roads are good we can easily travel seven miles an hour. In order to prevent too great shakings, our seats are suspended on wooden springs, — a simple but very useful mechanism. These inventions and (this) neatness we owe to the original Dutch settlers. . . .

The Dutch build them with timber which has been previously three years under water and then gradually seasoned.[93]

In 1794 William Strickland wrote about the Dutch wagons in New Jersey: "The people sit on benches going across the wagon, which has in general no awning or covering. A fat Dutchman and his fat wife, and two or three clumsy sons and daughters may frequently be seen thus driven and jolted by a not less fat negroe Slave."[94]

Thus, if Jenkins is right about the English farm wagon being derived from the Dutch wagon, then the Conestoga wagon, which became the famed covered wagon of the American West, was derived from the Dutch wagon by way of the English wagon. With its large rear wheels, the Conestoga wagon is more like the English wagon than the German continental wagon, which had four small wheels.[95]

In conclusion, Dutch-American farming was a mixed agricultural tradition with a distinct market orientation from an early date. Thus, it was a combination of the market-oriented, livestock agriculture of the western provinces and the self-sufficient, arable agriculture of the eastern provinces. Soon, however, differences from the Old World traditions developed in crops and livestock as Dutch breeds of livestock and strains of crops were mixed with English breeds and strains, and new crops, such as maize, pumpkins and squash, were borrowed from the American Indians. The use of both horses and oxen as draft animals located the Dutch-American culture area midway between New England and Pennsylvania. Certain Dutch tools and equipment, such as the hog plow, the sith, the mathook, and the Dutch wagon, continued to be used into the nineteenth century. Thus, Dutch-American farming, like the rest of Dutch-American culture, was a mixture of Dutch, English and American Indian elements.

CHAPTER 5

Family

In recent years there has been much scholarly interest in the history of the family in Europe and America. Much attention has been paid to the colonial farm families in Virginia and Massachusetts.[1] Less attention has focused on the Dutch-American farm family in New York and New Jersey.[2] Furthermore, few studies of the American farm family have attempted to relate it to the family structures of Europe and the British Isles.

Historians and sociologists classify family structure according to the makeup of the household. In the *nuclear family* the household consists of the husband, wife, and their offspring. In the *extended family* it consists of the husband, wife, and one or more married children. Two subtypes of the extended family are: the *stem family*, which consists of the husband, wife, and one married child and his or her spouse; and the *joint family*, which consists of the husband, wife, and two or more married children and their spouses or several married siblings living together in one household.

Until recently it was thought that the extended family characterized European and American family structure until the advent of the Industrial Revolution. This view, however, has been shown to be in error by studies indicating that the nuclear family antedates the Industrial Revolution in both Europe and America.[3] In her book, *The Dutch Family in Seventeenth and Eighteenth Centuries*, historian Bertha Mook writes that "the nuclear family had already begun to among the well-to-do in the seventeenth century; it became a more dominant family form towards the later part of the eighteenth century."[4] Furthermore, she states that "in the lower class, and possibly for the majority of the Dutch people, the old conditions of the extended family closely integrated within the neighborhood still prevailed."[5] She bases her conclusions on literary and artistic sources, which tend to reflect the middle and upper classes, and she defends her approach by stating that "the urban burghers were the leading group" and that "the farmers formed a separate but inconsequential group."[6] As we have seen, such an approach distorts the Dutch-American experience, which was drawn significantly from the rural European traditions.

Furthermore, while there were class differences in family structure, the nuclear family was common in rural areas both in England and on the continent. Historian Peter Laslett estimates that the percentage of extended-family households was only 8 percent in 1599 in the town of Ealing in Middlesex, England; only 17 percent in 1778 in Longuenesse in Pas-de-Calais, France; only 10 percent in 1687 in the town of Loffingen in Wurtemburg, Germany; only 5 percent in 1720 in Lesnica in Silesia, Poland; only 29 percent in 1733–34 in Belgrade, Serbia; and only 3 percent in 1689 in Bristol, Rhode Island.[7] He concludes that

in all the communities we are comparing, households of any form more complex than the simple family were in a minority, and a tiny minority in Ealing and Bristol; in fact, the classic nuclear family of man, wife, and children formed the household, with or without servants, in more than half of the Western European cases, and in a third of the others.[8]

Other historians argue that Laslett underestimates the incidence of the joint and stem families in Europe. Lutz Berkner and Robert Wheaton note that the extended family pertains only to certain stages of the life cycle of the family, that is, when the children are old enough to marry and the grandparents are still alive. Thus, the percentage of extended families at any one time fails to include those families that may have gone through an extended-family phase at some time during the life cycle of the family.[9] Furthermore, the extended family in Europe was associated with one class—the peasants. Statistics that group together the peasants with laborers, servants, and craftsmen tend to dilute the percentage of extended families. Berkner points out that Laslett's own figures on England show that 8 percent of the laborers had extended families as opposed to 7 percent of the yeoman farmers.[10]

There is also a geographical dimension to the topic, since the extended family was more common in some culture areas than in others. Berkner notes that the joint family tended to be common among the Slavic peoples of eastern Europe and the stem family tended to be predominant among the Germanic and Latin peoples of western Europe.[11] Robert Wheaton maintains that the joint family today existed until recently in a belt running from the Baltic Sea to the Balkan Peninsula. In some parts of Latvia, Finland, Estonia, Russia, Hungary, Serbia, Macedonia, and Albania, he states, the joint family was common at least into the nineteenth century.[12] One exception to this rule was the existence in southern France in the fourteenth century of a joint family subtype known as the *frereche*, which consisted of several couples of married siblings. However, as Wheaton cautions, this particular family type was a temporary response to the demographic crisis caused by the Great Plague, rather than an enduring family structure.[13]

Even within the Netherlands there was geographic variation in the makeup of the household. In the seventeenth and eighteenth centuries significant differences existed in household structure between the eastern provinces of the Netherlands as opposed to the northern and western provinces. A. M. van der Woude cites a study of the province of Overijssel in 1749 showing that 20.5 percent of the households were extended families. When this figure is broken down to distinguish between the villages and the countryside, the percentage of extended families was 15.3 percent in the villages and 22.6 percent in the countryside. Another study of the district of Veluwe in 1749 showed that the percentage of extended families was only 5 percent in the towns and 7 percent in the countryside. In one community in the province of Friesland in 1744 only 8 percent of the households were extended families. While he doesn't have percentages, van der Woude infers from a mean household size of 3.7 during the period 1622–1795 that the nuclear family must have predominated in Noorderkwartier in the province of Holland.[14] In the eastern provinces, it was the custom for newly married couples to live with the parents of one spouse. Even as recently as the 1950s, 18 out of 60 households in the

agricultural town of Anderen in the province of Drenthe had trigenerational families, consisting of one or both grandparents living
under the same roof with their children or grandchildren.[15]

However, as Berkner notes, the household is not always the same
as the family; the household might include such nonfamily members
as servants and lodgers. A servant was a person employed by the
family who received food and shelter as part of his or her wages. A
lodger was also a resident in the household, but he or she was not
usually a steady employee and had to pay for lodgings. Berkner notes
that servants were not necessarily a separate class, because the children, especially the daughters, of landed peasants were put out as
servants in other families.[16] The practice of putting out children as
servants in other households was more common in the eastern provinces of the Netherlands than in the western provinces. Van der
Woude estimates that the percentage of the population that was servants was 12 percent in Overijssel, 14 percent in the Veluwe, 9.4
percent in Friesland, and 5.9 percent in Noorderkwartier.[17]

Van der Woude sees the differences in family structure as correlated
to differences in the type of agriculture. In the eastern provinces and
in western Europe generally arable farming predominated. Cattle were
kept primarily for manure. Only production surpluses were sent to
market, and the household was mostly self-supporting. But in Holland, western Utrecht, and southwestern Friesland, dairying and livestock production predominated. Milk, butter, cheese, and cattle were
produced almost exclusively for market, which presupposes a mone-
tary economy and precludes self-sufficient families. Also livestock production is labor extensive, requiring little manpower. Since the farms
were generally small or medium-sized, there was no room for large
households with numerous servants and relatives.[18]

Other factors, such as settlement patterns and domestic architecture, affect family structure. According to Berkner, in central Europe,
parents living with a married child in a stem family often had a
separate retirement house known as an *Ausnahmshausel*. In the Prussian
province of Silesia and the Austrian province of Styria, there were
separate buildings some distance from the main farmhouse and often
on a separate parcel of land. But in the villages of the lower Austrian
Waldviertel, where the farmhouse, barn, stable, and sheds formed a

quadrangle around a central court, the retirement house, known as a *Stubl*, was located on one side of the main farmhouse, but separate from it. And in the Pays de Caux in Normandy, where the farmhouse, stable, barn, shed, and bakehouse were scattered throughout the enclosed parcel of land known as a *masure*, it is common for a widow to move into one of the sheds or the bakehouse or perhaps one room of the farmhouse.[19]

There is also a link between family structure and inheritance patterns. According to Berkner, those societies that had primogeniture (all the land was inherited by one son and other kinds of property were divided among the other siblings) tended to have stem families. Those societies that had partible inheritance (all the property was divided among the offspring equally) tended to have either joint or nuclear families. Under the lineage property system (the spouses maintained separate rights over whatever property they brought to the marriage), the eldest son was not required to stay at home to become an heir; he could not marry within the paternal household until the father died or decided to retire. Under the community property system, in which both spouses merged their property into a joint fund owned by both, the heir had to remain within the paternal household to inherit the farm; any children who left with a portion of his inheritance was excluded from the rest of the inheritance. Thus, according to Berkner, community property encouraged the stem family, and the lineage system encouraged the nuclear family.[20]

Emmanuel Le Roy Ladurie, the French historian, divided sixteenth century France into three culture areas based on inheritance custom. Preference legacy (one descendant inherited all the land) was common in the southern half of France and among the Walloons in Picardy and Belgium. The entire estate was divided equally among the heirs in western France (Normandy, Anjou, and Brittany) and among the Flemings in Flanders. This culture area had an inheritance custom known as "forced return," according to which all gifts given to the offspring prior to the death of the parent had to be returned.[21] Thus, in Flanders the tendency was toward the lineage property holdings, partible inheritance, and the nuclear family; in the Walloon provinces the system favored community property, primogeniture, and the stem family.

Finally, the household structure cannot be separated from the kinship system. Robert Wheaton suggests that societies with joint families and primogenitive tended also to have patrilinear kinship systems (kinship affiliation through the father's side of the family).[22] Thus, the extended family tended to be associated with primogeniture, the lineage system of property, and patrilinear kinship; the nuclear family with partible inheritance, community property and bilateral kinship.

When the above information about European family structure is combined with information about the places of origin of seventeenth-century Dutch settlers in New Netherland, we see that they came from different family traditions. Approximately 60 percent of the Dutch settlers came from those culture areas where the extended family was common. But only one-third of the Dutch settlers were from farming backgrounds. Assuming that the occupational distribution was equally distributed thoughout the culture areas, this would have meant that approximately one-fifth of the overall population would have come from the extended family tradition. More likely, however, this figure would have been higher, because the percentage of farmers would have been higher in those areas where the extended family was common, that is, predominantly agricultural areas.

Even though they came from regions in Europe with different family and inheritance patterns, a distinct Dutch-American family tradition emerged in America. Seventeenth-century ante-nuptial agreements show that the practice that became the rule among the Dutch in America was community property. For example, the ante-nuptial agreement of March 1, 1675, between Pieter Meuse Vrooman and Volkie Pieters in the court minutes of Albany, Rensselaerswyck, and Schenectady provided that the husband and wife "for the support of this marriage contributed and bring together all such present property and effects . . . which each of them has or is entitled to [and] possess the same in common."[23]

Furthermore, as historian David Narrett has noted, not only did the husband and wife own all property in common, they usually executed a mutual will, in which the wife inherited all property on the death of her husband. This Dutch custom was known as *boedelhouderschap*, this is, the retention of the estate or *boedel* by the widowed party. The children would not inherit the property until after the death of both their parents. In rural Ulster County, Narrett states, the widow needed her sons to work on the farm, and in some cases the sons actually leased the farm from their mother. However, if the widow remarried, the Dutch custom in America was to divide half the estate to the remarried widow and the other half among the children. This inheritance pattern was not the custom in New England. Under English common law, the wife became part of her husband. The husband upon marriage acquired full ownership of his wife's property. After the English conquest of New Netherland, English common law replaced Dutch custom. However, the Dutch inheritance patterns persisted for at least another generation in New York City and well into the eighteenth century in the rural areas of upstate New York. Narrett notes that the wealthy merchants tended to adopt the English inheritance customs more readily than the lower classes.[24]

A court battle cited by Narrett reveals the struggle between custom and individual desire. Igenas Dumon (Dumont) was a farmer from the rural area near Kingston, New York. In his will dated 1737, he provided that upon his death his wife, Catherine, should inherit his entire estate regardless of whether she remarried. His father, however, objected, arguing that his son's wife should have the farm only as long as she remained a widow. After his death, Igenas's wife remarried in 1741, and the will was contested in 1748 on the grounds that Igenas Dumon couldn't have intended to ignore local custom by allowing his remarried wife to retain possession of the entire estate. The court ruled in favor of his wife.[25]

Partible inheritance became the dominant pattern among the Dutch-Americans. For example, the will of Jacques Cortelyou dated 1693 provided that his sons, Jacques and Pieter, were to have the front end of his plantation named Najack, lying in New Utrecht, and his daughters, Helena and Maria, were to have the rear end of his plantation.[26] This tradition of dividing the estate equally among all the children, male and female, was called the custom of *Gavelkind*. Charles Wooley described it in 1701:

The Dutch in New York observe this custom, an instance of which I remember in one Frederick Philips, the richest *Mijn Heer* in that place, who was said to have whole Hogsheads of Indian Money or Wampam, who having one Son and Daughter, I was admiring what a heap of Wealth the Son would enjoy, to which a Dutch man replied that the Daughter must to halves, for so was the manner amongst them, they standing more upon Nature than Names; that as the root communicates itself to all its branches, so should the Parent to all his off-spring, which are the Olive branches round his Table.[27]

In fact, in his will, dated 1749, Frederick Philips bequeathed his manor at Philipsburgh to his oldest son "during his life, and after his death to his first-born son and his heirs male in succession forever." He divided a large, but less valuable, tract of land equally between his other son and three daughters. Each of his children received a house and lot in New York City.[28]

David Narrett contrasts the Dutch-American custom of partible inheritance to the English practice of primogeniture, under which the entire estate was inherited by the eldest son if the father died intestate (without a will). After 1683, primogeniture became the law in New York. Although the Dutch opposed primogeniture, Narrett notes that they often acknowledged in their wills that the eldest son deserved special treatment.[29] For example, when Marten Gerritsen van Bergen drew up his will in 1690, he willed his entire estate to his wife, Neeltje Mynders, except for fifty acres of land at Coxsackie, which he be-queathed to his sister's son, Claes Ziverse. When his youngest son, Myndert van Bergen, reached the age of majority or married, all his land, except the family farm, was to be equally divided among his children. The family farm was to be kept by his widow, and after her death his eldest son, Gerrit van Bergen, was to inherit it "in acknowl-edgement of his right of primogeniture." But Gerrit had to pay his brother, Myndert, two hundred pieces of eight in compensation.[30] Thus, van Bergen reconciled the English right of primogeniture with the Dutch custom of partible inheritance. However, William Mc-Laughlin notes that in Flatbush the principal heir who inherited the family farm was often the youngest son, because the estate often went to the oldest son living at home. Since the older sons usually left the home to set up their own families prior to the death of the father, this often meant the youngest son inherited the family farm. But he would have to reimburse the older brothers and sisters for their rights.[31]

As a consequence of partible inheritance, the estates got smaller and smaller with each generation. In 1794 William Strickland described how this resulted in Bergen County, New Jersey, in a loss of status for some families.

The country through which I have passed in the course of this expedition was formerly the property of great Dutch families, but in consequence of the division of property during several generations, it is now held almost entirely by small proprietors, who occupy it. The great families are either gone elsewhere, or are no longer in opulent circumstances. Except some good houses in Newark, I saw few or more which were likely to be inhabited by anyone above the rank of farmer.[32]

But this was not the case with all families. Those parents who could afford it bought land elsewhere for their other children to settle on, as can be seen in the case of Marten Gerritsen van Bergen mentioned above. According to McLaughlin, this tradition of neolocal residence contrasted to a pattern of patrilocal residence in New England. It resulted in a diffusion of the Dutch population he studied in Flatbush into Monmouth and Somerset counties in New Jersey and into parts of Pennsylvania and Delaware.[33] In 1708, Lord Cornbury, writing to the Lords of Trade, noted that

many are Removed lately, especially from King's County on Long Island; and the reasons why they remove are two kinds: The first is because King's County is but small and full of people, so as the young people grow up, they are forced to seek land further off, to settle upon; the land in the Eastern Division of New Jersey is good, and not very far from King's County, there is only a bay to crosse: The other reason that induces them to remove into New Jersey is because there they pay no taxes, nor no duties. . . .[34]

McLaughlin contrasts the relative independence afforded the children under the Dutch inheritance system, under which children were encouraged to establish their own nuclear families, to the situation in New England described by Philip Greven. In studying the family structure in Andover, Massachusetts, over four generations from 1650 to 1800, Greven found that in the first and second generations the fathers maintained control over their sons by delaying the transfer of property until after the fathers' deaths. This resulted in delayed marriages and extended families. But in the third generation these patriarchal controls loosened as fathers allowed sons to purchase their inheritances prior to the fathers' deaths.[35]

Another area of difference between Dutch-American and New England inheritance customs was that, while both practiced partible inheritance, the Dutch-Americans divided their estates equally among their sons and daughters, while the New Englanders tended to will land to their sons and provide their daughters with dowries, consisting of livestock, furniture, or money. According to Narrett, by the early eighteenth century, the Dutch began to acculturate to the English system. He found that in the seventeenth century the farmers in Ulster County divided their land among their sons and daughters, according to Dutch-American custom. But by the 1730s they willed all or most of their land to their sons, who in turn compensated their sisters for the value of the land.[36] By then, Narrett writes, "bearing a Dutch name no longer meant that the head of the household would almost invariably dispose of his property in a particular manner."[37] However, Narrett cautions, this was not merely the result of a decline in Dutch customs; both the Dutch-Americans and New Englanders were placing more emphasis on the rights of children.[38] But only the sons benefitted; wives and daughters fared better under the Dutch-American inheritance system.

Free blacks who lived in the Dutch culture area of New York and New Jersey adopted the Dutch-American inheritance pattern. Augustine van Donck II was a free black farmer who lived in the Hackensack Valley of New Jersey. In his will dated June 4, 1774, he bequeathed his entire farm to his wife, Rachel, the southwest fourth for her to have during her lifetime and the remaining three-fourths for her to have "during the time she shall continue [his] widow." After her death or remarriage, the northeast quarter of his farm was to go to his daughter Sophia; the southeast quarter to his daughter Annaitje; and the northwest quarter to be equally divided between his grandchildren, John, Augustine, Lewis, and Rachel.[39] This will demonstrates that both the Dutch-American customs of *boedelhouderschap* and *Gavelkind* survived longer among free blacks than among the Dutch themselves.

Like the New England family, the Dutch-American family tended to be large and nuclear, consisting of mother, father, and unmarried children. In 1744 Dr. Alexander Hamilton, the Scottish traveler, noted that the family of a Dutch farmer named Kaen Buiklaut consisted of eighteen children.[40] But at any one time, the number of children living at home was considerably smaller, because either the parents were young and just beginning to have children or the parents were old and some of the older children had married and moved away. A list of inhabitants of the town of Southampton, Long Island, in 1698 shows fourteen Dutch families, whose average size was 4.6 persons.[41] In 1702, the average number of children per Dutch household in Orange County, New York, was 2.6.[42] The average number of children per household in Flatlands in 1800 was 2.9.[43] While the nuclear family tended to be the rule, there were some trigenerational households. In 1786, Alexander Coventry described a Dutch family in upstate New York: "Tobias Legat house and homestead. His mother and Batzie (Miss Betsy Legat, a niece of Mr. Jacobus Legat) live with him. This is customary among the Dutch. Jacobus (Legat) has a wife and six children."[44]

It was also common for the farm household to include servants and slaves. During the colonial period, the Dutch, like their English neighbors, "put out" their children as servants in other households. A formal indenture was signed that spelled out the rights and obligations of both servant and master. This applied to girls as well as boys. In an indenture dated September, 1674, Barentie Stratsman, wife of Jacob Jansz Gardenier, "put out" her daughter, Johanna, in the household of Richard and Elizabeth Pretty. Johanna was then "over eight years old," and the period of her indenture was for eight years. The Prettys promised "to bring up the said girl . . . in the fear of the Lord as if she were their own child, to teach her to read, to keep her clothing, as well as woolen and linen." At the end of her period of indenture, the Prettys promised to provide her "with a new black grossgrained mantle and a black apron, a new skirt, three new chemises, three new aprons, a pair of new shoes and a pair of new stockings and furthermore other trifles which may be needful for her body, together with her old clothes which she then may have." In return, Barentie Stratsman promised that "this girl (with the help of God Almighty) shall serve out the aforesaid time with all diligence and faithfulness and that the said employers shall be to her as a father and mother and have the right to properly punish her for wrongdoing and disobedience, giving them full power to do so and trusting them to do all that is good."[45]

The comparison of the master-servant relationship to that of the parent and child suggests that children "put out" as servants were considered part of the household.

The indentures for boys differed little from those for girls. In 1677 Elisabeth de Honneur bound her ten-year-old son, Abraham Jansen, to Gerrit Visbeeck. The indenture stated that young Abraham will "perform all proper labor to the best of his ability with all diligence and faithfulness for the time of eight consecutive years, which time began on Amsterdam Fair-day 1677, and is to end on Amsterdam Fair-day 1685." In return, Gerrit Visbeeck promised "to furnish said youngster during said time with proper food and clothes, woolen and linen, to teach him to read and at the end of said term of service, besides his work day and Sunday suits, to give him a new suit of clothes, a new hat, a pair of stockings and shoes, six good new shirts, a cow three years old and six cravats."[46]

Despite the paternalistic attitude implicit in these indentures, the master-servant relationship was not necessarily always benign. Seventeenth-century court records show that it was not uncommon for servants to run away. In 1669, Peter van Alen sued Agniet, the wife of Leendert Philipsen, claiming that "he hired the defendant's son for one year and the boy without reason ran away from the farm. He demands that the boy shall reenter his service, as he is much handicapped, it being plowing season."[47] In some cases, the servant was evidently mistreated by his master. In 1669 Jan Alberts sued Albert Andriesz Bradt, claiming that "the defendant ill-treats his son by beating, cursing, and swearing at him, and that the latter earnestly complains that he can not live with him that way. He therefore demands wages for one year's service, such as a head-farmer is entitled to, as he has properly attended to his duties. He also requests payment for improvements, consisting of two new hay barracks."[48]

In addition to servants, the Dutch-American farm family in New York and New Jersey also had slaves within the household. New York and New Jersey did not abolish slavery until the early nineteenth century, and in both cases it was a gradual abolition. Only the children born to slave parents in 1804 or after were to be freed in New Jersey. Thus there were still some slaves in New Jersey at the outbreak of the Civil War. In 1787 Alexander Coventry visited some Dutch farm families in the vicinity of Coxsackie, New York, and noted that "each individual family had more or less black slaves who did all the work on the farm, and in the house."[49] Seven years later, William Strickland traveled through the same region and described the slaves of the Dutch farmers as follows:

Many of the old Dutch farmers in the county has 20 or 30 slaves about their house. To their care and management every thing is left; the oldest slave manages the lands, directs the cultivation of it and without consulting him the master can do nothing; he is in fact in general the more intelligent of the two; and so the master can exist in the enjoyment of contentment and ease, he is content to become the slave of this slave; nothing can exceed the state of indolence and ignorance in which these Dutchmen are described to live. Many of them are supposed to live and die without having been five miles from their own houses, unless compelled at any time to go to Albany or to their county town upon public business. I have several times called at Dutch houses to make inquiries, when the owner unable, though otherwise willing, to give the information, has called for Con, or Frank, his oldest slave to answer my questions, or point out the road to the place I was going not perhaps distant more than a very few miles.[50]

Generally, the slaves lived either in the garret above the kitchen, in the cellar, or in a separate slave quarters. Many of them were culturally Dutch—having Dutch names, speaking the Dutch language, and observing Dutch customs.[51] In most cases, the Dutch farmers had only one to five slaves, and there is evidence that the slaves lived in family units. McLaughlin notes that in 1698 slaves made up 15 percent of the population of Flatbush. Almost half the households owned slaves, and the largest number of slaves owned by a single family was five. Of the seventy-one slaves listed only twelve were the only slaves in the household, twenty were on farms with two slaves, and thirty-nine were on farms with three or more slaves. In 1738, only six black children under 10 years of age lived with a single older slave, a woman in each case. The other thirty-nine black children in Flatbush (80 percent) lived with at least two older slaves.[52]

The farm diary of Adriance Van Brunt, who had a farm near Brooklyn, provides a good picture of the work force on a typical Dutch-American family farm during the early nineteenth century. In the year 1828 his household consisted of himself, his wife, and his two daughters, Jane and Maria. In addition, he listed what he called his "kitchen family," which consisted of two hired men, Frank and Michel, who worked for him for $25 per year; three "bound boys" (indentured servants) named Robert, William, and Harry; two hired women, "Old Susan" and Isabelle; Isabelle's two children; and a bound girl named Nancy. Also, he hired four "Jersey-men" (John Dye Walling by the the year, John W. Walling by the month, Manuel Walling by the month, and Daniel Holmes by the month), two blacks (Dick by the month and Sam by the month), and one Virginian (William Walker by the month). He also hired five girls from "Jersey" to pick peas by the bushel. The total, he notes was "25 the Whole Number in the family."[53] It is significant that he included his own nuclear family and the hired help within his concept of the family.

The status of an unmarried woman in this rural society of nuclear families was uncertain. The nineteenth-century diary of Margaret Ten Eyck from North Branch, New Jersey, provides a good picture of how such a single woman had to fend for herself.

1 August. The last week I was quilting at Peggy Cox for Ellen. I quilted 4 days. September 22, 1838. Margaret Cox paid me 5 Dollars. She owes me 5 yet. She paid Dow[n] 2 dollars for me. March 19, 1837. I was at Mr. Timbrooks 3 days a quilting and at Mrs. Farratts 3 days. May 1, 1838—settled with Margaret Ten Eyk all accounts this day by me. I paid my Brother James 48 for my Board. James Ten Eyk 30 dollars interest he owed me and 10 I paid Easter accounts 75 cents. He gave me a note of 12 Dollars and a Bank note of 7 Dollars. I was abroad 24 weeks out of the year 1837.[54]

Margaret Ten Eyck was what was known as a "Spinster." She made her living from spinning, quilting, and sewing. She was continuously boarding out at different farm families. Even when she stayed with her brother's family at the place she called "home," she had to pay room and board.

The Dutch-American kinship system was bilateral, that is, relatives on both the maternal and paternal side of the family were recognized as kin. The naming system had both patrilinear and bilateral aspects. Instead of fixed surnames, the Dutch had patronymics, which literally means "father's names." In addition to his Christian name, the child took the name of his father with the addition of the suffix *son*, *sen*, *se*, or *s*, which means literally "son of." For example, Hendrick's son,

Teunis, would be named Teunis Hendrickson. Thus, the patronymic would change in each generation.

The patronymic naming system was applied to daughters as well as to sons. However, the daughter would take as her patronymic the Christian name of her father, not that of her mother. Thus, Gerrtie Brants and Lysbeth Brants were daughters of Brant Peelen van Nykerck. The fact that the daughter took the patronymic of her father indicates a degree of patrilinear descent within this bilateral naming system. On the other hand, Dutch-American women did not adopt their husband's patronymic upon marriage. Instead they continued to use their father's patronymic. Both Narrett and McLaughlin see this as a reflection of the communal property custom among Dutch-Americans.[55] By the mid-eighteenth century the Dutch-Americans in New York and New Jersey began to adopt English naming customs. They started using fixed surnames, and married women began to adopt the surnames of their husbands.

The naming of children also reflected the bilateral kinship system. The first son was named after the paternal grandfather, the second son after the maternal grandfather. The first daughter was named after the paternal grandmother, and the second daughter after the maternal grandmother. When a child died young, the next child born of the same sex was named after the deceased child. This took precedence over naming children after paternal and maternal relatives.[56]

There was a kind of fictive kinship involved in the godparent relationship. This too reflected a bilateral kinship system. When Jeremias van Rensselaer, the son of a Kiliaen van Rensselaer, the patroon of Rensselaerswyck, baptised his first son, Kiliaen, born in 1663, he chose his father-in-law, Oloff Stevensen van Cortlandt, as one godfather and his brother, Jan Baptist as another; he chose his mother and his mother-in-law as godmothers. Since neither his father-in-law, his brother, his mother-in-law, nor his mother could attend the baptism in person, he had stand-ins for them all.[57] When his fourth son, Joannes, was born in 1670, he again chose his father-in-law as one godfather and his uncle, Johan van Weely, as the other.[58] Thus, he made a conscious attempt to balance the godparent relationships so as to represent both the paternal and maternal sides of the family.

In summary, Dutch-Americans came from different culture areas in Europe with different inheritance patterns and different family structures. People from a tradition of nuclear families, partible inheritance, communal property, and bilateral kinship came in contact with people from a tradition of extended families, primogenture, linear property, and patrilinear kinship. The structure that emerged as the dominant Dutch-American family was the former. However, the dominant influence of the English lead to the gradual abandonment of communal property and the patronymic naming system by the early eighteenth century.

CHAPTER 6

Folklore and Folklife

Washington Irving has indelibly influenced the popular conception of Dutch-American folklore and folklife. He viewed the Dutch farmers of New York as quaint, isolated, and outside the mainstream of American life. In "The Legend of Sleepy Hollow," he wrote that

it is in such little retired Dutch valleys, found here and there embosomed in the great State of New York, that population, manners, and customs remain fixed; while the great torrent of migration and improvement, which is making such incessant changes in other parts of this restless country, sweeps by them unobserved.[1]

However, Irving's portrayal of the Dutch-American people and culture of the Hudson Valley is a comic stereotype, rather than an accurate picture. This stereotype infused Irving's view of Dutch-American folklore. He depicted "the old Dutch wives" and "their tales of ghosts and goblins, and haunted fields, and haunted brooks, and haunted bridges, and haunted houses, and particularly of the headless horseman, or galloping Hessian of the Hollow, as they sometimes called him."[2] Much of his "folklore" was drawn from German and other European written sources, rather than from Dutch-American oral tradition.[3] Thus, his writings are a source of information about Anglo-American attitudes toward the Dutch, rather than an authentic collection of Dutch-American folklore.

Today, little remains of Dutch-American folklore and folklife in New York and New Jersey, but it is possible to reconstruct from

149

written sources some of the Dutch traditions that survived through the end of the nineteenth century. Much of this folklore reflects Dutch-American farm life. In part this is because folk traditions tend to survive longer in isolated areas; in part it is because the urban merchants were more prone to adopt Anglo-American traditions. Contrary to Irving's image of a static folk tradition, there were many changes in the folklore and folklife that mirror the same cultural processes at work in other aspects of Dutch-American culture—cultural borrowings, survivals, and the emergence of a distinct Dutch-American regional culture.

The spoken language was part of Dutch-American folklore and reflects the changes that occurred in the culture. At the founding of New Netherland, numerous languages were spoken, because of the various places of origin of the settlers. In 1646 Father Isaac Joques observed that "on this Island of Manhate and its environs there may be four or five hundred men of different sects and nations; the Director General told me that there were persons there of eighteen different languages."[4] But Dutch was the dominant language and the dominant culture. After the English conquest of New Netherland in 1664, English became the official language of New York and New Jersey. Charles T. Gehring traced the changes that occurred in written Dutch in New York as a result of English influences. He documented examples of vocabulary borrowing and loan blends, especially in legal terminology, as, for example, *coerthuijs* (courthouse), *law sute* (law suit), and *justice van de peace* (justice of the peace). He also documented changes in the phonology (e.g., *vijf* became *vive*), morphology (e.g., English plurals, verb endings, and pronouns were introduced), and syntax (e.g., English word order). As English became the language of public life, Gehring stated, Dutch was relegated to the home.[5]

There was still much diversity of languages in New York in the eighteenth century. In 1785 Alexander Coventry wrote that "the farmers who came from the country . . . spoke in a different language called low Dutch. . . . The Low Dutch understood, and could talk English, though generally pronounced the 'th' as if 'd' or 'e.' But the language spoken by the well-bred was good English."[6] Linguists might argue with Coventry's distinction between "good" English and the dialect spoken by the Dutch; the important point, however, is that by this time the Dutch were bilingual.

By the nineteenth century two dialects developed. One was called "Jersey Dutch" or "Bergen County Dutch"; the other was "Hudson-Mohawk Dutch." The spoken language was called *Leeg Duits* in the Jersey Dutch dialect and *Lag Duits* in the Mohawk Valley dialect. Both are translated by Van Cleaf Bachman as "Low Dutch" (as opposed to "High Dutch," which was the eighteenth-century American term for German). Bachman notes that the Mohawk dialect was often referred to as *de Taal* (literally, "the language").[7] According to John Dyneley Prince, Jersey Dutch "was originally the South Holland or Flemish language, which, in the course of centuries (ca. 1630–1860), became mixed with and partially influenced by English, having borrowed also from the Minsi (Lenape-Delaware) Indian language a few animal and plant names."[8] "Hudson-Mohawk Dutch" was similar to Jersey Dutch in syntax, but the two dialects were different in vocabulary. Jersey Dutch contained some Algonkian Indian words; Mohawk-Hudson Dutch had Iroquois loan words.[9] For example, the word for "raccoon" in Jersey Dutch was *hespaan*, but in Mohawk Dutch it was *suikerdas*.[10]

What Gehring showed about the structural changes in the written language was also true about these spoken dialects. L. G. Van Loon wrote that "some speakers of Hudson-Mohawk Dutch really knew so little 'Dutch' that they spoke a jargon of mispronounced American with a hybrid syntax and no more than a fair sprinkling of words of a real Dutch origin."[11] He gave as an example the expression *"Weet je dat joe* was where *je gheen* business *had?"* ("Do you know where you had no business?"). This blending of English and Dutch was not really a corruption; it was a normal part of the formation of a creole dialect.

There was even a separate dialect of Dutch spoken by blacks. According to John B. H. Storms, "even colored people, for the most part children of slaves, without education, were proficient in the use of Jersey Dutch and had enough knowledge of English to converse in either."[12] This was confirmed by John Dyneley Prince who noted that "the negro slaves of the old settlers used an idiom tinged with their own peculiarities."[13]

Spoken Dutch began to disappear in the nineteenth century. Reli-

gious services in the Dutch Reformed churches continued to be con-
ducted in Dutch through the middle of the nineteenth century, but
the ministers used an educated form of Dutch, rather than the folk
speech. Bachman states that the Dutch in which the domines (pastors)
preached was known as *Nederduits*, and it became increasingly incom-
prehensible to the speakers of Low Dutch. Because the domines wanted
to be understood by their parishioners, Bachman argues, the abandonment of Dutch in the church service preceded the demise of the spoken
language by eighty to ninety years.[14]

Bachman states that the spoken language died out in the cities
before it did in the country.

By the 1820s and 1830s Dutch was long dead in New York City, a memory of
the older generation in Albany, and rapidly fading even in many rural districts
with long rooted Dutch populations (e.g., Somerset and Monmouth Counties,
New Jersey, and Kings County, New York). The principal areas where
children were still learning the *Taal* at this time seem to have been the rural
areas of Bergen and Passaic Counties, New Jersey; Ulster County, New York;
and the lower Mohawk Valley.[15]

He quotes a late nineteenth-century source, named Walter Hill, de-
scribing how the Mohawk dialect was spoken mainly by farmers who
were reluctant to speak it among outsiders.

Hill observed that "if a stranger be among them who will attempt to speak *De
Tawl* and he be not as fluent as his listeners they will change, almost at once,
into English. Any deliberate attempt then, to learn the *Tawl* will be thwarted
at once." Hill's Low Dutch acquaintances never gave him a very satisfactory
explanation for this reticence, simply professing great surprise that any non-
Dutchman would ever want to learn their dialect. Hill was forced to infer that,
despite the fact that the Mohawk Dutch were "to a man, a prideful people,"
they were "ashamed of what they considered a sign of Boorishness" and felt
they would "be called 'Boor Dauits' *(Boer Duits)* or 'farmer' and so looked down
upon by their urban cousins.[16]

James B. H. Storms of Park Ridge, New Jersey, one of the last
speakers of Jersey Dutch, died in the 1940s. Today only a few expres-
sions and fragments of rhymes remain in oral tradition.

The same creolization of Dutch and English culture that is observ-
able in architecture and language was also evident in folk music and
folk dance. In 1787, while staying at a tavern near Catskill, New York,

Alexander Coventry observed that the Dutchmen from that region sang in both English and Dutch.

Mr. Dubois treated us with some wine, and while drinking it, hearing the sound of song in the adjoining room, we followed ye customs of ye country, and walked in. Mr. Demun from Esopus, was singing a Bagatelle, first he sang it in Dutch and then he sang it in English, then Peter Yates sang what is called "The Song." Though his voice is not the very best, he sang scientifically, then he sang "The Debtor," also several Dutch songs; some in particular which flowed very smoothly.[17]

Coventry also mentioned that the Dutch were fond of dancing reels, but he took offense at the manner in which they monopolized the dance floor. "We were disgusted with the Dutch manner," he wrote. "They danced reels in which only four can be up at once, and the Dutch when once on the floor, never want to sit down and thus excluding the rest from participating in the pleasures."[18] The reference to reels indicates a borrowing of the music and dance tradition of the British Isles. Further evidence for this cultural borrowing is seen in Coventry's 1802 description of an outing he took with Jeremiah van Rensselaer and the latter's two sisters. "When we came to the waggon again Mr. V. R. desired me to take a seat at his side, which I did and had the pleasure of hearing the young ladies sing a number of songs, of which several were Scottish."[19] Acculturation was even greater in New Jersey. In an oral history interview published in 1955, centenarian Margaret Van Brunt Moore Gausmann, who was born in 1839 of Dutch parents in Bergen County, stated that she knew numerous Anglo-American and native American ballads (the term used by folklorists for ballads composed in America), including "Roy's Wife of Aldivalloch," "Polly, Won't You Ki' Me, Oh," "The Battle of the Constitution and the Guerriere," "Jimmy Polk," "Yankee Doodle," "Poor Old Horse," and a cante fable (half song, half story) about the Battle of Tripoli.[20]

Notwithstanding these cultural borrowings from the Anglo-American folk music tradition, a Dutch folk song tradition survived in oral tradition through the end of the nineteenth century. Considering the fact that the Dutch traditions tended to survive longer in the country than in the city, it is not surprising that many of the surviving folk songs reflected agricultural life. One such song was *De Pruttelarij*

Voerman ("The Grumbling Wagoner"), which was collected and translated in 1907 in Ulster County, New York, by local historian Benjamin Myer Brink.

Eens had ik mijn wagen verhuurd en dat aan oude wijven,
Toen zij op de kermis kwamen, gingen zij aan't kijven;
Nooit meer wil ik het wagen, oude wijven in mijn wagen.
Rijdt wat an, wagen, wagen, rijdt wat an, voerman.

Once had I my wagon hired and that to old gossips,
Soon as they reached the fair, all began to scold;
No more will hire the wagon, have old hags in my wagon.
Ride on, wagon, wagon, ride on, wagoner.

The following verses include "old curmudgeons" *(oude mannen)* who began "to plot together," "old maids" *(oude dochters)* who began "to groan," "old lords" *(oude heeren)* who began "to swear." In each case the singer resolves never to take this group of people in his wagon again. But in the last verse he takes "young women" *(jonge dochters)* to the fair.

Eens had ik mijn wagen verhuurd, en dat aan jonge dochters.
Toen zij op de kermis kwamen werden zij al verkocht er;
Verkocht al hier, verkocht al daar,

Jonge dochters is goede waar;
Ik wil wel laden op mijn wagen van de jonge dochters.
Rijdt wat an, wagen, wagen, rijdt wat an, voerman.

Once had I my wagon hired, and that to young women;
Soon as they reached the fair, every one was taken;
Were purchased here, were purchased there,
Young women are good weather;
I will load up my wagon with young women.
Ride on, wagon, wagon, ride on, wagoner.[21]

This song was known both in America and in the Netherlands. According to historian Herbert Rowen, the Dutch version has an anticlerical point of view missing from the Dutch-American version. While the Dutch-American version makes reference to the Dutch wagon, which continued to be used well into the nineteenth century, the references to the agricultural fair *(kermis)*, a tradition that did not survive beyond the seventeenth century in America, suggests that the setting of the song was the Netherlands, not America. Thus, the song is a survival in the folk memory of the culture of the old country. The attitudes expressed toward the young women in the song depart from the strict Calvinist teachings of the Dutch Reformed Church, suggesting that the folk attitudes did not always correspond with the official doctrine of the church.

Children's folklore also survived through the end of the nineteenth century. It is ironic that some folklore learned the earliest survived the longest. Here too agricultural references abound. An example is the following lullaby from upstate New York:

Slaap, kindje, slaap!	Sleep, little one, sleep!
Daar buiten loopt een schapt!	Out of doors there runs a sheep!
Een schapt met witte voetjes;	A sheep with four white feet;
Dat drink zijn melk zoo zoetjes;	That drinks its milk so sweet;
Slaap, kindje, slaap! toe;	Sleep, little one, sleep! so;
Slaap, kindje, slaap.	Sleep, little one, sleep.[22]

Perhaps the most famous Dutch nursery rhyme was *"Trip a Trop a Troontjes,"* which was recited while the child was bounced on the adult's knee. One version goes as follows:

Trip a trop a troontjes,	Trip a trop a troontjes,
De varkens in de boontjes.	The pigs are in the bean vines.
De koetjes in de klaver,	The cows are in the clover blooms,
De paarden in de haver.	The horses in the oat fields;
De eenjes in de water-plas,	The ducks are in the waterpond,
De kalf in de lange grass;	The calf is in the long grass;
So grott mijn kleine poppetje was.	So tall my little baby was.[23]

This nursery rhyme was known far and wide. It was collected in Flatbush in 1887, in Ulster County in 1905, and in Bergen County in the 1950s. It has been traced to the Netherlands, and it is also known in South Africa.[24] There are some people descended from Jersey Dutch families who still remember the rhyme, thus making this example of children's folklore the last surviving fragment of Dutch-American folklore in the Dutch language.

In another nursery rhyme the child also was bounced on an older person's knee, while the following was recited:

Zoo rijden de Heeren,	So ride the fine Lords,
Met hun mooije kleeren.	With their handsome clothes.
Zoo rijden de vrouwen,	So ride the ladies,
Met hun bonte mouwen.	With their calico sleeves.

Dan komt de akkerman,	Then comes the farmer,
Met zijn paardjes toppertan.	With his horses tandem.
Hij drift voorbij nauw Amsterdam,	He drives them on to Amsterdam,
Met zijn koetsier achteran,	With his coachman behind.
Schoe, schoe paardjes,	Shoe, shoe the horses,
Met zijn vlossa staartjes,	With their flossy tails,
Draf, draf, draf.	Trot, trot, trot.[25]

Here again the farmer and his wagon are mentioned, but again it is not in an American context, because the farmer and his wagon are contrasted to the fine lords and proud ladies, reflecting the European social structure. This too should not be seen as a literal portrayal of Dutch-American culture, but rather a survival of the Old World in America. Thus it represents an identification with the roots of Dutch-American culture in Europe.

Besides references to farming in Dutch-American folklore, there was also a folklore of farming. In the eighteenth century Dutch-American farmers believed in planting by the signs of the moon. Each of the twelve signs of the Zodiac was associated with a planet, a symbol, an element, a sex, and a part of the body. Each day was associated with one of these signs. There was an elaborate system to determine on which date to plant or harvest specific crops. Colonial almanacs contained a diagram, known as the Man of Signs, which showed these relationships, and also calendars, depicting which sign was associated with which day of the month. One such almanac specifically for the Dutch-American farmers in New York and New Jersey was the *Americaanse Almanac*. It was published in the Dutch language by Thomas More of Philadelphia.[26] With the exception of one or two Dutch holidays listed on the calendar, this Dutch-language almanac was virtually the same as the English-language almanacs. The folk belief in planting by signs was not distinctly Dutch, but Dutch farmers followed the advice of these almanacs as seen in the following entry from the 1760s in the farm book of Lambert Borghard, a Dutch farmer in Kinderhook, New York:

Soad my flax May the 10. New moon the 8th 1766. Begune to plant my Corn May 14, 1766. . . . May the 12 ye 1767. I Sowd my flex att full moon. Planted my punking Seeds. May the 25:26 Day att the Last Quarter. . . . May 19:1768. Soad my flax Seed. New Moon 16. . . . Planted my punking seeds May 25. 26:1768. Last Quarter 23 full mo[on] 31.[27]

There were rhymes that were recited to insure a good crop. The following is one example:

Klip, klop, bovenop,   Klip, klop, bovenop,
Zet je hoed al aan je kop.   Set your hat on your head.
Draaie, vleie, drie maal zaaie,   Turn, go, three times sow,
Pluk de veere van de kaaie.   Pick the ferry from the quay.[28]

The following variation was recited specifically for a good fruit crop.

Klip, klop, bovenop,   Klip, klop, bovenop,
Suiker stroop en appelsap.   Sugar syrup and apple cider.
Appelsap en roggestroo,   Apple cider and rye straw,
In 'n ghoed klein kerryboo.   In a good little carry-all.[29]

Another area of Dutch-American farm folklore was folk medicine, which included herb cures, home remedies, and even magic. As early as the seventeenth century, Adraien van der Donck noted the occurrence in New Netherland of healing herbs, which were used by both the Dutch and the Indians.

No reasonable person will doubt that there are not many medicinal and healing plants in New Netherlands. A certain chirurgeon, who was also a botanist, had a beautiful garden there, wherein a great variety of medicinal wild plants were collected. . . . The land is full of different kinds of herbs and trees besides those enumerated, among which there undoubtedly are good simplicia, with which discreet persons would do much good; for we know that the Indians with roots, bulbs, leaves, &c. cure dangerous wounds and old sores.[30]

Many of these folk remedies were used for livestock as well as humans, and many survived into the twentieth century. During the 1930s L. G. Van Loon collected the following remedies from Dutch farmers in upstate New York:

If a horse had worms, one took hold of it by the nose and shook its head three times, while saying: *"Hep je de worme, soo krygh ik je by de kop. Hullie moghe wel wit, bruine, of rood, soo sulle hullie ghaane dood"* ("Have you the worms, so I get you by the head. You may well be white, brown, or red, so will they die"). Or one could take the horse into the yard and stroke its abdomen while saying: *"Marie demoeder 's Heere, ghing over de land, se had drie worme in d'r hand, de een was wit, nander swaat, de derde was rood, soo gha je dood"* ("Mary mother of the

Lord, went over the land, she had three worms in her hand, the one was white, another black, and third was red, so you die"). If a horse had the heaves or hiccups, one stroked it three times and turned it around by its head in the sun while saying: *"De heiligh seght: Joseph ghing over'n Akker, daar vond hy drie worme; de een swaart, nander bruin, de derde was rood—je sal starveghaan dood"* ("The saint says: Joseph went over the field, there he found three worms; one was black, another was brown, the third was red—you shall drop dead").[31]

The references to "Mary, mother of the Lord," "the saint," and "Joseph" in the above charms are evidence of Catholic survivals in the folk belief of the Protestant Dutch. Folklorist Don Yoder has shown a similar phenomenon among the Pennsylvania "Dutch" (Germans). Despite their Protestantism, the Pennsylvania Dutch told legends about saints. "The Pennsylvania German folk-culture," Yoder writes, "which was built up in the eighteenth and early nineteenth century, reflects the passive continuance of much of the medieval Catholic world view and saint lore that marked the earlier European Protestantism."[32] The same was true about the Dutch-Americans in New York and New Jersey.

Dutch-American folklife was punctuated by ceremonies that marked the yearly calendar and the life cycle. Distinctive Dutch customs were associated with such holidays as New Year's, Shrove Tuesday, Easter, Whitsunday, and Saint Nicholas Day (December 6). There were also distinctive customs associated with weddings and funerals. Some of these customs survived into the nineteenth century, and were adopted by slaves and free blacks who lived in close proximity to the Dutch. But most of these customs either disappeared or were altered under the dominant influence of the English.

In seventeenth-century New Netherland New Year's and May Day were occasions for riotous behavior on the part of the rural segments of the population. In 1652 Director Slichtenhorst in Rensselaerswyck complained that soldiers "on New Year's Eve . . . shot burning fuses on the roof of the patroon's house and also on the house of the Director, which is covered with thatch, so that the fore part of the house seemed ablaze and the director's son, in the intense cold, was moved to spring naked out of bed to extinguish several papers."[33] The problem became so serious that in December 1655 the Director General and Council of New Netherland declared that

Whereas experience has manifested and shewn us, that on New Year's and May days much Drunkeness and other irregularities are committed besides other sorrowful accidents such as woundings frequently arising therefrom, by Firing, Mayplanting and Carousing, in addition to the unnecessary waste of powder, to prevent which for the future the Director and Council expressly forbid that from now henceforth there shall be, within this Province of New Netherland, on New Years or May Days, any Firing of Guns, or Planting of May Poles, or any beating of Drums, or any treating with Brandy, wine or Beer.[34]

The main folk activity associated with Shrove Tuesday (the day before Ash Wednesday and the beginning of Lent) was "riding the goose." This custom, common among the farmers' servants and country people in New Netherland, consisted of riding on horseback past a greased goose suspended by a rope and trying to pull off its head. The Dutch Reformed Church disapproved of the custom, and the Director General and Council banned it repeatedly. Nevertheless, like most folk customs, it continued despite official disapproval. In 1654 the Burgomasters and a majority of the Schepens of New Amsterdam complained that the Director General and Council had "without their knowledge interdicted and forbidden certain farmers' servants to ride the goose on the feast of Bacchus at Shrove-tide." They contended that "it is moreover altogether unprofitable, unnecessary and censurable for subjects and neighbors to celebrate such pagan and popish feasts and to practise such evil customs in this Country." They noted that it was never practised in New Netherland until it was banned. The moral was, according to the Burgomasters and Schepens, that the Director General and Council shouldn't forbid the "rabble to celebrate the feast of Bacchus without the advice, knowledge and consent of the Burgomasters and Schepens."[35] The political significance of this points to a jurisdictional conflict between the Burgomasters and Schepens, on the one hand, and the Director General and the Council, on the other. But the cultural significance indicates the survival of pre-Reformation customs in New Netherland, as we have seen previously in folk beliefs.

The custom of riding the goose continued in New Amsterdam through the Dutch period. In February 1655 the court in New Amsterdam was informed that "the country people intended Riding the Goose again as they did last year." The court again declared that the custom was illegal to no apparent avail.[36] Riding the goose was also practised in the smaller agricultural towns of the Hudson River Valley. In 1664 a petition was submitted by the Consistory of Wildwyck (Kingston today) to prohibit "the public, sinful and scandalous Baccanalian days of Shrovetide (descended from the Heathen from their idol Bacchus, the God of wine and drunkenness: being also a leaven of Papacy, which the Apostle, I Cor. 5, has warned us to cast off)." The petition stated further the "if people will still indulge in the pleasures of such scandalous sins as those of the Shrovetide, they will more and more provoke God and bring his punishment on us again."[37] There is no evidence that the custom of riding the goose continued past the seventeenth century.

The Dutch traditions associated with Easter and Whitsunday, on the other hand, survived much longer. The Dutch name for Easter was *Paas*, which they celebrated for two days. The two-day celebration of Easter continued in upstate New York into the 1780s. Alexander Coventry noted this in his diary, as follows: "Sunday 12 April 1789. Paas (Easter Sunday) . . . 13 Monday . . . This is a holiday amongst the Dutch; they call it Paas."[38] Even the slaves of the Dutch observed the holiday for two days, according to Coventry.

Saturday 11 April . . . Van Curen's negro Cuff came to me the morning. I asked if he would live with me. He said he would; he helped to drive the cows home to fodder, and when we got home, Van Curen was there at the house, and i agreed to purchase his negro at the price agreed upon yesterday. Cuff wanted to go over the creek to get some hoop poles which he had there, and he wanted two days next week to keep Paas.[39]

As with other European Christian groups, colored eggs, symbolizing Christ's resurrection, were part of the Dutch-American Easter festival. This too was noted by Coventry. "Sunday. April 16, 1789. Hudson. This is a festival among the Dutch called Paas. It is the custom to have plenty of colored boild eggs . . . 17. All the world idle keeping Paas."[40]

Another part of the Dutch-American Easter was the preparation of Paas cakes. The batter was made of eggs and flour beaten lightly. The cakes were fried on an iron spider (a skillet with legs) usually by the slaves. When the cake was browned on one side, it was flipped over. Elizabeth L. Gebhard, writing in 1909 about life in an old Dutch parsonage in upstate New York, stated that "there was a great rivalry among the colored people as to which could throw the Paas-cakes the highest and still successfully catch them."[41] She noted that stories were told about the preparation of these cakes. "In the competition over tossing the cakes, the stories reached large proportions, it having been told on good authority that one Paascake had been seen going out the top of a chimney only to turn in the air, and descend through the chimney's wide mouth on its right side in the spider."[42]

Pentecost or Whitsunday was know as *Pinkster* among the Dutch. Its religious significances was to commemorate the appearance of the Holy Ghost to the Apostles after Christ's crucifixion. In its folk manifestation it became a springtime carnival festival, consisting of colored eggs and frolics. It too was celebrated by both the Dutch and their slaves. In 1786 Alexander Coventry described a *Pinkster* celebration in upstate New York as follows:

It is all frolicing to-day with the Dutch and the Negro. This is a holy day, Whitsunday, called among the Dutch 'Pinkster,' and they have eggs boiled in all sorts of colors, and eggs cooked in every way, and everybody must eat all the eggs he can. And the frolicing is still kept up among the young folks, so that little else is done to-day but eat eggs and be jolly.[43]

Two days later Coventry noted in his diary that they were "still frolicing Dutch Pinkster."[44] In 1797 William Dunlap described a Pinkster celebration among the Dutch farmers along the Passaic River Valley in New Jersey.

The settlements along the River are dutch. It is the holiday they called pinkster and every public house is crowded with merry makers and waggon's full of rustic beaux and bells met us at every mile. The blacks as well as their masters were frolicking and the women and children look'd peculiarly neat and well dressed.[45]

In the early nineteenth century the blacks in Albany and from the surrounding countryside would assemble on the day following Pinkster on "Pinkster Hill" under the leadership of a slave known as King Charles. The celebration was described in a poem written by Absalom

Aimwell (probably a *nom de plume*) titled "A Pinkster Ode for the Year 1803. Most Respectfully Dedicated to Carolus Africanus Rex: Thus Rendered in English: King Charles, Captain-General and Commander in Chief of the Pinkster Boys." The poem indicates that Pinkster was a rite of spring.

> When leaves the fig tree putteth out,
> When calves and lambs for mothers cry,
> When toads begin to hop about,
> We know of truth that summer's high.

It associates it with flowers and love.

> At Pinkster, flow'rs will deck the field,
> And pleasures sweet will banish pain;
> Love-broken hearts shall all be heal'd,
> Although they may be crack'd again.

It notes that the holiday was celebrated by blacks and whites as a celebration of liberty.

> Every colour revels there,
> From ebon black to lilly fair.
> Ah! how much happiness they see,
> In one short day of Liberty!

And it describes King Charles as the ruling monarch of the celebration.

> And now they move around the the ring,
> To see again the jovial king;
> Charles rejoices at the sight,
> And dances, bowing most polite.[46]

The poem states that King Charles was "nobly born" in Africa and was brought to America as a slave, although still retaining his "native majesty." It describes how at Pinkster time he would lead "the Guinea dance," dressed in his "Pinkster clothes" with his "hat of yellow lace." It mentions the instruments played, including the fiddle, the flute, the fife, the Jew's harp, the pipe, the drum, the banjo, and the tabor.[47] Another source described King Charles as a "Guinea man" from Angola, who lived to the age of 125. His costume was that of a British soldier: "He was nearly barelegged, wore a red military coat trimmed profusely with variegated ribbons, and a small black hat with a pom-

pom stuck on one side." The dances were "the original Congo dances as danced in their native Africa." One of the dances was called the "Toto Dance." The drums were "eel-pots covered with dressed sheep-skin" and a song was sung with the African refrain "Hi-a-bomba-bomba-bomba."[48]

From this description it seems that Pinkster in Albany was an Afro-Dutch celebration with certain African cultural survivals. Thus, it was akin to the carnival celebrations in New Orleans, the Caribbean, and South America.[49] On April 28, 1811, the Albany Common Council banned the Pinkster celebration; the implication was that not only was it not in keeping with the tenets of the Dutch Reformed Church, but there was something subversive about the Afro-Dutch Pinkster crews. Ironically, Pinkster survived longer among the blacks than among the whites. In 1874 Gabriel Furman wrote that on Long Island "poor *Pinckster* has lost its rank among the festivals, and is only kept by the negroes; with them, however, especially on the west end of the island, it is still much of a holiday."[50]

Saint Nicholas is the patron saint of Amsterdam, and his saint's day is celebrated in the Netherlands on December 6. He appears on the eve of the holiday dressed as a bishop on horseback and accompanied by his servant Zwarte Piet (Black Peter). Children receive gifts in their shoes, which they set out overnight. There is some doubt, however, whether this saint's day was ever celebrated in Dutch colonial America. Charles W. Jones argues that the celebration was not introduced in America until after the American Revolution.[51] In a research report for Sleepy Hollow Restorations, Field Horne argues that there are no contemporary descriptions of St. Nicholas Day in either New Netherland or colonial New York, but the day is listed in some colonial almanacs. However, Horne notes that there is evidence that St. Nicholas cakes were baked and a folk song about St. Nicholas was sung.[52] One version of that song was as follows:

Santa Klaus, goedt heilig man, Santa Claus, good holy man,
Loop ye weg van Amsterdam. Go your way from Amsterdam.
Van Amsterdam na Spanje, From Amsterdam to Spain,
Van Spanje na Oranje, From Spain to Orange,
En breng deze kindjes einige graps. And bring these little children toys.
Sint Nicholas, myn goeden vriend, Saint Nicholas, my good friend,

Ik had u altyd wel gediend.   To serve you ever was my end.
Als gy mij ny wat wilt given,   If you me now something will give,
Zal ik u dienen myn leven.   Serve you I will as long as I live.[53]

Again, the continued veneration of Saint Nicholas by the Protestant Dutch is a survival of pre-Reformation traditions.

In the nineteenth century, St. Nicholas became associated with the holiday of Christmas. This association of a Dutch patron saint with a celebration that was German in origin and English by adoption is another example of the cultural syncretism that occurred in America. Gabriel Furman remembered his Dutch family's celebration of Christmas circa 1805, when he was a boy. "I recollect perfectly well," he wrote, "the delight which I experienced when a small boy in hanging up my stocking, and in emptying it of its load in the morning and I recollect well that one Christmas Eve I unfortunately sat up later than usual, and saw my father come home with a parcel of St. Nicholas' holiday presents which he had been purchasing to put in my own and my sister's stocking."[54] It was about this time that Washington Irving wrote his description of St. Nicholas in *The Knickerbocker History of New York*, in which he associated St. Nicholas with Christmas.[55] Yet some Dutch-Americans retained the custom of placing gifts in children's shoes, but on Christmas, not St. Nicholas Day. For example, in the 1830s Henry Van Der Lyn of Chenango County, New York, described in his diary his family's Christmas celebrations as follows:

December 24, 1830. I put my Christmas presents in the shoes of Mary, Henry & Peter.

. . .

December 25, 1838. Snow began to fall in the begin. of the evening. We had a rich feast on Turkey, roast fowl, pumpkin & Mince pies, a glass of Champaign. & Syllabub at tea of the best kind. The boys presents of candies, Almonds, raisins &c. gave them much comfort. This evening Their presents are renewed again, according to the old Dutch custom. These Yankies know no holidays & work all day to day.[56]

There were also distinctive Dutch customs associated with weddings and funerals. At Dutch weddings, the ceremony was followed by a frolic (party) that would sometimes last all night. In 1791 Alexander Coventry described one such wedding frolic.

Thurs. 7 April. Thomas Van Alstine and Mabel Butler being married (today). Betsey and I were invited to the wedding. Set put after sunset: found a multitude there. We had wine and other drink enough; also a good supper, and all felt well. Never saw so many Dutchmen in a frolic before. They seemed an open hearted (noisy) cheery set. (Much for friendship and wine.) Friday 8 April. Remained at Van Alstine's all last night until 7 A.M. today dancing (and drinking) etc. They had a horse race this morning for a gallon of wine, and that was produced and used.[57]

The traditional Dutch funerals were formal and elaborate, but they were followed by a reception that was more like a party. The deceased was laid out in the best room of the house, which was known as the *dood-kamer* (death room). The church sexton performed the role of *dood graver* (inviter). Wearing a black coat and a mantle decorated with black material and carrying a watchman's staff, he delivered formal invitations to friends and relatives. Each person who was invited received a linen scarf, a pair of black silk gloves, a bottle of Madeira wine, and two funeral cakes. On the day of the funeral the friends and relatives gathered at the home of the deceased. Women were not allowed to accompany the funeral procession. The body was taken to the graveyard on the shoulders of the pall bearers, who wore gloves and long scarves of either black or white material. The pall bearers were given gifts, usually mourning rings or spoons. When they returned home, there was a reception with cakes, spiced wine, beer, and brandy, which continued into the night.[58]

A young traveler described a late-eighteenth-century Dutch funeral in New York State for a member of the Van Rensselaer family.

1783, Feb. 24. Had the curiosity to attend a Dutch funeral,—the remains of Col. Van Renslear a man rich, old, and universally beloved. He lived on the other side of the river from town, but the whole city & 14 or 15 miles round were invited; and also all Claverac, as they were his tenants. The ice was gone, so we were obliged to ferry, but yet there were many present. The house in every room had as many as could sit with convenience, & servants at the doors to direct people according to their appearance. No ladies were present. The procession began about 3 o'clock. The corpse preceded, upon a coach, converted into a hearse by taking off the box, &c. The horses were white, but covered with black cloth, and the coachman all in black. Next followed 10 persons with scarfs of white, the mourners without scarfs, and the ministers and doctors with. After these the people who attended walked in a long train by pairs. All were invited to return to the house and take a glass of wine.

Tables were set in every room of a very large house, with bottles of wine, glasses, pipes, & tobacco, with candles ready lighted & servants, with each a white napkin round their arm, stood ready to replace anything that was wanted. The wine was pretty good, & I'm sure many drank of it very freely. Their merriment was apparent. In a word, the whole scene had rather the appearance of a jovial meeting than the tender sympathetic feelings of humane condolence. There was no prayer, & the conversation was upon news, horse-jockeying & other indifferent subjects. I'm sure I did not hear a word adapted to the occasion or a house of mourning, & in reality the appearance is rather of joy and feasting.[59]

This was obviously the funeral of a wealthy Dutch landowner, but many of the traditions were the same for the Dutch farmer of more modest means. For example, the elaborate invitation ritual was part of a funeral on Long Island, described in June 1829 in the Van Brunt farm journal.

23 . . . Mrs. Berry came. Mr. and Mrs. Wyckoff, Mr. and Mrs. Polhemus, Mrs. Widow C. Van Wyck, Mr. Denton, Mr. Mrs. and Miss Schoonmaker. Mr. A. Cortelyou took a list of the names of those persons to be invited to Mr. Denton's, who sent it on to Mr. Spader Sexton. Albert Nicholas and John came. We made arrangements for the funeral. 24. Mr. Peter Wyckoff sen. took our little wagon and horse and invited our friends in N. Utrecht. Mr. Polhemus our friends in Flatbush, Flat-lands and Gravesend, Nicholas attended to inviting in N.Y.—Rev. Mathaus N.Y. Strong Flatbush Cruikshank. Rev. Mr. Rouse performed funeral services at 4 P.M.—a great many friends attended.[60]

According to Gabriel Furman, when the head of a family died, it was the custom among the Dutch farmers on Long Island to kill an ox or steer and to buy a barrel of wine for a great feast among the relatives and friends.[61] By the end of the nineteenth century, these traditions had died out. The farm diary of David Voorhees, who had a farm near Blawenburg, New Jersey, describes the death and funeral in 1875 of his baby son. The funeral was not distinctively Dutch in any way.[62]

Several Dutch traditional foods were introduced to America, especially those that had correspondents in either the English or the American Indian tradition. Historian Fernand Braudel described the Dutch diet in the Netherlands until the end of the eighteenth century as consisting of beans, salt meat, bread made from barley or rye, fish, bacon, and occasionally game. The national dish, known as *hutsepot*, was a stew containing finely minced beef or mutton. The evening meal typically was a gruel made from left-over bread soaked in milk.[63] The latter had a correspondent in New Netherland in a dish that the Dutch adopted from the Indians. It was a corn-meal porridge, but the Dutch prepared it in a distinctive manner, that is, mixed with milk, rather than in the Indian manner of mixing it with water. In the 1740s the Swedish traveler Peter Kalm described it as follows:

In the evening they made a porridge of corn, poured it as customary into a dish, made a large hole in the center into which they poured fresh milk, but more often buttermilk. They ate it taking half a spoonful of porridge and half of milk. As they ordinarily took more milk than porridge, the milk in the dish was soon consumed. Then more milk was poured in. This was their supper.[64]

To make this more tasty, they would add some sugar or syrup. Kalm noted that the Dutch used the Algonkian word *sappaen* for this dish.

Kalm also described the typical Dutch-American meals of the mid-eighteenth century. Breakfast consisted of tea, bread, butter, radishes, and slices of dried beef. Tea was served with sugar, but without milk. They would take a bite of sugar and then sip the tea. Kalm noted that forty years earlier the Dutch colonists had only bread and butter or bread and milk for breakfast. Sometimes they also had small round cheeses, which Kalm did not find very tasty. These they cut into small slices and spread on the bread. They ate breakfast at seven o'clock. At noon they had another meal, but Kalm did not think there was anything distinctive about it. For supper they usually had *sappaen* and meat or bread and butter with cheese. The cheese was grated into the consistency of coarse flour, which they thought improved the taste. If any porridge was left over, in the morning it was boiled with buttermilk until it reached the consistency of gruel. Meat was sometimes served with turnips and cabbage. With this meal they drank water or weak beer. For dinner they had a large salad, with a dressing that was mostly vinegar and little or no oil. Sometimes they had chocolate, but seldom the English dishes of pie or pudding. Since they were devout Calvinists, the head of the family said grace before meals. Kalm felt that the Dutch were more frugal in their food habits than the English. They never put on their tables more food than they were going to consume, nor did they drink as much as the English.[65] The Dutch foodways were not that different from those of the English in New

England; both relied heavily on dairy products as their main source of protein.[66]

The preparation and consumption of *sappaen* survived well into the nineteenth century. In his 1887 notebook, Rufus A. Grider noted that in the Schoharie Valley of New York State the Dutch consumed a "Mush & Milk Dish for their evening meal, which they called 'Mush Sapahn.' " It was served in a distinctive manner.

Until abt 1830 to 1840 the inhabitants of the rural districts of Schohaier—which were settled by Dutch & Germans—eat their meals from a large pewter dish placed by the house wife in the center of a round top table . . . Mush was prepared in the fall & winter of the year.—It was boiled in the afternoon and about one hour before mealtime poured from the Iron Pot into the Pewter Dish and set in a cold place, cooling stiffens it. Near meal time the House Wife made as many excavations as there were guests—piling on heaping up the Centre, & filling the hollows with Cold milk . . .—as many Pewter Table Spoons as milk Ponds were supplied. After Grace was said by the head of the family—Everyone began to diminish the banks & increase the size of his White Lake by feeding on its banks and Centre—but there were limits beyond those no one could go—if for instance any one tapped his neighbor's Milk Pond it was ill manners.[67]

Mrs. Peter G. Rose, who included this reference in her introduction to a seventeenth-century Dutch cookbook she translated, notes that eating from a communal dish survived in certain parts of the Netherlands well into the twentieth century. But this was fairly late for America. Archeologist James Deetz notes that in seventeenth-century Anglo-America, food was served directly from pots and eaten in wooden trenchers (small wooden trays with shallow depressions in the center), and beverages were drunk from common containers made of leather, pewter, or pottery. By the 1760s, Deetz states that this communal eating tradition was replaced by greater individualism "with each person having his own plate and chamber pot."[68]

In conclusion, Dutch-American folklore and folklife demonstrated the same cultural process by which Dutch culture became Dutch-American. There were cultural borrowings, first from the Indians and then from the English. There were also survivals of pre-Reformation Dutch traditions and beliefs. Eventually, the folklore and folklife became unlike anything in the Netherlands. Yet Dutch survivals in language, music, lore, and customs persisted through the late nineteenth century. Ironically, some of these survivals persisted longer among blacks than among the Dutch-Americans themselves. While Dutch-American culture was really a regional variant of American culture, these survivals gave the culture its distinct identity.

CONCLUSION

The Meaning of Dutch-American

The mid-eighteenth century was a turning point for the Dutch in New York and New Jersey. A new farmhouse architecture that was structurally different from the Dutch architectural tradition that was dominant until that time was emerging, not only in New York and New Jersey, but in the other English colonies in North America. At the same time, major changes were occurring in the Dutch Reformed Church. It is no accident that these changes in religious institutions paralleled changes in architecture, given the interrelated web of behavioral, institutional, and material structures that constitute a regional culture. A brief look at the religious changes helps us understand the changes in other aspects of the culture, such as the farmhouse architecture. It also helps us understand why the term Dutch-American, rather than Georgian or Anglo-American, is the term that best explains the significance of this change.

In the winter of 1720 a twenty-seven-year-old Dutch Reformed domine named Theodorus Jacobus Frelinghuysen arrived in America to become the minister of several congregations in the Raritan Valley of New Jersey. The congregations included the town of New Brunswick as well as several rural congregations at Three-Mile Run and Six-Mile Run (both in North Brunswick today) and in North Branch (later known as the Readington Church). As we have seen in regard to the place of origin of the Dutch in America generally, Frelinghuysen, like many of the ministers in the Dutch Reformed Church in America, did not come from the Netherlands. His family was from Westphalia, he was educated at the University of Lingen, and his first pastorate was in East Friesland, all places in Germany that bordered on the Netherlands. East Friesland and Lingen had close ties to the Netherlands. In fact, the district of Lingen had once been the personal possession of the Dutch House of Orange, but reverted to the German state of Prussia in 1702. The Reformed Church in the region was more closely tied to the Dutch Reformed Church than the German Reformed Church, and the University of Lingen was under the influence of a movement known as Pietism as it was manifested in the theology of the Utrecht theologican Gisbertus Voetius (1589–1676), which stressed personal religious experiences of regeneration.[1] The religious factionalism between the followers of Voetius, the so-called Voetians, and those of the Leiden theologian Johannes Cocceius (1603–1669), known as Cocceians, has been seen as a major factor in explaining Leisler's Rebellion of 1689.[2] Giuliam Bertholf, who between 1683 and 1724 was the pastor of congregations at Bergen (now Jersey City), Aquackanonk (now Passaic), Hackensack, and who preached and administered the sacraments in Raritan, the Ponds (Oakland), Pompton Plains, Schraalenburgh (Bergenfield), and Second River, New Jersey and Tappan, Tarrytown, and Staten Island, New York, was a follower of Jacobus Koelman, who was a student of Voetius.[3] According to one scholar, Guiliam Bertholf "prepared the ground" for Theodorus Jacobus Frelinghuysen.[4]

When he first arrived in America, Frelinghuysen immediately ran afoul of Domines Gualtherus DuBois and Henricus Boel, pastors of the Dutch Reformed Church in New York City. Boel disagreed with Frelinghuysen's view that the Lord's Prayer was not an essential part of the worship service and was offended by what was termed Frelinghuysen's "howling prayers," referring to his emotional preaching style. Furthermore, Frelinghuysen made the mistake of criticizing DuBois for having a large wall mirror in his house. Then once he was settled in the Raritan Valley, Frelinghuysen caused a furor in his own congregations by denying communion to some of his congregants who did not show signs of having had a religious experience of regeneration. The congregants complained to Domine Bernardus Freeman, who was the pastor of the Dutch Reformed Churches of New Utrecht, Bushwick, Flatbush, and Brooklyn. But Freeman was also a Pietist, and he sided with Frelinghuysen, as did Domine Bertholf in Bergen County, New Jersey. Then they went to Domine Boel in New York City, who took their side against Frelinghuysen.[5] The result was a schism within the Dutch Reformed Church in America, which historians have seen as being over the issue of the autonomy of individual congregations, namely the rural churches on Long Island, Bergen County, and the Raritan Valley resisting Domine Boel in New York City.[6]

A dispute also arose over the ordination of Domine John Henry Goetschius, the son of a German Reformed minister from Switzerland, who came to Philadelphia with his father in 1735 and began to preach at area churches, despite the fact that he was not ordained. He was finally ordained in 1741 by Frelinghuysen; Gilbert Tennent, a New-Light Presbyterian minister who like Frelinghuysen also had a congregation in New Brunswick; and Peter Henry Dorsius, who, although he was born in Germany, became the pastor of the Dutch Reformed Church in Neshaminy, Bucks County, Pennsylvania, not far from the so-called Log College run by Gilbert Tennent's father William Tennent. Goetschius then became the minister of four Dutch Reformed congregations in Jamaica, Newtown, Success, and Oyster Bay, Long Island. Later, Goetschius would become the pastor at Hackensack and Schraalenburgh, New Jersey. Goetschius's ordination was challenged by Domine Boel in New York City and the Classis of Amsterdam, the church body made up of ministers and elders at the organizational level between the local consistory and the provincial synod, under whose jurisdiction came all the Dutch Reformed congregations in America. After a prolonged dispute that soon involved not only Frelinghuysen, but also Domine Freeman as well, the matter was finally resolved in 1748 by a reordination of Domine Goetschius by a delegation of ministers approved by the Classis of Amsterdam.[7]

Frelinghuysen and Tennent became the two foremost New Jersey proponents of the revival of religion that swept through the colonies in the 1740s known as the Great Awakening. It was prompted by the visit to America in 1739 of the Anglican evangelical minister, George Whitefield. In November 1739, on his first visit to New Brunswick, Whitefield preached in Tennent's church in New Brunswick. In April 1740, on his second visit, he preached from a wagon in front of

Frelinghuysen's church to an assembly of two thousand.[8] Historian
Randall H. Balmer notes that "for the pietist Dutch in New Jersey the
revival functioned as an assimilating force which brought them into
contact with other ethnic groups."[9] It was a movement in which
participated not only Frelinghuysen, who was Dutch Reformed; Tennent, who was Presbyterian; Whitefield, who was Anglican; but also
Henry Melchior Muhlenberg, who was Lutheran. "In the ferment of
revival," writes Balmer,

ethnic distinctiveness and denominational identities began quickly to erode, as
evangelicalism provided the common language for their discourse. Contact
with Huguenots, Quakers, Moravians, Lutherans, and especially Presbyteri-
ans functioned as an Americanizing force among the Jersey Dutch.[10]

Balmer also notes that Frelinghuysen was opposed by the ministers
in the older areas of Dutch settlement, such as Domines Vincentius
Antonides on Long Island, Petrus Van Driessen of Albany, Petrus
Vas of Kingston, and DuBois and Boel of New York. Frelinghuysen's
opponents in the Raritan Valley, according to Balmer, all owned
sizeable estates and characterized his supporters as "stupid farmers"
who were "wholly illiterate."[11] Balmer quotes Domine Johannes Ritz-
ema's description of the religious divisions upon his arrival in America
in 1744:

I soon found to my great sorrow that an extensive dispute and division had
arisen in the Dutch Reformed churches here. It does not exist so much in the
city, where, since my stay, everything has gone on in a fairly quiet way; but it
rages principally in the country districts, and especially on Long Island.[12]

The dispute over the ordination of John Henry Goetschius pointed
to a problem of the training of Dutch Reformed ministers in America
that eventually led to a full-fledged schism. Starting in the 1730s
numerous Dutch Reformed ministers in America felt the need for a
new church body between the local consistories and the classis that
would have the authority to examine and ordain Dutch Reformed
ministers in America, a power reserved by the classis. There was a
precedent for a body known as a "coetus" in the Dutch Reformed
churches in the East Indies, South Africa, Surinam, Brazil, and East
Friesland, Germany. In 1736 a group of ministers and elders met in
New York City to seek approval from the Classis of Amsterdam for

such a coetus. Theodorus Jacobus Frelinghuysen had favored the establishing of a coetus, as did son Theodore, who was the minister of the Dutch Reformed Church in Albany, and was one of the leaders of the movement. Henricus Boel led the opposition, insisting on continued loyalty to the Classis of Amsterdam. The ministers who opposed the Coetus met periodically in an assembly known as the Conferentie (literally, the "conference"). Thus, the schism became known as the Coetus-Conferentie schism. The Coetus supporters tended to be evangelicals, and the opponents tended to come from the older areas of Dutch settlement such as New York City, Kingston, and Albany. Finally, in 1747, the Classis of Amsterdam agreed to the establishment of a Coetus with limited authority for the examination and ordination of ministers.[13]

Despite the establishment of the Coetus, the ordinations of ministers continued to be sent to the Classis of Amsterdam for their approval and the problem of training Dutch Reformed ministers in America still remained. Thus, the two issues of the establishment of an American classis to ordain ministers and the founding of a college in America to train ministers became linked. In 1754 the Coetus decided to request the full status of a classis. The New York Dutch Reformed Church opposed an American classis and decided to support the idea advanced by Anglicans to establish a college, known as King's College (now Columbia University) founded in that same year, providing there was a professorate of divinity from the Dutch Reformed Church. The Coetus in 1755 commissioned Theodore Frelinghuysen to go to the Netherlands to seek support for a separate Dutch Reformed college in New Jersey. At the same time, the Coetus transformed itself into a classis, without waiting for the approval of the Classis of Amsterdam. Frelinghuysen wasn't able to go to the Netherlands until four years later. He stayed two years, but did not gain approval for a college in New Jersey. On his return voyage he perished at sea. However, the cause was taken up by others, including John Henry Goetschius and Jacob Rutsen Hardenburgh, who was the protégé of Theodore Frelinghuysen's brother, John Frelinghuysen of Raritan, New Jersey. Finally, in November 1766, Governor William Franklin of New Jersey granted the charter to Queens College (today Rutgers University).[14]

The schism between the Coetus and the Conferentie continued for eighteen years. It split congregations such as the Dutch Reformed Church of Hackensack that had two ministers, two consistories, and two congregations that alternately used the church building. Finally, the schism was resolved in 1777 by the establishment of a General Assembly to replace the Coetus. Historian Gerald F. De Jong interprets the significance of the schism as a disagreement over the "Americanization of the church." He notes that at about the same time the issue of an American college to train and an American classis to ordain Dutch Reformed ministers was dividing the church, the New York Dutch Reformed Church was debating whether the ministers should preach in English or Dutch.[15] It is significant that the division between the Coetus faction and the Conferentie faction correlated to which side one took during the American Revolution. The Coetus supporters tended to become Whigs and the Conferentie became Loyalists.[16]

Thus, while the Great Awakening divided the Dutch into two factions, for those who participated in the revival it had several effects. As a widespread movement that involved many colonies, religious denominations, and ethnic groups, it integrated the Dutch into a common movement. While the Great Awakening had its parallels in evangelicalism on the British Isles and in Pietism on the European continent, in the American context and especially for the Dutch, it was tied to other factors, such as the establishment of an American classis and a separate Dutch Reformed college, that involved breaking institutional ties with the Netherlands and establishing separate American institutions. While historians generally have noted the connection between the anti-authoritarianism of the Great Awakening and the American Revolution, the correlation was even greater for the Dutch than for other ethnic groups in America.[17] Furthermore, the Dutch-American experience during the Great Awakening provides some insight into the difference between Anglicanization and Americanization. According to Balmer, the Conferentie faction of the Dutch Reformed Church, which had shown a willingness to adopt English ways during the regime of Governor Cornbury, was further Anglicized during the Great Awakening, by allying itself with the Anglican Church, which also opposed the religious enthusiasm of the evangelicals.[18] This is what lay behind the willingness of the New York Dutch Reformed

Church to support the establishment of King's College and to oppose Queen's College.

These dramatic changes in the religious life of the Dutch in America were contemporaneous with the advent of the new architecture that has been termed English Georgian. Scholars in the field of material culture have argued that this was not simply a new style of architecture. Folklorist Henry Glassie noted that in middle Virginia and the Delaware Valley, where Georgian architecture started to become part of the building tradition in the late eighteenth century, it represented a violent break or revolution, not just in building traditions, but in the culture generally, resulting in a new mentality.[19] Archeologist James Deetz has called this mentality "the Georgian world view" as opposed to the medieval world view.[20] Yet it is a misnomer to give it the name of the English king at the time, because neither the architecture nor the mentality were exclusively English. Glassie calls it an "international Renaissance style," that has parallels throughout western Europe, the British Isles, and America.[21] He associates it with the advent of the modern mind. "More utilitarian than aesthetic, more analytical than organic, more individualistic than communitarian, emphasizing precise repetition, mechanical line, and geometric objectification, this mind, though rural and agrarian, was a cause of the industrial revolution, not a result of it."[22] Thus, this house type is not necessarily an example of Anglicanization and should not be termed Anglo-American any more than it should be termed English Georgian.

Glassie notes that this new architecture was generally associated with a prosperous, landed gentry. He interprets the central hallway, which was one of the characteristics of the new house type, not only as protection from the weather (that is, a transitional space between the outside and the inside), but also as an expression of the need for control, a new sense of privacy, and a desire to be fashionable.[23] Folklorist Bernard Herman, in writing about similar changes in central Delaware, argues that this architecture involved the social implications of individualism, a separation of public and private space, and increased specialization of room, which constitute "a conservative revolution designed to consolidate in housing the importance of landed and monied power."[24] Architectural historian Dell Upton sees the same architecture in Virginia as embodying "social formality as an assertion of local and political control" by Virginia's local elite, whose domination of their neighbors had been limited by England.[25]

Such class-conscious interpretations may work for Virginia and Delaware, but they are less useful in understanding the Dutch in New York and New Jersey. This is not to suggest that the Dutch were any more egalitarian than the English. They too owned slaves, although perhaps not in such large numbers per household as in the South. Rather, it is that the events taking place in the religious sphere of Dutch culture at the same time suggest that another factor better explains the cultural revolution that the Dutch were undergoing. This was the development of a Dutch-American subculture, as distinct from adaptations of Dutch culture to an American environment, on the one hand, or cultural borrowings from the neighboring English culture, on the other.

Architectural historian Edward A. Chappell describes a similar process among the Swiss and German settlers who moved from Pennsylvania into the Shenandoah Valley of Virginia. Toward the end of the eighteenth century they abandoned their traditional house types in favor of the so-called I-house, which was distinctly nineteenth century and Anglo-American. At about the same time there was a decline in the public use of the German language. Yet certain ethnic traits continued, such as the Rhenish cellar and first-floor kitchens. Thus for the Germans of the Shenandoah Valley, Chappell argues, the I-house "provided a highly visible evidence of at least partial entrance into an acceptable regional culture."[26]

This insight opens the door to the meaning of the distinction between the Dutch farmhouse and the Dutch-American farmhouse and why the term Dutch-American is preferable to Anglo-American or English Georgian. The Dutch farmhouse is one whose floorplan and/or framing can be traced back to the Netherlands. Just as there are a number of dialects of Dutch in the Netherlands, so too are there a number of farmhouse types. The linguistic culture areas spill over the political boundaries of the Netherlands into the adjacent provinces of Belgium, France, and Germany. For example, the dialect spoken in East Friesland, Germany, is similar to that spoken in the Dutch province of Friesland. And, as we have seen, the Dutch Reformed church was also present in East Friesland as well. So too the farmhouse culture areas extend beyond the boundaries of the Netherlands into adjacent areas. And, as we have also seen, the people who have become known as the Dutch in America came from not only the Netherlands, but also from these adjacent areas. Thus, we must remember that the term Dutch must be seen in the sense of drawing upon the variety of regional cultural traditions. The process of transplanting these traditions in America was one of selecting those traditions thought to be most suitable and adapting them to a new environment. This occurred during the so-called Dutch period between 1624 and 1664, when the colony of New Netherland existed.

When the English conquered New Netherland in 1664 and subdivided it into New York and New Jersey, important changes occurred in both the language and the architecture. English was made the official language of the colonies, and the Dutch began to acculturate to English traditions. The wealthy merchants in the cities, such as New York, and the owners of the large estate, such as Philipsburg Manor, were quick to adopt English ways. The smaller independent farmers in northern New Jersey and western Long Island and the Dutch tenants on the large estates were somewhat slower. During this period between 1664 and about 1750 regional differences in the architecture developed, seen primarily in different building materials available in the Upper Hudson Valley, the Middle Hudson Valley, northern New Jersey and Rockland County, and Long Island and Monmouth County, New Jersey. Also, during this period the Dutch settlers became bilingual, speaking English in public and Dutch at home. And just as there developed regional differences in architecture, distinct dialects arose that distinguished Mohawk-Hudson Valley Dutch and Jersey Dutch.

Then, in the mid-eighteenth century, a major structural change occurred in Dutch architecture in America. The new houses had Dutch-English framing and floorplans that have been called Georgian. The Dutch features, such as the Dutch door, the stoop, and the jambless fireplace, were continued as secondary characteristics, along with certain English secondary characteristics, such as the gambrel roof. The net result was something that was regionally distinct. It was not English and not Dutch; it could only be found in America in the Dutch culture area. That is why I term it Dutch-American. The new architecture developed at about the same time there were institutional changes in the Reformed Church that have been characterized as an Americanization process. These religious changes resulted in the establishment of separate Dutch-American religious and educational institutions and are correlated with support for the American Revolution.[27]

Here lies the meaning of the term Dutch-American. It refers to a regional subculture of American culture. The English language was the dominant language of the new country, but American English is a dialect different from "the King's English." Similarly, the so-called English Georgian architectural tradition became the common denominator in the British American colonies. While it integrated the various regional and ethnic subcultures into a national culture, regional differences continued that distinguished the New England Georgian Saltbox from the Mid-Atlantic and Southern I-House. The Dutch-American farmhouse is such a regional subtype. In linguistic terms, it is comparable to a dialect. What gave the Dutch-American subculture its identity were the survivals of Dutch culture in architecture (the Dutch barn and hay barrack), language (Jersey Dutch and Mohawk-Hudson Dutch), tools and equipment (the Dutch plow, the sith and mathook, and the Dutch wagon), and folklife (Dutch folk songs, rhymes, and the Pinkster celebration). These survivals continued to flourish in rural areas of New York and New Jersey through the end of the nineteenth century. One by one, these survivals began to disappear, until only the farmhouses remained on the landscape in mute testimony to the making of an American regional subculture.

Notes

Introduction

1. John A. Kouwenhoven, "American Studies: Words or Things?" in *American Studies in Transition*, Marshall W. Fishwick, ed. (Philadelphia: University of Pennsylvania Press, 1964), pp. 15–35.

2. E. McClung Fleming, "Early American Decorative Arts as Social Documents," *Mississippi Valley Historical Review* 45 (1958): 276.

3. William B. Hesseltine, "The Challenge of the Artifact," in *Material Culture Studies in America*, Thomas J. Schlereth, ed. (Nashville: American Association for State and Local History, 1982), p. 97.

4. James Deetz, *In Small Things Forgotten: The Archeology of Early American Life* (Garden City, N.Y.: Doubleday-Anchor, 1977), p. 161.

5. For an example of this approach, see Alan Gowans, *Images of American Living: Four Centuries of Architecture and Furniture as Cultural Expression* (Philadelphia and New York: J. B. Lippincott Co., 1964).

6. Henry Glassie, *Folk Housing in Middle Virginia: A Structural Analysis of Historic Artifacts* (Knoxville: University of Tennessee Press, 1975), p. 12.

7. Matthew Arnold, *Culture and Anarchy*, J. Dover Wilson, ed. (1869; Reprint, Cambridge: Cambridge University Press, 1963), p. 6.

8. Fred Kniffen, "Folk Housing: Key to Diffusion," *Annals of the Association of American Geographers* 55 (1965): 549.

9. Kniffen and Henry Glassie, "Building in Wood in the Eastern United States: A Time-Place Perspective," *Geographical Review* 56 (1966): 40–66.

10. Frederick Jackson Turner, "The Significance of the Frontier in American History," in *The Frontier in American History* (New York: Henry Holt & Co., 1920), pp. 1–38.

11. Kniffen, "Folk Housing," p. 558.

12. Glassie, *Pattern in the Material Folk Culture of the Eastern United States* (Philadelphia: University of Pennsylvania Press, 1968), p. 558.

13. Langdon C. Wright, "Local Government and Central Authority in New Netherland," *New York Historical Society Quarterly* 57 (1973): 7–29.

14. For discussions about how tolerant the Dutch in New Netherland were, see John Webb Pratt, *Religion, Politics, and Diversity: The Church-State Theme in New York History* (Ithaca: Cornell University Press, 1967) and George Smith, *Religion and Trade in New Netherland* (Ithaca: Cornell University Press, 1973).

15. Thomas J. Condon, *New York Beginnings: The Commercial Origins of New Netherland* (New York and London: New York University Press and University of London Press, 1968), p. vii.

16. Joan Huizinga, *Dutch Civilization in the Seventeenth Century*, Arnold J. Pomerans, trans. (New York: Frederick Ungar, 1968); Pieter Geyl, *The Netherlands in the Seventeenth Century* (London and New York: Ernest Benn Ltd. and Barnes and Noble, 1961), 2 vols.

17. Alice P. Kenney, *Stubborn for Liberty: The Dutch in New York* (Syracuse: Syracuse University Press, 1975); Donna Merwick, "Dutch Townsmen and Land Use: A Spatial Perspective on Seventeenth-Century Albany, New York," *William and Mary Quarterly* 3rd. ser. 37 (1980): 53–78; idem, *Possessing Albany, 1630–1710: The Dutch and English Experiences* (Cambridge: Cambridge University Press, 1990); Condon, *New York Beginnings.*

18. Van Cleaf Bachman, *Peltries or Plantations: The Economic Policies of the Dutch West India Company in New Netherland, 1623–1639* (Baltimore: Johns Hopkins Press, 1969).

19. Charles Theodore Gehring, "The Dutch Language in Colonial New York: An Investigation of a Language in Decline and its Relationship to Social Change" (Ph.D. diss., Indiana University, 1973); David Evan Narrett, "Patterns of Inheritance in Colonial New York City, 1664–1775" (Ph.D. diss., Cornell University, 1981); William John McLaughlin, "Dutch Rural New York: Community, Economy, and Family in Colonial Flatbush" (Ph.D. diss., Columbia University, 1981); Randall H. Balmer, *A Perfect Babel of Confusion: Dutch Religion and English Culture in the Middle Colonies* (New York and Oxford: Oxford University Press, 1989); Joyce D. Goodfriend, *Before the Melting Pot: Society and Culture in Colonial New York City, 1664–1730* (Princeton: Princeton University Press, in press).

1. Origins

1. Johan Huizinga, "The Spirit of the Netherlands," in *Dutch Civilization in the Seventeenth Century*, Arnold J. Pomerans, trans. (New York: Frederick Ungar, 1968), p. 112.

2. Pieter Geyl, *The Netherlands in the Seventeenth Century* (London and New York: Ernest Benn Ltd. and Barnes and Noble, 1961) I:248.

3. Huizinga, "Dutch Civilization in the Seventeenth Century," in *Dutch Civilization*, p. 14.

4. Simon Schama, *The Embarrassment of Riches: An Interpretation of Dutch*

Culture in the Golden Age (Berkeley: University of California Press, 1988), pp. 4, 7.

5. Alice P. Kenney, "Dutch Patricians in Colonial Albany," *New York History* 49 (1968): 253; quoted in Alice Kenney, *Stubborn for Liberty: The Dutch in New York* (Syracuse: Syracuse University Press, 1975), p. 69.

6. Donna Merwick, "Dutch Townsmen and Land Use: A Spatial Perspective on Seventeenth-Century Albany, New York," *William and Mary Quarterly* 3rd ser. 37 (1980): 53–78; idem, *Possessing Albany, 1630–1710: The Dutch and English Experiences* (Cambridge: Cambridge University Press, 1990). However, Albert S. McKinley noted that "town life developed late and with difficulty among the Dutch [in New Netherland.]" He cites instructions dated July 7, 1645, sent to the Director and Council at New Amsterdam that "they shall endeavor as much as possible, that the colonists settle themselves with a certain number of families in some of the most suitable places, in the manner of villages, towns, and hamlets, as the English are in the habit of doing, who thereby live more securely." McKinley, "English and Dutch Towns of New Netherland," *American Historical Review* 6 (1900): 1–18.

7. Thomas J. Condon, *New York Beginnings: The Commercial Origins of New Netherland* (New York and London: New York University Press and University of London Press, 1968), p. 120.

8. Ibid., p. 178. For a different interpretation see Van Cleaf Bachman, *Peltries or Plantations: The Economic Policies of the Dutch West India Company in New Netherland, 1623–1639* (Baltimore: Johns Hopkins University Press, 1969).

9. Alan Gowans, *Architecture in New Jersey* (Princeton: D. Van Nostrand, 1964), p. 19; idem, *Images of American Living: Four Centuries of Architecture and Furniture as Cultural Expression* (Philadelphia and New York: J. B. Lippincott, 1964), p. 60.

10. Rosalie Fellows Bailey, *Pre-Revolutionary Dutch Houses and Families in Northern New Jersey and Southern New York* (1936; Reprint, New York: Dover, 1968); idem, "Emigrants to New Netherland, Account Book, 1654 to 1664," *New York Genealogical and Biographical Record* 94 (1963): 193–200; Henry G. Bayer, *The Belgians: First Settlers in New York and the Middle States* (New York: Devin-Adair, 1925); Van Brunt Bergen, "A List of Early Immigrants to New Netherland, 1657–1664," Holland Society of New York. *Yearbook* (1896): 141–158; John O. Evjen, *Scandinavian Immigrants in New York, 1630–1674* (Minneapolis, Minn.: K. C. Holter, 1916); Cornelius Burnham Harvey, *Genealogical History of Hudson and Bergen Counties, New Jersey* (New York: New Jersey Genealogical Publishing Co., 1900); "List of Passengers, 1654–1664," Holland Society of New York. *Yearbook* (1902): 5–37; I. N. P. Stokes, *The Iconography of Manhattan Island, 1498–1909* (New York: R. H. Dodd, 1915–1928)II; Helen Wilkinson Reynolds, *Dutch Houses in the Hudson Valley Before 1776* (1929; Reprint, New York: Dover, 1965); A. J. F. Van Laer, ed., *Van Rensselaer-Bowier Manuscripts* (Albany: University of the State of New York, 1908), pp. 805–846.

11. Edmund B. O'Callaghan, ed., *Documents Relative to the Colonial History of the State of New York* (Albany: Weed, Parsons and Co., 1853–1887) I: 44; Peter O. Wacker, *Land and People: A Cultural Geography of Preindustrial New Jersey* (New Brunswick: Rutgers University Press, 1975), pp. 129–130.

12. Compiled from "List of Passengers, 1653–1664," pp. 5–57; Bailey, "Emigrants to New Netherland," pp. 193–200.

13. Oliver A. Rink, *Holland on the Hudson: An Economic and Social History of Dutch New York* (Ithaca and London: Cornell University Press; Cooperstown, N.Y.: New York State Historical Association, 1986), p. 150; idem, "The People of New Netherland: Notes on Non-English Immigration to New York in the Seventeenth Century," *New York History* 62 (1981): 22–23.

14. Mildred Campbell, "Social Origins of Some Early Americans," in *Seventeenth-Century America: Essays in Colonial History*, James Morton Smith, ed. (Chapel Hill: University of North Carolina Press, 1959), pp. 71, 73. Campbell's findings have been questioned by David W. Galenson, " 'Middling People' or 'Common Sort'? : The Social Origins of Some Early Americans Reexamined," *William and Mary Quarterly* 3d. ser. 35 (1978): 499–524. Campbell replied in *ibid.*, pp. 525–540, and Galenson responded to her reply in *ibid.*, 36 (1979): 264–286.

15. Van Laer, *Van Rensselaer-Bowier Manuscripts*, pp. 841–842; *Philipsburgh Manor* (Tarrytown: Sleepy Hollow Restorations, 1969), pp. 8–9; Evjen, *Scandinavian Immigrants*, p. 145; Stokes, *Iconography* II: 240, 243–244, 249; Bailey, *Pre-Revolutionary Dutch Houses*, p. 504.

16. Robert G. Wheeler, "The House of Jeremias Van Rensselaer, 1658–1666," *New York Historical Society Quarterly* 45 (1961): 79.

17. Most previous studies of the origins of the settlers in New Netherland have been either genealogies solely of antiquarian interest or exercises in ethnic chauvinism trying to prove which nationality came first or contributed most. See Bailey, *Pre-Revolutionary Dutch Houses*; Harvey, *Genealogical History*; Bayer, *The Belgians*; and Evjen, *Scandinavian Immigrants*. Yet national origin is elusive, because the national boundaries have changed considerably since the seventeenth century. Territory that was then part of the Spanish Netherlands (Belgium) is today part of France. Furthermore, cultural boundaries tend to cut across political boundaries. There was little difference in either language or house types between peasants in Friesland in the Netherlands and peasants in East Friesland in Germany. Therefore, I listed places of origin by provinces, duchies, and principalities, using the political boundaries that existed in the seventeenth century. I utilized gazetteers to determine the town, province, duchy, or principality in which each place was located in the seventeenth century. See Angelo Heilprin and Louis Heilprin, eds., *Lippincott's New Gazetteer* (Philadelphia: J. B. Lippincott, 1906); Leon E. Speltzer, ed., *The Columbia Lippincott Gazetteer of the World* (New York: Columbia University Press, 1962).

18. The Palatinate was the domain of the Electors Palatine, who were high

princes of the Holy Roman Empire. It consisted of two geographically separate territories. The Lower Palatinate, situated on the Rhine, was divided into Baden, Hesse, and Nassau in the nineteenth century. The Upper Palatinate, situated to the southeast, became part of Bavaria in the eighteenth century. The town of New Paltz, New York, was named after the Palatinate (*Pfalz* or *Pfalts* in German).

19. Evjen, *Scandinavian Immigrants*, pp. 402, 434–35; Reynolds, *Dutch Houses*, p. 220; E. B. O'Callaghan, ed., *Documentary History of the State of New York* (Albany: Weed, Parsons & Co., 1850) III: 36; Bailey, *Pre-Revolutionary Dutch Houses*, pp. 89–90; Morton Wagman, "The Rise of Pieter Claessen Wyckoff: Social Mobility on the Colonial Frontier," *New York History* 52 (1972): 5–24.

20. Reynolds, *Dutch Houses*, pp. 203–4; Katherine Bevier, *The Bevier Family* (New York: T. A. Wright, 1916), p. 15; Bailey, *Pre-Revolutionary Dutch Houses*, pp. 284–85; Adrian C. Leiby, *The Huguenot Settlement of Schraalenburgh* (Bergenfield, N.J.: Bergenfield Free Public Library, 1964), pp. 6–8; Stokes, *Iconography*, II: 273–74; Bayer, *The Belgians*, pp. 175–78.

21. Katherine Bevier, *The Bevier Family* (New York: T. A. Wright, 1916), pp. 11–13; Bayer, *The Belgians*, pp. 70, 96, 163–165, 175, 178, 190, 194, 221.

22. Bailey, *Pre-Revolutionary Dutch Houses*, pp. 210, 265, 314; Evjen, *Scandinavian Immigrants*, pp. 167–181, 276.

23. Evjen, *Scandinavian Immigrants*, p. 12.

24. Ibid., pp. 19–36; Reynolds, *Dutch Houses*, p. 64.

25. Bayer, *The Belgians*, pp. 174–175; Bailey, *Pre-Revolutionary Dutch Houses*, pp. 293, 312; O'Callaghan, *Documentary History* III: 35; Evjen, *Scandinavian Immigrants*, pp. 214–215; Van Laer, *Van Rensselaer-Bowier Manuscripts*, p. 812.

26. Van Laer, *Van Rensselaer-Bowier Manuscripts*, pp. 805, 809; Alvin Page Johnson, *Franklin D. Roosevelt's Colonial Ancestors* (Boston: Lothrop, Lee and Shepard, 1933), pp. 16–18.

27. Van Laer, *Van Rensselaer-Bowier Manuscripts*, p. 817; Bailey, *Pre-Revolutionary Dutch Houses*, p. 523; O'Callaghan, *Documentary History* III: 35.

28. Adrian Leiby, *The Early Dutch and Swedish Settlers of New Jersey* (Princeton: D. Van Nostrand, 1964), pp. 41–42; Bailey, *Pre-Revolutionary Dutch Houses*, pp. 180–181, 270, 277, 281, 320; Reynolds, *Dutch Houses*, p. 376; O'Callaghan, *Documentary History* III: 39; Van Laer, *Van Rensselaer-Bowier Manuscripts*, p. 824.

29. Conrad M. Arensberg, "A Comparative Analysis of Culture and Community: Peoples of the Old World," in *Culture and Community*, by Conrad M. Arensberg and Solon T. Kimball (New York: Harcourt, Brace, and World, 1965), p. 79.

30. Ibid., p. 80.

31. Audrey M. Lambert, *The Making of the Dutch Landscape: A Historical Geography of the Netherlands* (London and New York: Seminar Press, 1971), pp. 18, 48.

32. Ibid., p. 67.

33. Ibid., pp. 124–125.

34. Ibid., p. 232; For an account of how the market economy developed in the western provinces of the Netherlands, see Jan de Vries, *The Dutch Rural Economy in the Golden Age, 1500–1700* (New Haven: Yale University Press, 1974).

35. R. C. Hekker, "Historical Types of Farms," *Atlas van Nederland*, Foundation for the Scientific Atlas of the Netherlands ('s Gravenhage: Staatsdrakkerij en Uitgeverijdedrijf, 1963–), Plate X-1; Hekker, "De Ontwikkeling van de Boerderijvormen in Nederland," *Duizend Jaar Bowen in Nederland*, edited by S. J. Fockema Andreae, E. H. Ter Kuile, and R. C. Hekker (Amsterdam: Allert de Lange, 1956) II: 294–301, 309–316; Hekker, *De Zeeuwse Hofstede* (Middleburg: J. C. & W. Alterffere, 1951), pp. 37–39.

36. Karl Baumgarten, "Studies in Rural Buildings in Mecklenburg," *Technology and Culture* 5 (1964): 234–240; Hans Riediger and Johan Ulrich Folkers, *Stammestude von Schleswig-Holstein und Mecklenburg* (Potsdam: Adademische Verlagsge Athenaion, 1942); Adolf Helbok, "Die Deutschen Stamme und die Moderne Volksforschung," *Volkskundliche Gabe*, John Meier, ed. (Berlin und Leipzig: Walter De Gruyter und Co., 1934), pp. 54–67; Bruno Schmidt, *Das Sachsiche Bauernhaus und Seine Dorfgenossen* (Dresden: Holzeund Pahl, n.d.); Wilhelm Pessler, *Das Altsachsiche Bauernhause in Seiner Geographische Verbreitung* (Braunsschweig: F. Vieweg und Soh, 1906).

37. William Z. Shetter, *Introduction to Dutch* (The Hague: Martinus Nijhoff, 1975), p. 2.

38. Piet van Wijk, "Form and Function in the Netherlands' Agricultural Architecture," in *New World Dutch Studies*, Roderic Blackburn and Nancy A. Kelley, eds. (Albany: Albany Institute of History and Art, 1987), pp. 165–169.

39. L'Abbe J. Lemire, "L'habitat dans la Flandre Francaise," *Annales du Comite Flamand de France* 20 (1892): 17–18.

40. John Y. Keur and Dorothy L. Keur, *The Deeply Rooted: A Study of a Drents Community in the Netherlands* (Seattle: University of Washington Press, 1955), pp. 49–50.

41. Sumner Chilton Powell, *Puritan Village: The Formation of a New England Town* (1963; Reprint, Garden City: Doubleday and Co., 1963), p. xvi. Historian David Grayson Allen has modified Powell's thesis somewhat by noting that it is an oversimplification to say that Massachusetts colonists came from only three types of English communities. For example, Allen notes that there were differences between open field manors in Yorkshire and Hampshire. Furthermore, in some New England towns the inhabitants came from a single locality and reconstructed its agricultural system; in other New England towns the settlers were from several different localities in England, but one tradition became dominant. See David Grayson Allen, *In English Ways: The Movement of Societies and the Transferral of English Local Law and Custom to Massachusetts Bay in*

the Seventeenth Century (Chapel Hill: University of North Carolina Press, 1981), pp. 16, 82.

2. Farmhouse

1. Rosalie Fellows Bailey, *Pre-Revolutionary Dutch Houses and Families in Northern New Jersey and Southern New York* (1936; Reprint, New York: Dover, 1968), p. 20.

2. Ibid.; Helen Wilkinson Reynolds, *Dutch Houses in the Hudson Valley Before 1776* (1929; Reprint, New York: Dover, 1968).

3. Bailey, *Pre-Revolutionary Dutch Houses*, p. 20.

4. Hugh Morrison, *Early American Architecture from the First Colonial Settlement to the National Period* (New York: Oxford University Press, 1951), p. 123.

5. Thomas Jefferson Wertenbaker, *The Old South*, The Founding of American Civilization (1942; Reprint, New York: Cooper Square, 1963), pp. 82, 88 facing.

6. J[ohn] Frederick Kelly, *The Early Domestic Architecture of Connecticut* (New Haven: Yale University Press, 1924), pp. 59–60.

7. Thomas Jefferson Wertenbaker, *The Middle Colonies*, The Founding of American Civilization (1938; Reprint, New York: Cooper Square, 1963), pp. 66–74.

8. Alan Gowans, *Images of American Living; Four Centuries of Architecture and Furniture as Cultural Expression* (Philadelphia and New York: J. B. Lippincott, 1964), p. 55.

9. Michel Lessard et Huguette Marquis, *Encyclopedia de la Maison Quebecoise: 3 Siecles d'Habitations* (Montreal: Les Editions de l'Homme, 1972).

10. Gowans, *Images of American Living*, p. 59.

11. Ibid., p. 56.

12. Ibid., p. 59.

13. Ibid., p. 60.

14. Ibid., pp. 46–47.

15. John L. Cotter and J. Paul Hudson, *New Discoveries at Jamestown* (Washington, D.C.: U.S. Government Printing Office, 1957), pp. 21, 23.

16. Wertenbaker, *The Old South*, p. 81; Morrison, *Early American Architecture*, p. 158.

17. Henry Glassie, *Pattern in the Material Folk Culture of the Eastern United States* (Philadelphia: University of Pennsylvania Press, 1968), pp. 7–11.

18. Kelly, *Early Domestic Architecture of Connecticut*.

19. Henry Glassie, *Folk Housing in Middle Virginia: A Structural Analysis of Historic Artifacts* (Knoxville: University of Tennessee Press, 1975), pp. 17, 19–21, 36, 39, 71, 162, 185.

20. Ricardo Torres-Reyes describes the Wick House as a "transitional Dutch-English type" because it lacks summer beams. *The Wick House: Historic Structure Report* (Washington, D.C.: U.S. Department of the Interior, National

Park Service, 1971), pp. 15–16. However, the summer beam is only one architectural feature. The frame of the Wick House is basically English, not Dutch, and it has a central-chimney floor plan similar to houses in New England. Thus, by the methodology suggested in this chapter, the house is clearly English, because its primary characteristics are English.

21. M[aurice] W. Barley, *The English Farmhouse and Cottage* (London: Routledge and Kegan Paul, 1961), pp. 21–37; L. F. Saltzman, *Building in England down to 1540; A Documentary History* (1952; Reprint, London: Oxford University Press, 1967), pp. 195–222.

22. John Fitchen, *The New World Dutch Barn* (Syracuse: Syracuse University Press, 1968), pp. 13–16; 115–137.

23. Marvin D. Schwartz, *The Jan Martense Schenck House* (Brooklyn: The Brooklyn Museum, 1964).

24. In the New World Dutch barn, the H-bent forms the center aisle, and secondary posts, connected to the H-bents by means of transverse struts form the two outside aisles. Fitchen, *The New World Dutch Barn*, pp. 26–31.

25. Theodore H. M. Prudon, "The Dutch Barn in America: Survival of a Medieval Structural Frame," *New York Folklore* 2 (1976): 125–130.

26. Henry Glassie, "The Variation of Concepts Within Tradition: Barn Building in Otsego County, New York," in *Man and Cultural Heritage; Papers in Honor of Fred B. Kniffen*, ed. H. J. Walter and W. G. Haag, *Geoscience and Man*, vol. 5 (Baton Rouge: School of Geoscience, Louisiana State University, 1974), pp. 229–230.

27. James Deetz, *In Small Things Forgotten: The Archeology of Early American Life* (Garden City: Doubleday-Anchor, 1977), p. 93.

28. Joel Munsell, ed. *The Annals of Albany* (Albany: J. Munsell, 1850–1859) VI: 20.

29. "From the 'Historisch Verhael,' by Nicholaes van Wassenaer, 1624–1630," in *Narratives of New Netherland*, J. Franklin Jameson, ed. (New York: Charles Scribner's Sons, 1909), p. 83.

30. E. B. O'Callaghan, ed., *The Documentary History of the State of New York* (Albany: Charles van Benthuysen, 1851) IV: 31.

31. Isaac Newton Phelps Stokes, ed., *The Iconography of Manhattan Island, 1498–1909* (New York: R. H. Dodd, 1915–1928) I: 14.

32. John Fitchen, *The New World Dutch Barn* (Syracuse: Syracuse University Press, 1968), pp. 3–4.

33. Arnold J. F. Van Laer, ed., *Van Rensselaer-Bowier Manuscripts* (Albany: University of the State of New York, 1908), pp. 308, 309.

34. Reginald McMahon, "The Achter Col Colony on the Hackensack," *New Jersey History* 89 (1971): 228–229.

35. Arnold J. F. Van Laer, trans., *New York Historical Manuscripts: Dutch*, Kenneth Scott and Kenn Stryker-Rhodda, eds. (Baltimore: Genealogical Publishing Co., 1974) II: 16–17.

36. A. J. F. Van Laer, trans., *Register of the Provincial Secretary, 1638–1642*, Kenneth Scott and Kenn Stryker-Rhodda, eds. (Baltimore: Genealogical Publishing Co., 1974) I: 82.

37. E. B. O'Callaghan, *History of New Netherland* (New York: D. Appleton and Co., 1848), p. 458.

38. New York State Division for Historic Preservation, *Archeology at the Schuyler Flatts, 1971–1974* (Colonie, N.Y.: Town of Colonie, 1974).

39. Paul Huey, "Archeology in Seventeenth-Century Dutch Sites in Rensselaerswyck," a lecture presented at the Seminar on Rensselaerswyck, New York State Library, Albany, N.Y., April 7, 1979.

40. Van Laer, *New York Historical Manuscripts*, I: 28.

41. O'Callaghan, *History of New Netherland*, p. 473.

42. H. J. Zantkuyl, "De Houten Huizen van Holysloot," *Bulletin van de Koninklijke Oudheidkundige Bond* 67 (1968): 11–27.

43. Idem, "Reconstructive van Enkele Nederlandse Huizen in Nieuw-Nederland uit de Zeventiende Eeuw," *Bulletin van de Koninklijke Oudheidkundige Bond* 84 (1985): 166–179.

44. Isaac Newton Phelps Stokes, *The Iconography of Manhattan Island, 1498–1909* (New York: R. H. Dodd, 1915–1928) II: 219, 225, 249, 259, 280, 282, 295, 300, 314, 316, 323, 326, 327; A. J. F. Van Laer, ed., *Van Rensselaer-Bowier Manuscripts* (Albany: University of the State of New York, 1908), pp. 835, 836, 839, 840–841, 843, 826, 809, 810, 812, 813, 816, 821, 825, 830, 832, 833.

45. Augustus Van Buren, *A History of Ulster County Under the Dutch* (Kingston, N.Y.: n.p., 1923), p. 50.

46. A. J. F. Van Laer, ed., *Minutes of the Court of Albany, Rensselaerswyck, and Schenectady, 1668–1680* (Albany: University of the State of New York, 1926–1932) I: 106.

47. Historic American Building Survey, New Jersey, NJ-16, Sheet 23.

48. Peter Kalm, *The America of 1750: Peter Kalm's Travels in North America*, Adolph B. Benson, ed. (New York: Wilson Erickson, 1937) I: 356.

49. " 'Novum Belgium' by Father Isaac Joques, 1646," in Jameson, ed., *Narratives of New Netherland*, p. 261.

50. In 1790 Dr. Alexander Coventry, a Scottish physician living at Hudson, New York, visited the house of Lambert Burgherts, which he described as being "built of small irregular stones; then plastered over with lime mixed with charcoal, which gives it a blue limestone appearance in colour. Then this is painted white, so as to resemble square stones." Alexander Coventry, Diary, p. 462. New York State Library, Albany, New York.

51. Joques, "Novum Belgium," p. 262.

52. Van Laer, *New York Historical Manuscripts*, II: 200–201.

53. Quoted in Christopher Ward, *The Dutch and Swedes on the Delaware, 1609–64* (Philadelphia: University of Pennsylvania Press, 1930), p. 116.

54. Kalm, *Travels in America*, I: 341.

55. "Letter of Reverend Jonas Michaelius, 1628," in Jameson, ed., *Narratives of New Netherland*, p. 131.

56. Van Laer, *Van Rensselaer-Bowier Manuscripts*, pp. 575, 606.

57. N. R. Ewans, *Early Brickmaking in the Colonies: A Common Fallacy Corrected* (Camden, N.J.: Camden County Historical Society, 1938), pp. 1, 10.

58. Van Laer, *Register of the Provincial Secretary*, II: 109.

59. "From the 'Kort Historiael Ende Journaels Aaenteyckeninge,' by David Pietersz. de Vries, 1633–1643," in Jameson, *Narratives of New Netherland*, p. 198.

60. Van Laer, *Register of the Provincial Secretary*, II: 200–201.

61. Ibid., III: 213.

62. [Alexander Hamilton,] *Gentleman's Progress: The Itinerarium of Dr. Alexander Hamilton, 1744*, Carl Bridenbaugh, ed. (Chapel Hill: University of North Carolina Press, 1948), p. 39.

63. Roderic H. Blackburn and Ruth Piwonka, *Remembrance of Patria: Dutch Arts and Culture in Colonial America, 1609–1776* (Albany: Albany Institute of History and Art, 1988), p. 147.

64. Glassie, "Variation of Concepts," pp. 229–230.

65. Kalm, *Travels in North America*, I: 356.

66. Joseph W. Hammond, "An Historical Analysis of the Bronck House, Coxsackie, New York," *De Halve Maen* 55 (1980): 5–8, 17–18.

67. Anne McVicar Grant, *Memoirs of an American Lady* (New York: Samuel Campbell, 1809), pp. 85–89.

68. Roger G. Kennedy, *Architecture, Men, Women and Money in America, 1600–1860* (New York: Random House, 1985), pp. 60–72.

69. Zantkuyl, "Reconstructive van Enkele Nederlandse Huizen," pp. 176–179.

70. Paul Huey and John G. Waite, *Washington's Headquarters: The Hasbrouck House: An Historic Structure Report* (n.p.: New York State Historic Trust, 1971).

71. Marquis de Chastellux, *Travels in North America in the Years 1780, 1781, and 1782*, Howard C. Rice, ed. (Chapel Hill: University of North Carolina Press, 1963), pp. 513–514.

72. Helen Wilkinson Reynolds, *Dutch Houses in the Hudson Valley Before 1776* (1929; Reprint, New York: Dover Publications, 1965), pp. 203–204; Kenneth E. Hasbrouck, *A Guide to Huguenot Street and Preservation Efforts of the Huguenot Historical Society, New Paltz, N.Y.* (New Paltz: Huguenot Historical Society, 1974), pp. 20–24.

73. Robert Blair St. George, "A Retreat from the Wilderness: Patterns in the Domestic Environments of Southeastern New England, 1630–1730" (Ph.D. diss., University of Pennsylvania, 1982), p. 159.

74. [Jasper Danckaerts,] *Journal of Jasper Danckaerts*, Bartlett Burleigh James and J. Franklin Jameson, eds. (New York: Charles Scribner's Sons, 1913), p. 58.

75. Rosalie Fellows Bailey, *Pre-Revolutionary Dutch Houses and Families in*

Northern New Jersey and Southern New York (1936; Reprint, New York: Dover Publications, 1968), pp. 88–91; Maud Esther Dilliard, *Old Dutch Houses of Brooklyn* (New York: Richard R. Smith, 1945), n.p.; Milner (John) Associates, "Historical Structure Report on the Pieter Claesen Wyckoff House, Brooklyn, New York," Preliminary Report (New York City Department of Parks and Recreation and New York City Landmarks Commission, 1979), n.p.

76. Milner Associates, "The Pieter Claesen Wyckoff House," n.p.

77. Marvin D. Schwartz, *The Jan Martense Schenck House* (Brooklyn: The Brooklyn Museum, 1964).

78. Letter from Marvin D. Schwartz and Daniel M. C. Hopping to H. J. Zantkuyl, April 19, 1963, Jan Martense Schenck Notebooks, vol. 1, Brooklyn Museum, Brooklyn, N.Y.

79. H. J. Zantkuyl, "De Houten Huizen van Holysloot," *Bulletin van de Koninklijke Nederlandse Oudheidkundige Bond* 67 (1968): 11–27.

80. Bailey, *Pre-Revolutionary Dutch Houses*, pp. 404–405, 421; Clifford W. Zink, "Dutch Framed Houses in New York and New Jersey," *Winterthur Portfolio* 22 (1987): 289.

81. "The Minnie Schenck House in Nassau County, L.I.," *De Halve Maen* 50 (April 1975): 11–12.

82. James Thacher, *A Military Journal During the American Revolutionary War* (Boston: Cottons and Barnard, 1872), p. 154.

83. George Olin Zabriskie, "The Zabriskie-von Steuben House," *De Halve Maen* 38 (1963): 11–12; idem., "Bergen County Landmark to be Re-Named," ibid. 42 (1967): 11–12.

84. Firth Haring Fabend, "The Yeoman Ideal: A Dutch Family in the Middle Colonies, 1660–1800" (Ph.D. diss., New York University, 1988), pp. 111–112; idem, *A Dutch Family in the Middle Colonies, 1660–1800* (New Brunswick and London: Rutgers University Press, 1991), pp. 242–244.

85. Henry Glassie, "Eighteenth-Century Cultural Process in Delaware Valley Folk Building," *Winterthur Portfolio* 7 (1972): 42–43.

86. Coventry, Diary, p. 124.

87. Ibid., p. 125.

88. Ibid., p. 129.

89. Ibid., p. 130.

90. Ibid.

91. Ibid., p. 161.

92. Van Laer, *Register of the Provincial Secretary*, III: 267–272.

93. Estate inventory of Jacques Cortelyou, New Utrecht, January 20, 1694, New York State Library Mss., Albany, N.Y.

94. Simon Schama, *The Embarrassment of Riches: An Interpretation of Dutch Culture in the Golden Age* (Berkeley: University of California Press, 1988), pp. 316–320.

95. John Demos, *A Little Commonwealth: Family Life in Plymouth Colony* (New York: Oxford University Press, 1970), pp. 36–51; James Deetz, *In Small*

Things Forgotten: The Archeology of Early American Life (Garden City, N.Y.: Anchor Books, 1977), pp. 51–52, 59–60.

96. These conclusions are based on the following estate inventories in the New Jersey State Archives, Trenton, New Jersey: Joseph Sigler, Bloomfield Township, Essex County, December 14, 1800; Cornelius Lozier, Township of Franklin, Bergen County, 1815; Jacob Van Ness, Township of Caldwell, Essex County, May 15, 1821; George Doremus, New Barbadoes, Bergen County, June 2, 1830; Abraham Staats, Franklin Township, Somerset County, May 10, 1821; Martin T. Cook, Montville Township, Morris County, October 11, 1880; Symen Van Wickle, Franklin Township, Somerset County, March 24, 1757; and the following estate inventory in the New York State Library, Albany, N.Y.: Hezekiah Van Orden, Catskill, Albany County, November 1, 2, and 4, 1796.

97. Van Laer, *Correspondence of Jeremias Van Rensselaer, 1651–1674* (Albany: University of the State of New York, 1932), p. 387n.

98. Ibid., p. 386.

99. Hanson, "Interior Architecture and Housing," p. 124.

100. Abbott Lowell Cummings, "Inside the Massachusetts House," in *Common Places: Readings in American Vernacular Architecture*, Dell Upton and John Michael Vlach, eds. (Athens: University of Georgia Press, 1986), p. 227.

101. Ibid., p. 224.

102. The term parlor occurs in Massachusetts and Virginia in the seventeenth century, but there too it had multiple uses, including the room for the best furniture, a bedroom for the parents, and a room for entertaining guests. Ibid., pp. 220, 222. See also Mark R. Wenger, "The Central Passage in Virginia: Evolution of an Eighteenth-Century Living Space," in *Perspectives in Vernacular Architecture, II*, Camille Wells, ed. (Columbia: University of Missouri Press, 1986) and Dell Upton, "Vernacular Domestic Architecture in Eighteenth-Century Virginia," in Upton and Vlach, eds., *Common Places*, p. 320.

3. Landscape

1. John R. Stilgoe, *Common Landscape of America, 1580 to 1845* (New Haven and London: Yale University Press, 1982), p. 7.

2. Adriaen van der Donck, *A Description of the New Netherlands*, Thomas F. O'Donnell, ed. (1655; Reprint, Syracuse: Syracuse University Press, 1968), pp. 17–19.

3. Stilgoe, *Common Landscape*, p. 143.

4. E. B. O'Callaghan, *Documentary History of the State of New York* (Albany: Charles van Benthuysen, 1851) IV: 30.

5. Stilgoe, *Common Landscape*, pp. 171–173.

6. A. J. F. Van Laer, ed., *Documents Relating to New Netherland, 1624–1626, in the Henry E. Huntington Library* (San Marino, Calif.: Huntington Library, 1924), pp. 2–17.

7. Ibid., pp. 40, 43.

8. Ibid., p. 118.

9. Van Cleaf Bachman, *Peltries and Plantations: The Economic Policies of the Dutch West India Company in New Netherland, 1613–1639* (Baltimore: Johns Hopkins University Press, 1969), p. 70.

10. Van Laer, ed., *Van Rensselaer-Bowier Manuscripts* (Albany: University of the State of New York, 1908), p. 149.

11. John Y. Keur and Dorothy L. Keur, *The Deeply Rooted: A Study of a Drents Community in the Netherlands* (Seattle: University of Washington Press, 1955), p. 71.

12. Isaac Newton Phelps Stokes, *The Iconography of Manhattan Island, 1498–1909* (New York: Robert H. Dodd, 1916) II: 183–208.

13. Audrey M. Lambert, *The Making of the Dutch Landscape: A Historical Geography of the Netherlands* (London and New York: Seminar Press, 1971), pp. 66–67.

14. Van Laer, *Van Rensselaer-Bowier Manuscripts*, p. 139.

15. Ibid., p. 141.

16. Ibid., p. 157.

17. Ibid., pp. 306–312.

18. Ibid., pp. 740–743.

19. Lambert, *The Making of the Dutch Landscape*, pp. 89–106.

20. See Anthony N. B. Garvan, *Architecture and Town Planning in Colonial Connecticut* (New Haven: Yale University Press, 1951).

21. Albert E. McKinley, "The English and Dutch Towns of New Netherland," *The American Historical Review* 5 (1900): 6.

22. Donna Merwick, "Dutch Townsmen and Land Use: A Spatial Perspective on Seventeenth-Century Albany, New York," *William and Mary Quarterly* 3rd ser. 37 (1980): 53–78.

23. E. B. O'Callaghan, *History of New Netherland* (New York: D. Appleton, 1848) I: 392–393.

24. O'Callaghan, ed., *Documents Relative to the Colonial History of the State of New York* (Albany: Weed, Parsons and Co., 1856) I: 160–162.

25. McKinley, "The English and Dutch Towns," pp. 6, 6n., 10, 10n, 12n; Langdon C. Wright, "Local Governmental and Central Authority in New Netherland," *New York Historical Society Quarterly* 57 (1973): 7–29; Dixon Ryan Fox, *Yankees and Yorkers* (New York: New York University Press, 1940).

26. Frederick Van Wyck, *Kreskechauge, or the First White Settlement on Long Island* (New York: G. P. Putnam's Sons, 1924), pp. 59–60, 67–68, 70–80.

27. [Jasper Danckaerts,] *Journal of Jasper Danckaerts*, Bartlett Burleigh James and J. Franklin Jameson, eds. (New York: Charles Scribner's Sons, 1913), pp. 52, 60, 62.

28. James Riker, *Revised History of Harlem: Its Origin and Early Annals* (New York: New Harlem Publishing Company, 1904), pp. 184–206.

29. Lambert, *The Making of the Dutch Landscape*, pp. 52–60.

30. Peter O. Wacker, *Land and People: A Cultural Geography of Preindustrial New Jersey: Origins and Settlement Patterns* (New Brunswick: Rutgers University Press, 1975), pp. 239–242.

31. Sung Bok Kim, *Landlord and Tenant in Colonial New York: Manorial Society, 1664–1775* (Chapel Hill: University of North Carolina Press, 1978), p. 41.

32. George H. Budke, "The History of the Tappan Patent," in *The Rockland Record*, George H. Budke, ed. (Nyack, N.Y.: Rockland County Society of the State of New York, 1931) II: 35–42.

33. Peter O. Wacker, *Land and People: A Cultural Geography of Preindustrial New Jersey: Origins and Settlement Patterns* (New Brunswick: Rutgers University Press, 1975) p. 242.

34. Richard Bayles, *History of Richmond County (Staten Island), New York, From Its Discovery to the Present Time* (New York: L. E. Preston, 1887), p. 95.

35. [Danckaerts,] *Journal of Jasper Danckaerts*, pp. 69–70, 72.

36. Patricia Bonomi, *A Factious People: Politics and Society in Colonial New York* (New York: Columbia University Press, 1971); David Maldwyn Ellis, *Landlords and Farmers in the Hudson-Mohawk Region, 1670–1850* (Ithaca: Cornell University Press, 1946); Fox, *Yankees and Yorkers*; Kim, *Landlord and Tenant*; idem, "A New Look at the Great Landlords of Eighteenth-Century New York," *William and Mary Quarterly* 3rd ser. 27 (1970): 581–614; Staughton Lynd, *Anti-Federalists in Dutchess County, New York* (Chicago: Loyala University Press, 1962); idem, "Who Should Rule at Home? Dutchess County, New York, in the American Revolution," *William and Mary Quarterly* 3rd. ser. 27 (1961): 330–359.

37. Kim, *Landlord and Tenant*, p. 183.

38. Ibid., p. 234.

39. Ellis, *Landlords and Farmers*, pp. 309–312.

40. H. F. Raup, "The Fence in the Cultural Landscape," *Western Folklore* 6 (1947): 1.

41. Wilbur Zelinsky, "Walls and Fences," *Landscape* 8 (1959): 14–15; Eugene Cotton Mather and John Fraser Hart, "Fences and Farms," *The Geographical Review* 44 (1954): 208–209.

42. Raup, "The Fence," p. 2.

43. Adriaen van der Donck, *A Description of the New Netherlands*, Thomas F. O'Donnell, ed. (1655; Reprint, Syracuse: Syracuse University Press, 1968), pp. 29–30.

44. A. T. F. Van Laer, trans. *Register of the Provincial Secretary, 1638–1642* (Baltimore: Genealogical Publishing Co., 1974) I: 28.

45. Berthold Fernow, ed., *The Record of New Amsterdam from 1653 to 1674, Anno Domini* (New York: The Knickerbocker Press, 1897) I: 3.

46. Ibid., p. 4.

47. A. T. F. Van Laer, *Minutes of the Court of Albany, Rensselaerswyck, and*

Schenectady, 1668–1673 (Albany: University of the State of New York, 1926) I: 16–17.

48. Quoted in Frederick van Wyck, *Kreskachauge, or the First White Settlement on Long Island* (New York and London: G. P. Putnam's Sons, 1924), p. 118.

49. Van Laer, *Register of the Provincial Secretary*, II: 89.

50. Ibid., p. 214.

51. Ibid., p. 127.

52. William Strickland, *Journal of a Tour in the United States of America, 1794–1795*, Rev. T. E. Strickland, ed. (New York: New York Historical Society, 1971), p. 76.

53. Adriances Van Brunt, Diary and Journal Kept on his Farm near Brooklyn, New York, June 8, 1828 to March 20, 1830, Manuscript Division, New York Public Library, New York, N.Y.

54. Alexander Hamilton, *Itinerarium* . . . , Albert Bushnell Hart, ed. (St. Louis: William K. Bixby, 1907), p. 47.

55. Coventry, Diary, p. 472.

56. Zelinsky, "Walls and Fences," p. 17.

57. Peter Kalm, *Travels in North America*, Adolph B. Benson, ed. (New York: Wilson-Erickson, 1937) I: 352.

58. Strickland, *Journal*, p. 91.

59. Raup, "The Fence in the Cultural Landscape," pp. 3–4.

60. J. Le Francq van Berkhey, *Natuurlijke Historie van Holland* (Te Amsterdam en te Leyden: Yntema en Tieboel, P. H. Trap, 1769–1810) Afb. 9.

61. Don McTernan, "The Barrack, A Relict Feature on the North American Landscape," Pioneer America Society, *Transactions* (1978): 57.

62. R. C. Hekker, "Het Hooiberggebied," *Volkskunde* 9 (1950): 31–40.

63. Alfred L. Schoemaker, "Barracks," *Pennsylvania Folklife* 9 (1958): 3.

64. *Olde Ulster* 5 (1909): 41.

65. Kristin Lunde Gibbons, "The Van Bergen Overmantel" (M.A. thesis, State University of New York at Oneonta, 1966), pp. 49–50.

66. Ibid., p. 54.

67. Van Laer, *Van Rensselaer-Bowier Manuscripts*, pp. 308, 309.

68. A. T. F. Van Laer, trans., *Register of the Provincial Secretary, 1638–1642*, Kenneth Scott and Kenn Stryker-Rodda, eds. (Baltimore: Genealogical Publishing Co., 1974) I: 38.

69. Ibid., II: 134, 136.

70. Ibid., 127.

71. Gibbons, "The Van Bergen Overmantel."

72. Peter Kalm, *Travels in North America*, Adolph B. Benson, ed. (New York: Wilson-Erickson, 1937) I: 264–265.

73. Ibid., p. 332.

74. Quoted in Hubert G. Schmidt, *Rural Hunterdon: An Agricultural History* (New Brunswick: Rutgers University Press, 1945), p. 95.

75. *Harper's Magazine* (November 1854), p. 849, quoted in Shoemaker, "Barracks," p. 6.

76. Coventry, Diary, pp. 200–204.

77. Verplanck Family Mss., vol. 1, pp. 41–42, New York Historical Society, New York, N.Y.

78. A Treatise on Agriculture and Practical Husbandry, Farm and Garden Notebooks I, Verplanck Family Mss., pp. 39–40.

79. Gibbons, "The Van Bergen Overmantel," pp. 50–52.

80. Verplanck Family Mss., I: 40–41.

81. Estate Inventory of John Parleman, Pequannock Township, Morris County, N.J., 1805, New Jersey State Archives, Trenton, N.J.

82. Estate Inventory of John Day, English Neighborhood, Bergen County, N.J., 1816, New Jersey State Archives, Trenton, N.J.

83. Estate Inventory of William Colfax, Pompton, Passaic County, N.J., 1830, New Jersey State Archives, Trenton, N.J.

84. Estate Inventory of John H. Van Dien, Bergen County, N.J., 1878, New Jersey State Archives, Trenton, N.J.

85. Peter O. Wacker, "Folk Architecture as an Indicator of Culture Areas and Culture Diffusion: Dutch Barns and Barracks in New Jersey," *Pioneer America* 5 (1973): 42, 44.

86. Ibid., p. 39.

87. McTernan, "The Barrack," p. 57.

88. Patrick Campbell, *Travels in the Interior Inhabited Parts of North America in the Years 1791 and 1792*, H. H. Langton, ed. (Toronto: The Champlain Society, 1937), p. 133.

89. Verplanck Family Mss, I: 39.

90. Van Laer, *Register of the Provincial Secretary*, III: 267–276.

91. Ibid., I: 28.

92. John Fitchen, *The New World Dutch Barn* (Syracuse: Syracuse University Press, 1968), pp. 76–77; Theodore H. M. Prudon, "The Dutch Barn in America: Survival of a Medieval Structural Frame," *New York Folklore* 2 (1976): 123–142.

93. A. T. F. Van Laer, ed., *Early Records of the City and County of Albany and Colony of Rensselaerswyck* (Albany: University of the State of New York, 1918) III: 425.

94. "From the 'Korte Historiael Ende Journaels Aenteyckeninge,' by David Pieterze de Vries, 1633–1643 (1655)," in *Narratives of New Netherland, 1607–1664*, J. Franklin Jameson, ed. (New York: Charles Scribner's Sons, 1909).

95. Joseph Depuy, Account Book, 1770–1801, Albany Institute of History and Art, Albany, N.Y.

96. Juljan U. Niemcewicz, *Under Their Vine and Fig Tree: Travels in America in 1797–1799, 1805, with Some Further Account of Life in New Jersey* (Elizabeth, N.J.: New Jersey Historical Society, 1965), p. 180.

97. [Danckaerts,] *Journal of Jasper Danckaerts*, p. 58.

98. Kalm, *Travels in North America*, I: 118–119.

99. Ibid., p. 351.

100. Coventry, Diary, p. 392.

101. Ibid., p. 394.

102. Ibid., p. 468.

103. Ibid., p. 1185.

104. Mrs. Anne Grant, *Memoirs of an American Lady* (New York: Samuel Campbell, 1809), pp. 91–94.

105. Estate Inventory of Joseph Sigler, Essex County, N.J., 1800, New Jersey State Archives, Trenton, N.J.

106. Estate Inventory of Cornelius Lozier, Franklin Township, N.J., 1815, New Jersey State Archives, Trenton, N.J.

107. Estate Inventory of George Doremus, New Barbadoes, N.J., 1830, New Jersey State Archives, Trenton, N.J.

4. Farming

1. Alice P. Kenney, *Stubborn For Liberty: The Dutch in New York* (Syracuse: Syracuse University Press, 1975), p. 92.

2. Berthold Fernow, trans., *Records of New Amsterdam from 1653 to 1674 Anno Domini* (New York: Knickerbocker Press, 1897) I: 23.

3. Jasper Danckaerts, *Journal of Jasper Danckaerts*, Bartlett Burleigh James and J. Franklin Jameson, eds. (New York: Charles Scribner's Sons, 1913), p. 221.

4. Rodney C. Loehr, "Self-Sufficiency on the Farm, 1759–1819" *Agricultural History* 26 (1952): 37–42; James T. Lemon, *Best Poor Man's Country: A Geographical Study of Early Southeastern Pennsylvania* (Baltimore and London: Johns Hopkins Press, 1972), p. 6.

5. Adriaen van der Donck, *A Description of the New Netherlands*, Thomas F. O'Donnell, ed. (Syracuse: Syracuse University Press, 1968), pp. 30–31.

6. Ibid., p. 31.

7. Ibid., p. 33.

8. Ibid.

9. Ibid., p. 24.

10. Ibid., pp. 24–25.

11. Ibid., p. 68.

12. Ibid.

13. Peter Kalm, *Travels in North America*, Adolph B. Benson, ed. (New York: Wilson-Erickson, 1938), I: 335.

14. A Treatise on Agriculture and Practical Husbandry, Verplank Farm and Garden Notebook, Verplank Family Papers, c. 1800, vol. 1, pp. 77–79, New York Historical Society, New York, N.Y.

15. Kalm, *Travels*, I: 335.

16. Alexander Coventry, Recollections and Diary, July 1783–August 1789, p. 123, New York State Library, Albany, New York.

17. Quoted in Joel Munsell, *The Annals of Albany* (Albany: J. Munsell, 1850–1859) IV: 231.

18. Kalm, *Travels*, pp. 335–336.

19. Ibid., p. 335.

20. William Strickland, *Journal of a Tour in the United States of America, 1794–1795*, Rev. T. E. Strickland, ed. (New York: New York Historical Society, 1971), pp. 72–73.

21. Hubert G. Schmidt, *Agriculture in New Jersey: A Three-Hundred Year History* (New Brunswick: Rutgers University Press, 1973), p. 181.

22. Kalm, *Travels*, p. 336.

23. Coventry, Diary, p. 72.

24. Strickland, *Journal*, p. 72.

25. Kalm, *Travels*, p. 124.

26. Ibid., pp. 334–335.

27. Ibid., p. 135.

28. Abraham Lott, Diary of a Trip to Albany from New York City and Return, June 22–July 19, 1774, n.p., Albany Institute of History and Art, Albany, N.Y.

29. Joseph Depuy, Account Book, n.p., Albany Institute of History and Art, Albany, N.Y.

30. Schmidt, *Agriculture in New Jersey*, pp. 118–132, 166–190.

31. D. W. Meinig, "Geography of Expansion, 1785–1855," in *Geography of New York State*, John H. Thompson, ed. (Syracuse: Syracuse University Press, 1966), p. 166.

32. Adriance Van Brunt, Diary, June 8, 1828–March 20, 1830, n.p., Manuscript Division, New York Public Library, New York, N.Y.

33. Benjamin Myer Brink, *The Early History of Saugerties, 1660–1825* (Kingston: R. W. Anderson, 1902), p. 222.

34. "From the 'Historisch Verhael,' by Nicolaes van Wassenaer, 1624–1630," in *Narratives of New Netherland, 1609–1664*, J. Franklin Jameson, ed. (New York: Charles Scribner's Sons, 1909), pp. 79–80.

35. Van der Donck, *A Description of the New Netherlands*, p. 40.

36. Ibid.

37. Coventry, Diary, p. 72.

38. Strickland, *Journal*, p. 123.

39. Lemon, *The Best Poor Man's Country*, p. 164.

40. Van der Donck, *A Description of the New Netherlands*, p. 41.

41. Strickland, *Journal*, p. 93.

42. Van der Donck, *A Description of the New Netherlands*, pp. 40–41.

43. Coventry, Diary, p. 72.

44. Strickland, *Journal*, p. 93.

45. Ibid., p. 74.

46. Van der Donck, *A Description of the New Netherlands*, p. 41.

47. Ibid., p. 42.

48. Strickland, *Journal*, pp. 92–93.

49. Van der Donck, *A Description of the New Netherlands*, pp. 42–43.

50. Arnold J. F. Van Laer, *Register of the Provincial Secretary, 1638–1642* (Baltimore: Genealogical Publishing Co., 1972) I: 28.

51. Quoted in John O. Evjen, *Scandinavian Immigrants in New York, 1630–1674* (Minneapolis: K. C. Holter, 1916), pp. 178–179.

52. Van Laer, *Register of the Provincial Secretary*, III: 275.

53. Quoted in John Van Zandt Cortelyou, *The Cortelyou Genealogy* (Lincoln, Neb.: Brown, 1942), pp. 63–64.

54. A. T. F. Van Laer, *Van Rensselaer-Bowier Manuscripts* (Albany: University of the State of New York, 1908), pp. 308–309.

55. Ibid., pp. 732–740.

56. Ibid., pp. 775–776.

57. James Riker, *History of Harlem* (New York: New Harlem Publishing Co., 1881), pp. 250–251.

58. Danckaerts, *Journal*, p. 70.

59. Kalm, *Travels*, I: 334.

60. Coventry, Diary, p. 123.

61. Percy Wells Bidwell and John I. Falconer, *History of Agriculture in the Northern United States, 1620–1860* (Washington, D.C.: Carnegie Institution of Washington, 1925), pp. 26–32.

62. Estate Inventory of William Colfax, Pompton, New Jersey, 1830, New Jersey State Archives, Trenton, N.J.

63. Estate Inventory of Adrian Van Houten, Passaic County, New Jersey, February 19, 1855, New Jersey State Archives, Trenton, N.J.

64. Meinig, "Geography of Expansion," p. 166.

65. Peter H. Cousins, *Hog Plow and Sith: Cultural Aspects of Early Agricultural Technology* (Dearborn, Mich.: Greenfield Village and Henry Ford Museum, 1973), pp. 1–5.

66. Ibid., pp. 3–4.

67. Hector St. John de Crevecoeur, *Sketches of Eighteenth Century America*, Henri L. Bourdin, Ralph H. Gabriel, and Stanley T. Williams, eds. (New Haven: Yale University Press, 1925), pp. 139–140, quoted in Cousins, *Hog Plow and Sith*, p. 6.

68. Cousins, *Hog Plow and Sith*, p. 7.

69. Van Laer, *Register of the Provincial Secretary*, I: 28.

70. Richard Smith, *A Tour of Four Great Rivers: The Hudson, Mohawk, Susquehanna and Delaware in 1769*, Francis W. Halsey, ed. (New York: Scribner's, 1906), p. 21, quoted in Cousins, *Hog Plow and Sith*, p. 7.

71. J. Dutcher to T. B. Wakeman in *Transactions of the New York State Agricultural Society* 27 (1867): 474–475, quoted in Cousins, *Hog Plow and Sith*, p. 6.

72. Estate inventory of Jacob Van Ness of Caldwell, N.J., May 15, 1821, New Jersey State Archives, Trenton, N.J.; Estate inventory of Henry Berry

of Pequannock, N.J., July 25, 1833, New Jersey State Archives, Trenton, N.J.

73. Cousins, *Hog Plow and Sith*, pp. 6–7.

74. Ibid., pp. 11–14.

75. Van Laer, *Van Rensselaer-Bowier Manuscripts* (Albany: University of the State of New York, 1908), p. 204.

76. Ibid., p. 264.

77. Van Laer, *Register of the Provincial Secretary*, II: 135–136.

78. Ibid., III: 273–274.

79. Smith, *A Tour of Four Great Rivers*, p. 21, quoted in Cousins, *Hog Plow and Sith*, p. 13.

80. Estate inventory of Hezekiah Van Orden of Catskill, N.Y., November 1, 2, and 4, 1796, New York State Library, Albany, N.Y.

81. Coventry, Diary, p. 116.

82. Schmidt, *Agriculture in New Jersey*, p. 141.

83. Ibid.

84. J. Geraint Jenkins, *The English Farm Wagon: Origins and Structure* (Lingfield, England: Published by the Oakwood Press for the Museum of English Rural Life, 1961), pp. 8–9, 56.

85. Ibid., pp. 3–6; Hans Kurath, *A Word Geography of the Eastern United States*. Studies in American English, no. 1 (Ann Arbor: University of Michigan Press, 1949), p. 58.

86. Jenkins, *The English Farm Wagon*, pp. 10, 43–47.

87. Van Laer, *Register of the Provincial Secretary*, I: 28.

88. Ibid., II: 134; III: 275.

89. A. J. F. Van Laer, ed., *Early Records of the City of Albany and the Colony of Rensselaerswyck*, vol. 3 *Notarial Papers 1 and 2, 1660–1696* (Albany: The University of the State of New York, 1918), p. 473.

90. Isaac Newton Phelps Stokes, *The Iconography of Manhattan Island, 1498–1909* (New York: R. H. Dodd, 1915–1928) I: Plate 18, cited by Kristin Lunde Gibbons, "The Van Bergen Overmantel," (M.A. thesis, Cooperstown Graduate Program, State University of New York, College at Oneonta, 1966), p. 55.

91. Gibbons, "The Van Bergen Overmantel," pp. 55–60.

92. *New Jersey Archives, Documents Relating to the Colonial History of the State of New Jersey*, William Nelson, ed. 1st. ser., vol. 12 *Newspaper Extracts*, vol. 2 *1740–1750* (Paterson, N.J.: The Press Printing and Publishing Co., 1895), p. 629.

93. Crevecoeur, *Sketches of Eighteenth Century America*, pp. 138–139, quoted in Gibbons, "The Van Bergen Overmantel," pp. 56–57.

94. William Strickland, *Journal of a Tour in the United States of America, 1794–1795*, Rev. J. E. Strickland, ed. (1795; Reprint, New York: The New-York Historical Society, 1971), pp. 123, 74.

95. George Schumway and Howard C. Frey, *Conestoga Wagon, 1750–1850*

(n.p.: George Schumway, 1968); John Omwake, *The Conestoga Six-Horse Bell Teams of Eastern Pennsylvania* (Cincinnati: Ebbert & Richardson, 1930).

5. Family

1. John Demos, *A Little Commonwealth: Family Life in Plymouth Colony* (London: Oxford University Press, 1970); Philip J. Greven, Jr., *Four Generations: Population, Land, and Family in Colonial Andover, Massachusetts* (Ithaca: Cornell University Press, 1970); Edmund S. Morgan, *Virginians at Home: Family Life in the Eighteenth Century* (Charlottesville: The University Press of Virginia, 1952).

2. David Evan Narrett, "Patterns of Inheritance in Colonial New York City, 1664–1775: A Study in the History of the Family" (Ph.D. diss., Cornell University, 1981); William John McLaughlin, "Dutch Rural New York: Community, Economy, and Family in Colonial Flatbush" (Ph.D. diss., Columbia University, 1981).

3. Demos, *A Little Commonwealth*; Greven, *Four Generations*; Peter Laslett and Richard Wall, eds., *Household and Family in Past Time* (London: Cambridge University Press, 1972).

4. Bertha Mook, *The Dutch Family in the Seventeenth and Eighteenth Centuries: An Explorative-Descriptive Study* (Ottawa: University of Ottawa Press, 1977), p. 94.

5. Ibid.

6. Ibid., p. 3.

7. Peter Laslett, "Introduction: The History of the Family," in Laslett and Wall, eds., *Household and Family*, p. 61.

8. Ibid., pp. 59–60.

9. Lutz K. Berkner, "The Stem Family and the Developmental Cycle of the Peasant Household: An Eighteenth-Century Austrian Example," *American Historical Review* 77 (1972): 398–418; Robert Wheaton, "Family and Kinship in Western Europe: The Problem of the Joint Family Household," *Journal of Interdisciplinary History* 5 (1975): 601–628.

10. Berkner, "The Stem Family," p. 409.

11. Lutz K. Berkner, "Rural Family Organization in Europe: A Problem in Comparative History," *Peasant Studies Newsletter* 1 (1972): 148.

12. Wheaton, "Family and Kinship," pp. 612–613.

13. Ibid., pp. 616.

14. A. M. van der Woude, "Variations in the Size and Structure of the Household in the United Provinces of the Netherlands in the Seventeenth and Eighteenth Centuries," in Laslett and Wall, eds., *Household and Family*, pp. 306–309.

15. John Y. Keur and Dorothy L. Keur, *The Deeply Rooted: A Study of a Drents Community in the Netherlands* (Seattle: University of Washington Press, 1955), pp. 106–107.

16. Berkner, "The Stem Family," pp. 411–412.

17. Van der Woude, "The Household in the United Provinces," pp. 314, 318.

18. Ibid., pp. 303–304.

19. Berkner, "Rural Family Organization," pp. 147–148.

20. Ibid., pp. 150–153.

21. Emmanuel Le Roy Landurie, "A System of Customary Law: Family Structures and Inheritance Customs in Sixteenth-Century France," in *Family and Society: Selections from the Annales Economies, Societies, Civilisations*, Robert Forster Orest Ranum, ed. (Baltimore: Johns Hopkins University Press, 1976), pp. 77–78, 87–89, 96–101.

22. Wheaton, "Family and Kinship," pp. 616, 618, 624–628.

23. A. J. F. van Laer, ed. *Minutes of the Court of Albany, Rensselaerswyck, and Schenectady, 1668–1680* (Albany: The University of the State of New York, 1926–1932) II: 118–119.

24. Narrett, "Patterns of Inheritance," pp. 114–116, 122–124, 336–338, 142.

25. Ibid., pp. 139–141.

26. John van Zandt Cortelyou, *The Cortelyou Genealogy* (Lincoln, Neb.: Brown Printing Service, 1942), p. 62.

27. Charles Wooley, "A Two Years' Journal in New York and Part of its Territories in America," in *Historical Chronicles of New Amsterdam, Colonial New York and Early Long Island*, ed. Cornell Taray (Port Washington, N.Y.: Ira T. Friedman, n.d.) I: 58.

28. Narrett, "Preparation for Death and Provision for the Living: Notes on New York Wills (1665–1760)," *New York History* 57 (1976): 424.

29. Narrett, "Patterns of Inheritance," p. 223.

30. Van Laer, ed., *Early Records*, vol. 4 *Mortgages 1, 1658–1660, and Wills 1–2, 1680–1681*, pp. 130–132.

31. McLaughlin, "Dutch Rural New York," pp. 270–271.

32. William Strickland, *Journal of a Tour in the United States of America, 1794–1795*, Rev. T. E. Strickland, ed. (New York: New York Historical Society, 1971), p. 73.

33. McLaughlin, "Dutch Rural New York," pp. 89–90, 270.

34. Quoted in Peter O. Wacker, *Land and People: A Cultural Geography of Preindustrial New Jersey: Origins and Settlement Patterns* (New Brunswick: Rutgers University Press, 1975), p. 135.

35. McLaughlin, "Dutch Rural New York," p. 318; Greven, *Four Generations*, pp. 7–8, 130–136.

36. Narrett, "Preparation for Death," p. 422; idem, "Patterns of Inheritance," pp. 343–344.

37. Ibid., p. 142.

38. Ibid., pp. 173, 336.

39. David Steven Cohen, *The Ramapo Mountain People* (New Brunswick: Rutgers University Press, 1974), pp. 40–41.

40. [Alexander Hamilton,] *Gentleman's Progress: The Itinerarium of Dr. Alexander Hamilton, 1744*, ed. Carl Bridenbaugh (Chapel Hill: University of North Carolina Press, 1948), p. 78.

41. E. B. O'Callaghan, ed. *The Documentary History of the State of New York* (Albany: Charles van Benthuysen, 1851) I: 665ff.

42. Ibid., pp. 366–367.

43. "Federal Census, 1800—Kings County, Long Island, New York," *The New York Genealogical and Biographical Record* 55 (1924): 25.

44. Alexander Coventry, Recollections and Diary, July 1783–August 1789, New York State Library Mss., p. 115.

45. Van Laer, *Early Records*, vol. 3 *Notarial Papers 1 and 2, 1660–1696*, p. 474.

46. Ibid., p. 415.

47. Ibid., p. 474.

48. Van Laer, *Court Minutes*, I: 99.

49. Coventry, Diary, p. 145.

50. Strickland, *Journal*, p. 143.

51. David Steven Cohen, "In Search of Carolus Africanus Rex: Afro-Dutch Folklore and Folklife in New York and New Jersey," *Journal of the Afro-American Historical and Genealogical Society* 5 (1984): 149–162.

52. McLaughlin, "Dutch Rural New York," pp. 193–194.

53. Adriance van Brunt, Diary and Journal Kept on his Farm near Brooklyn, N.Y., June 8, 1828–March 20, 1830, New York Public Library, New York, N.Y.

54. Quoted in Cohen, *The Folklore and Folklife of New Jersey* (New Brunswick: Rutgers University Press, 1983), p. 151.

55. Narrett, "Patterns of Inheritance," p. 123; McLaughlin, "Dutch Rural New York," pp. 302–303.

56. Cohen, *The Folklore and Folklife of New Jersey*, pp. 19–20.

57. A. T. F. van Laer, trans. & ed., *Correspondence of Jeremias van Rensselaer, 1651–1674* (Albany: The University of the State of New York, 1932), pp. 326–329.

58. Ibid., pp. 432–433.

6. Folklore and Folklife

1. Washington Irving, "The Legend of Sleepy Hollow," in *The Sketch Book* (1820; Reprint, New York: Signet Classics, 1961), p. 331.

2. Ibid., p. 336.

3. Sara Puryear Rodes, "Washington Irving's Use of Traditional Folklore," *Southern Folklore Quarterly* 19 (1956): 143–153.

4. "Novum Belgium, by Father Isaac Joques, 1646," in *Narratives of New*

Netherland, 1609–1664, J. Franklin Jameson, ed. (New York: Charles Scribner's Sons, 1909), p. 259.

5. Charles T. Gehring, "The Dutch Language in Colonial New York: An Investigation of Language in Decline and its Relationship to Social Change," (Ph.D. diss., Indiana University, 1973), pp. 101–102, 114.

6. Alexander Coventry, Diary, July 1782–August 1789, p. 69. New York State Library, Albany, N.Y.

7. Van Cleaf Bachman, "What Is Low Dutch?" *De Halve Maen* 57 (1983): 14.

8. John Dyneley Prince, "The Jersey Dutch Dialect," *Dialect Notes* 3(1910): 459.

9. L. G. Van Loon, *Crumbs from an Old Dutch Closet: The Dutch Dialect of Old New York* (The Hague: Matinus Nijhoff, 1938), p. 47.

10. Bachman, "What Is Low Dutch?" p. 16.

11. Van Loon, *Crumbs from an Old Dutch Closet*, p. 25.

12. James B. H. Storms, *A Jersey Dutch Vocabulary* (Park Ridge, N.J.: Pascack Historical Society, 1964), n.p.

13. Prince, "Jersey Dutch," p. 460.

14. Van Cleaf Bachman, "The Story of the Low Dutch Language: I," *De Halve Maen* 56 (1982): 2.

15. Bachman, "What Is Low Dutch?" p. 15.

16. Ibid., pp. 15–16.

17. Coventry, Diary, p. 178.

18. Ibid., p. 179.

19. Ibid., p. 1015.

20. Anna Gausmann Noyes, *Three Petticoats* (Leonia, N.J.: n.p., 1955), pp. 20–21, 62, 65–70, 82.

21. "De Pruttelarij Voerman," *Olde Ulster* 3(1907): 136–139.

22. *Olde Ulster* 3(1906): 368.

23. "Various Versions of 'Trip a Trop a Troontjes,' " *Olde Ulster* 1(1905): 234–237.

24. Benjamin Myer Brink, *The Early History of Saugerties, 1660–1825* (Kingston, N.Y.: R. W. Anderson and Sons, 1902), p. 324; Mrs. John King Van Rensselaer, *The Goede Vrouw of Mana-ha-ta* (New York: Charles Scribner's Sons, 1898), p. 59; Gertrude Lefferts Vanderbilt, *The Social History of Flatbush* (New York: P. Appleton and Co., 1882), p. 93; Noyes, *Three Petticoats*, pp. 70–71.

25. Brink, *History of Saugerties*, p. 325.

26. Marion Barber Stowell, *Early American Almanacs: The Colonial Weekday Bible* (New York: Burt Franklin, 1977), pp. 17–25.

27. Lambert Borghard, Diary and Daybook, 1763–1788, pp. 4, 14, Albany Institute of History and Art, Albany, N.Y.

28. Van Loon, *Crumbs from an Old Dutch Closet*, p. 43.

29. Ibid.

30. Adriaen van der Donck, *A Description of the New Netherlands,* Thomas F. O'Donnell, ed. (Syracuse: Syracuse University Press, 1968), p. 28.

31. Van Loon, *Crumbs from an Old Dutch Closet,* p. 40.

32. Don Yoder, "The Saint's Legend in Pennsylvania German Folk-Culture," in *American Folk Legend: A Symposium,* Wayland D. Hand, ed. (Berkeley, Los Angeles, and London: University of California Press, 1971), p. 159.

33. A. T. F. Van Laer, ed. *Court Minutes, 1648–1652,* p. 189.

34. Berthold Fernow, *The Records of New Amsterdam from 1653 to 1674,* vol. 1 *Court Minutes of New Amsterdam* (New York: Knickerbocker Press, 1897), p. 420.

35. Ibid., p. 172.

36. Ibid., p. 286.

37. Quoted in Esther Singleton, *Dutch New York* (New York: Dodd, Mead, and Co., 1909), pp. 304–305.

38. Coventry, Diary, p. 211.

39. Ibid.

40. Ibid., p. 94.

41. Elizabeth L. Gebhard, *The Parsonage Between Two Manors: Annals of Clover-Reach* (Hudson, N.Y.: Bryan Printing Co., 1909), pp. 224–225.

42. Ibid., p. 225.

43. Coventry, Diary, p. 108.

44. Ibid.

45. William Dunlap, "Diary of William Dunlap," New York Historical Society, *Collections* 62 (1929): 65.

46. "Pinkster Ode, Albany, 1803," *New York Folklore Quarterly* 13 (1952): 32, 42.

47. Ibid.

48. Quoted in Alice Morse Earle, *Colonial Days in Old New York* (New York: Empire State Book Co., 1926), pp. 196–198.

49. David Steven Cohen, "In Search of Carolus Africanus Rex: Afro-Dutch Folklore in New York and New Jersey," *Journal of the Afro-American Historical and Genealogical Society* 5 (1984): 149–162.

50. Gabriel Furman, *Antiquities of Long Island* (New York: J. W. Bouton, 1874), pp. 265–266.

51. Charles W. Jones, "Knickerbocker Santa Claus," *The New York Historical Society Quarterly* 38 (1954): 357–383.

52. Field Horne, "Winter Holidays," Sleepy Hollow Restorations Research Report, No. 23, November 12, 1976, n.p.

53. Dekay, "Der Colonie Nieu Nederland," p. 252.

54. Gabriel Furman Mss., New York Historical Society, p. 12, quoted in Horne, "Winter Holidays," n.p.

55. Washington Irving, *A History of New York* (1809; Reprint, New Haven: College and University Press, 1964), pp. 132–133.

56. Henry Van Der Lyn, Diary, II: 170; IV:219, New York Historical Society, New York, N.Y., quoted in Horne, "Winter Holidays," n.p.

57. Coventry, Diary, p. 524.

58. Kenneth Scott, "Funeral Customs in Colonial New York," *New York Folklore Quarterly* 15 (1959): 274–282; Berthold Fernow, ed., *Calendar of Court Minutes, Fort Orange, Beverwyck, Albany, 1652–1685* (New York: C. A. Hollenbeck, 1905), p. 17; Kenney, *Stubborn for Liberty*, pp. 84–85; Furman, *Antiquities of Long Island*, pp. 160ff.

59. Simon E. Baldwin, "A Young Man's Journal of a Hundred Years Ago," New Haven Colony Historical Society, *Papers* 4 (1888): 197–198.

60. Adriances Van Brunt, Diary and Journal Kept on his Farm near Brooklyn, N.Y., 1828 June 8–1830 March 20, Manuscript Division, New York Public Library, New York, N.Y.

61. Furman, *Antiquities of Long Island*, p. 167.

62. David C. Voorhees, Diary, 1875, n.p. Special Collections, Rutgers University Library, New Brunswick, N.J.

63. Fernand Braudel, *Capitalism and Material Life, 1400–1800*, Miriam Kochen, trans. (1967; Reprint, New York: Harper Colophon, 1973), pp. 132–133.

64. Peter Kalm, *Travels in North America*, Adolph B. Benson, ed. (New York: Wilson Erickson, 1937) II: 602.

65. Ibid. I: 346–347; II: 602–603, 614–615, 628–629.

66. James Deetz, *In Small Things Forgotten* (Garden City, N.Y.: Anchor Books, 1977), pp. 52–55.

67. Rufus A. Grider, Notebooks (1887), quoted in Peter G. Rose, trans., *The Sensible Cook* (Syracuse: Syracuse University Press, 1989), p. 32.

68. Deetz, *In Small Things Forgotten*, pp. 59–60.

Conclusion

1. Gerald F. DeJong, *The Dutch Reformed Church in the American Colonies*, Historical Series of the Reformed Church in America, no. 5 (Grand Rapids: Wm. B. Eerdman, 1978), p. 106; James Tanis, *Dutch Calvinistic Pietism in the Life and Theology of Theodorus Jacobus Frelinghuysen* (The Hague: Martinus Nijhoff, 1967), pp. 11–12, 27–28, 30–37, 46–47; Randall H. Balmer, *A Perfect Babel of Confusion: Dutch Religion and Culture in the Middle Colonies* (New York and Oxford: Oxford University Press, 1989), p. 108.

2. David William Voorhees, " 'In Behalf of the True Protestant Religion': The Glorious Revolution in New York" (Ph.D. diss., New York University, 1988).

3. De Jong, *The Dutch Reformed Church*, pp. 75–76; Adrian C. Leiby, *The United Churches of Hackensack and Schraalenburgh, New Jersey, 1686–1822* (River Edge, N.J.: Bergen County Historical Society, 1976), p. 12.

4. Balmer, *A Perfect Babel of Confusion*, p. 133.

5. Ibid., pp. 109–111; Tanis, *Dutch Calvinistic Pietism*, pp. 42–43.

6. Balmer, *A Perfect Babel of Confusion*, pp. 132–133.

7. Ibid., pp. 123–127; Tanis, *Dutch Calvinistic Pietism*, pp. 71–72; De Jong, *The Dutch Reformed Church*, pp. 8, 181.

8. Tanis, *Dutch Calvinistic Pietism*, pp. 81–82.

9. Balmer, *A Perfect Babel of Confusion*, p. 140.

10. Ibid., p. 139.

11. Ibid., pp. 111, 115.

12. Quoted in ibid., p. 126.

13. Ibid., pp. 127–128; De Jong, *The Dutch Reformed Church*, p. 188; Tanis, *Calvinistic Pietism*, pp. 78, 91.

14. Richard P. McCormick, *Rutgers: A Bicentennial History* (New Brunswick: Rutgers University Press, 1966), pp. 2–5.

15. De Jong, *The Dutch Reformed Church*, pp. 188–210, 211–227.

16. Adrian C. Leiby, *The United Churches*, p. 150; idem, "The Conflict Among the Jersey Dutch During the Revolution," in *New Jersey in the American Revolution: Political and Social Conflict*, William C. Wright, ed. (rev. ed., Trenton: New Jersey Historical Commission, 1970), pp. 26–39; Richard P. McCormick, *New Jersey From Colony to State, 1609–1789*, New Jersey Historical Series (New Brunswick: Rutgers University Press, 1964), p. 129; Balmer, *A Perfect Babel of Confusion*, pp. 149–152.

17. William W. Sweet, *Revivalism in America* (New York: Charles Scribner's Sons, 1944), pp. 24–27; William G. McLaughlin, " 'Enthusiasm For Liberty': The Great Awakening as the Key to the Revolution," in *Preachers and Politicians: Two Essays on the Origins of the American Revolution* (Worcester, Mass.: American Antiquarian Society, 1977), pp. 66, 67; Jerald C. Brauer, "Puritanism, Revivalism, and the Revolution," in *Religion and the American Revolution*, by Jerald C. Brauer, Sidney E. Mead, and Robert E. Bellah (Philadelphia: Fortress Press, 1976), p. 25.

18. Balmer, *A Perfect Babel of Confusion*, pp. 139–140.

19. Henry Glassie, *Folk Housing in Middle Virginia: A Structural Analysis of Historic Artifacts* (Knoxville: University of Tennessee Press, 1975), p. 185; idem, "Eighteenth-Century Cultural Process in Delaware Valley Folk Building," *Winterthur Portfolio* 7 (1972): 37.

20. James Deetz, *In Small Things Forgotten: The Archeology of Early American Life* (New York: Anchor Books, 1977), pp. 40–43.

21. Glassie, *Folk Housing in Middle Virginia*, p. 190; idem, "Eighteenth-Century Cultural Process," p. 37.

22. Glassie, *Folk Housing in Middle Virginia*, p. 188.

23. Ibid., p. 189.

24. Bernard L. Herman, *Architecture and Rural Life in Central Delaware, 1700–1900* (Knoxville: University of Tennessee Press, 1987), p. 131.

25. Dell Upton, "Vernacular Domestic Architecture in Eighteenth-Cen-

tury Virginia," in *Common Places: Readings in American Vernacular Architecture*, Dell Upton and John Michael Vlach, eds. (Athens: University of Georgia Press, 1985), p. 332.

26. Edward A. Chappell, "Acculturation in the Shenandoah Valley: Rhenish Houses in the Massanutten Settlement," *Proceedings of the American Philosophical Society* 124 (1980): 55–56, 63, 76.

27. It is no coincidence that the same forces that were transforming the countryside were also changing the relationships between the Dutch and other ethnic groups in New York City. See, Joyce D. Goodfriend, *Before the Melting Pot: Society and Culture in Colonial New York City, 1664–1730* (Princeton: Princeton University Press, in press). However, rather than representing the demise of ethnic pluralism or the eclipse of Dutch culture by British culture, it was the rise of a new American culture with regional variants.

Bibliography

Ackerson, Cornelius. "Agriculture in New Netherland's History." *De Halve Maen* 35 (1961): 4.

Allen, David Grayson. *In English Ways: The Movement of Societies and the Transferal of English Local Law and Custom to Massachusetts Bay in the Seventeenth Century.* Chapel Hill: University of North Carolina Press, 1981.

De Americaanse Almanacke 1 (1754).

Archdeacon, Thomas J. *New York City, 1664–1710: Conquest and Change.* Ithaca: Cornell University Press, 1976.

Arensberg, Conrad and Solon Kimball. *Culture and Community.* New York: Harcourt, Brace and World, 1965.

Arnold, Matthew. *Culture and Anarchy.* Edited by J. Dover Wilson. 1869. Reprint. Cambridge: Cambridge University, 1963.

Atlas of Bergen County, New Jersey. Philadelphia: C. C. Pease, 1876.

Bachman, Van Cleaf. *Peltries or Plantations: The Economic Policies of the Dutch West India Company in New Netherland, 1623–1639.* Johns Hopkins University Studies in Historical and Political Science. Baltimore: The Johns Hopkins Press, 1969.

———. "The Story of the Low Dutch Language." *De Halve Maen* 56 (1982): 1–3, 21; 57 (1983): 10–13.

———. "What Is Low Dutch?" *De Halve Maen* 57 (1983): 14–17, 23–24.

———, Alice P. Kenney, and Lawrence G. Van Loon. " 'Het Poelmeisie': An Introduction to the Hudson Valley Dutch Dialect." *New York History* 61 (1980): 161–185.

Bailey, Rosalie Fellows. *Pre-Revolutionary Dutch Houses and Families in Northern New Jersey and Southern New York.* 1936. Reprint. New York: Dover Publications, 1968.

Balmer, Randall H. *A Perfect Babel of Confusion: Dutch Religion and English*

Culture in the Middle Colonies. New York and Oxford: Oxford University Press, 1989.

Barley, M. W. *The English Farmhouse and Cottage*. London: Routledge and Kegan Paul, 1961.

Baumgarten, Karl. "Probleme der Mecklenburgisches Hausforschung." *Deutsches Jahrbuch* 153 (1953): 24 ff.

———. "Probleme Mecklenburgischer Niedersachsenhausforschung." *Deutsches Jahrbuch fur Volkskunde* (1955): 169–182, *Driemaandelijkse Bladen* II (1959).

———. "Studies of Rural Buildings in Mecklenburg." *Technology and Culture* 5 (1964): 234–240.

Bayer, Henry G. *The Belgians: First Settlers in New York and in the Middle States*. New York: Devin-Adair, 1925.

Bayles, Richard. *History of Richmond County (Staten Island), New York, From its Discovery to the Present Time*. New York: L. E. Preston & Co., 1887.

Beekman, George C. *Early Dutch Settlers of Monmouth County, New Jersey*. Freehold, N.J.: Moreau Brothers, 1901.

Bennit, Dorothy V. "Albany Preserves its Dutch Lore." *New York Folklore Quarterly* 11 (1955): 246–255.

Bergen, Tunis G. "More About the Dutch Settlers." *Our Home* 1 (1873): 400–403, 460–463.

Bergen, Van Brunt. "A List of Early Immigrants to New Netherland, 1654–1664." *New York Genealogical and Biographical Record* 14 (1883): 181–190; 15 (1883): 34–40, 72–77.

Berkner, Lutz K. "Rural Family Organization in Europe: A Problem in Comparative History." *Peasant Studies Newsletter* 1 (1972): 145–156.

———. "The Stem Family and the Developmental Cycle of the Peasant Household: An Eighteenth-Century Austrian Example." *American Historical Review* 77 (1974): 398–418.

Bernt, Adolf und Gunther Binding. *Das Deutsche Burgerhaus*. 27 vols. Tubingen: Verlag Ernst Wasmuth, 1959–1977.

Bevier, Katherine. *The Bevier Family*. New York: T. A. Wright, 1916.

Bidwell, Percy Wells and John I. Falconer. *History of Agriculture in the Northern United States, 1620–1860*. Washington, D.C.: Carnegie Institution of Washington, 1925.

Black, William N. "Colonial Building in New Jersey." *Architectural Record* 3 (1894): 245–262.

Blackburn, Roderic H. "Dutch Domestic Architecture in the Hudson Valley." *Tijdschrift van de Koninklijke Nederlandse Oudheidkundig Bond* 84 (1985): 151–165.

———. "Dutch Material Culture: Architecture." *De Halve Maen* 57 (1982): 1–5.

———. "Dutch Material Culture: Furniture." *De Halve Maen* 54 (1979): 3–5.

——— and Ruth Piwonka, eds. *Remembrance of Patria: Dutch Arts and Culture in Colonial America, 1609–1776.* Albany: Albany Institute of History and Art, 1988.

Blanchard, Raoul. *La Flandre.* Lille: Danel, 1906.

Boer, Louis P. de. "Passenger List of Colonists to the South River (Delaware Colony of New Netherland), 1661." *New York Genealogical and Biographical Record* 60 (1929): 68–70.

Bonomi, Patricia. *A Factious People: Politics and Society in Colonial New York.* New York: Columbia University Press, 1971.

Bonney, Mrs. Catharina V. [van] R[ensselaer]. *A Legacy of Historical Gleanings.* 2 vols. Albany: J. Munsell, 1875.

Borghard, Lambert. Diary and Daybook, 1763–1788. Albany Institute of History and Art, Albany, N.Y.

Boyd, John T., Jr. "Some Early Dutch Houses in New Jersey." *Architectural Record* 36 (1914): 31–48; 148–158, 220–230.

Braudel, Fernand. *Capitalism and Material Life, 1400–1800.* Translated by Miriam Kochen. 1960. Reprint, New York: Harper Colophon, 1973.

Brauer, Jerald C. "Puritanism, Revivalism, and the Revolution," in *Religion and the American Revolution,* by Jerald C. Brauer, Sidney E. Mead, and Robert N. Bellah, pp. 1–27. Philadelphia: Fortress Press, 1976.

Brink, Benjamin Myer. *The Early History of Saugerties, 1660–1825.* Kingston: R. W. Anderson & Son, 1902.

Budke, George H. "The History of the Tappan Patent." In *The Rockland Record.* Edited by George H. Budke. II: 35–42. Nyack, N.Y.: Rockland County Society of the State of New York, 1931.

Burke, Gerald L. *The Making of Dutch Towns.* New York: Simmons-Boardman, 1960.

Campbell, Mildred. "Social Origins of Some Early Americans." In *Seventeenth-Century America: Essays in Colonial History.* Edited by James Morton Smith, pp. 63–89. Chapel Hill: University of North Carolina Press, 1959.

Campbell, Patrick. *Travels in the Interior Inhabited Parts of North America in the Years 1791–1792.* Edited by H. H. Langton. Toronto: The Champlain Society, 1937.

Cazenove, Theophile. *Cazenove Journal, 1794; A Record of the Journey of Theophile Cazenove Through New Jersey and Pennsylvania.* Edited by Rayner Wickersham Kelsey. Haverford, Pa.: The Pennsylvania History Press, 1922.

Chappell, Edward A. "Acculturation in the Shenandoah Valley: Rhenish Houses of the Massanutten Settlement." *Proceedings of the American Philosophical Society* 124 (1980): 55–89.

Chastellux, Marquis de. *Travels in North America in the Years 1780, 1781, and 1782.* Edited by Howard C. Rice, Jr. 2 vols. Chapel Hill: University of North Carolina Press for the Institute of Early American History and Culture, 1963.

Coad, Oral Sumner. *New Jersey in Travelers' Accounts, 1524–1971.* Metuchen: Scarecrow Press, 1972.

Cohen, David Steven. "Dutch-American Farming: Crops, Livestock, and Equipment, 1623–1900." In *New World Dutch Studies: Dutch Arts and Culture in Colonial America, 1609–1776*. Edited by Roderic H. Blackburn and Nancy A. Kelley, pp. 185–200. Albany: Albany Institute of History and Art, 1987.

———. *The Folklore and Folklife of New Jersey*. New Brunswick: Rutgers University Press, 1984.

———. "How Dutch Were the Dutch of New Netherland?" *New York History* 62 (1981): 43–60.

———. "In Search of Carolus Africanus Rex: Afro-Dutch Folklore and Folklife in New York and New Jersey." *Journal of the Afro-American Historical and Genealogical Society* 5 (1984): 149–162.

———. *The Ramapo Mountain People*. New Brunswick: Rutgers University Press, 1974.

Collier, Edward A. *A History of Old Kinderhook*. New York and London: G. P. Putnam's Sons, 1914.

Condon, Thomas J. *New York Beginnings: The Commercial Origins of New Netherland*. New York: New York University Press; London: The University of London Press Ltd., 1968.

Cortelyou, John Van Zandt. *The Cortelyou Genealogy: A Record of Jacques Cortelyou and the Many of his Descendants*. Lincoln, Neb.: Brown Printing Service, 1942.

Cotter, John L. and J. Paul Hudson. *New Discoveries at Jamestown: Site of the First Successful English Settlement in America*. Washington, D.C.: U.S. Government Printing Office, 1957.

Cousins, Peter H. *Hog Plow and Sith: Cultural Aspects of Early Agricultural Technology*. Dearborn, Mich.: Greenfield Village and Henry Ford Museum, [1973].

Coventry, Alexander. Recollections and Diary, July 1783–August 1789. New York State Library, Albany, N.Y.

Crevecoeur, Hector St. John de. *Sketches of Eighteenth-Century America*. Edited by Henri L. Bourdin, Ralph H. Gabriel, and Stanley T. Williams. New Haven: Yale University Press, 1925.

———. *Journey into Northern Pennsylvania and the State of New York*. Translated by Clarissa Spencer Bostelmann. Ann Arbor: The University of Michigan Press, 1964.

Cummings, Abbott Lowell. *The Framed Houses of Massachusetts Bay, 1625–1725*. Cambridge: The Belknap Press, Harvard University Press, 1979.

———. "Inside the Massachusetts House." In *Common Places: Readings in American Vernacular Architecture*. Edited by Dell Upton and John Michael Vlach, pp. 219–239. Athens: University of Georgia Press, 1986.

Danckaerts, Jasper. *Diary of our Second Trip from Holland to New Netherland, 1683*. Translated by Kenneth Scott. Upper Saddle River, N.J.: Gregg Press, 1969.

————. *Journal of Jasper Danckaerts, 1679–1680*. Edited by Bartlett Burleigh James and J. Franklin Jameson. New York: Charles Scribner's Sons, 1913.

Daniel, Robert. Diary. April 1–July 5, 1859. New York Historical Society, New York City, N.Y.

Deetz, James. *In Small Things Forgotten: The Archeology of Early American Life*. Garden City, N.Y.: Anchor Books, 1977.

De Groot, A. D. "The Myth of Sinterklaas." *Delta: A Review of Arts, Life and Thought in the Netherlands* 2 (1959): 5–13.

De Jong, Gerald F. *The Dutch Reformed Church in the American Colonies*. Historical Series of the Reformed Church in America, no. 5. Grand Rapids: Wm. B. Eerdmans, 1978.

De Jonge, C. H. and W. Vogelsang. *Hollandische Mobel und Raumkunst von 1650–1780*. Stuttgart: Julius Hoffman, 1922.

De Kay, Eckford J. "Der Colonie Nieu Nederland." *New York Folklore Quarterly* 9 (1953): 245–254.

Demarest, Mary and William Demarest. *The Demarest Family*. New Brunswick: Thatcher-Anderson, 1938.

Demarest, Voorhess D. *The Demarest Family*. 2 vols. Hackensack, N.J.: Demarest Family Association, 1964.

Demos, John. *A Little Commonwealth: Family Life in Plymouth Colony*. New York: Oxford University Press, 1970.

Denton, Daniel. *A Brief Description of New-York*. 1670. Reprint. New York: Columbia University Press for the Facsimile Text Society, 1937.

Depuy, Joseph. Account Book. 1770–1804. Albany Institute of History and Art, Albany, N.Y.

de Vries, Jan. *The Dutch Rural Economy in the Golden Age, 1500–1700*. New Haven: Yale University Press, 1974.

Dilliard, Maud Esther. *An Album of New Netherland: Dutch Colonial Antiques and Architecture*. New York: Bramhall House, 1963.

————. *Old Dutch Houses of Brooklyn*. New York: Richard R. Smith, 1945.

Dorson, Richard M. "The Eclipse of Solar Mythology." *Journal of America Folklore* 68 (1955): 393–416.

Dunlap, William. *Diary of William Dunlap . . .* New York Historical Society Collections. 3 vols. New York: New York Historical Society, 1929–1931.

"Dutch Five-Finger Rhymes." *Old Ulster* 2 (1906): 365–368.

"Early Immigrants to New Netherland, 1657–1664." Holland Society of New York. *Yearbook* (1896): 141–158.

Eberlein, Harold Donaldson. *The Architecture of Colonial America*. Boston: Little, Brown, & Co., 1915.

————. *Manor Houses and Historic Homes of Long Island and Staten Island*. Philadelphia and London: J. B. Lippincott, 1928.

———— and Cortlandt Van Dyke Hubbard. *Historic Houses of the Hudson Valley*. New York: Architectural Book Publishing Co., 1942.

Eitzen, Gerhard von. "Die Alteren Hallenhausgefugen in Niedersachsen." *Zeitschrift fur Volkskunde* 51 (1954): 37–76.

Ellis, Rowland C. *Colonial Dutch Houses in New Jersey* . . . Newark: The Carteret Book Club, 1933.

Ellis, David Maldwyn. *Landlords and Farmers in the Hudson-Mohawk Region, 1790–1850.* Ithaca: Cornell University Press, 1946.

Elting, Irving. *Dutch Village Communities on the Hudson River.* Johns Hopkins University Studies in History and Political Science, ser. 4, no. 1. Baltimore: The Johns Hopkins Press, 1886.

Eno, Joel N. "New York 'Knickerbocker' Families: Origin and Settlement." *New York Genealogical and Biographical Record* 45 (1914): 387–391.

Erixon, Sigurd. "Western European Connections and Culture Relations." *Folk-Liv* 2 (1938): 137–172.

Evjen, John O. *Scandinavian Immigrants in New York, 1630–1674.* Minneapolis: K. C. Holter, 1916.

Ewans, N. R. *Early Brickmaking in the Colonies: A Common Fallacy Corrected.* Camden: Camden County Historical Society, 1938.

Fabend, Firth Haring. "The Yeoman Ideal: A Dutch Family in the Middle Colonies, 1660–1800." Ph.D. dissertation, New York University, 1988.

———. *A Dutch Family in the Middle Colonies, 1660–1800.* New Brunswick and London: Rutgers University Press, 1991.

Fairbridge, Dorothea. *Historic Houses of South Africa.* London: Oxford University Press, 1922.

"Federal Census, 1800—Kings County, Long Island, New York," *The New York Genealogical and Biographical Record* 55 (1924): 25.

Feister, Lois M. "Linguistic Communication Between the Dutch and Indians in New Netherland, 1609–1664." *Ethnohistory* 20 (1973): 25–38.

Fernow, Berthold, trans. *Calendar of Court Minutes of Old Fort Orange, Beverwyck and Albany.* . . . Albany: C. A. Hollenbeck, 1905.

———, ed. *The Records of New Amsterdam from 1653 to 1674 Anno Domini.* 7 vols. New York: The Knickerbocker Press, 1897.

Fiske, John. *The Dutch and Quaker Colonies in America.* Boston and New York: Houghton, Mifflin & Co., 1899.

Fitchen, John. *The New World Dutch Barn: A Study of Its Characteristics, Its Structural System, and Its Probable Erectional Procedure.* Syracuse: Syracuse University Press, 1968.

Fleming, E. McClung. "Early American Decorative Arts as Social Documents." *Mississippi Valley Historical Review* 45 (1958): 276–284.

Fockema Andreae, Synbrandus Johannes, E. H. Terkuile, and M. D. Ozinga, eds. *Duizend Jaar Bouwen in Nederland.* 2 vols. Amsterdam: Allert de Lange, 1948–1957.

Folkers, Johann Ulrich. "Die Schichtenfulge in alten Bestand Niedersachsicher Bauernhauser Mecklenburgs." In *Festschrift Richard Wossildo*, pp. 112–132. Newmunster: K. Wachsholtz, 1939.

Foundation for the Scientific Atlas of the Nederlands. *Atlas van Nederland*. 's Gravenhage: Staatsdrukkerij en Uitgeverijbedrijf, 1963– .

Fox, Dixon Ryan. *Yankees and Yorkers*. New York: New York University Press, 1940.

Furman, Gabriel. *Antiquities of Long Island*. New York: J. W. Bouton, 1874.

Gadourek, Ivan. *A Dutch Community: Social and Cultural Structure and Process in a Bulb-Growing Region in the Netherlands*. Gronigen: J. B. Wolters, 1961.

Galenson, David W. " 'Middling People' or 'Common Sort'?: The Social Origins of Some Early Americans Reexamined." *William and Mary Quarterly* 3d ser. 35 (1978): 499–524.

Garvan, Anthony N. B. *Architecture and Town Planning in Colonial Connecticut*. New Haven: Yale University Press, 1951.

Gebhard, Elizabeth L. *The Parsonage Between Two Manors: Annals of Clover-Reach*. Hudson, N.Y.: Bryan Printing Co., 1909.

Gehring, Charles T. "The Dutch Language in Colonial New York: An Investigation of Language in Decline and Its Relationship to Social Change." Ph.D. dissertation, Indiana University, 1973.

Geyl, Pieter. *History of the Low Countries: Episodes and Problems*. London: Macmillan, 1964.

––––––. *The Netherlands in the Seventeenth Century*. 2 vols. 1936. Reprint. London: Ernest Benn Ltd.; New York: Barnes and Noble, 1961.

Gibbons, Kristin Lunde. "The Van Bergen Overmantel." M.A. thesis, Cooperstown Graduate Program, State University of New York, College at Oneonta, 1966.

Glassie, Henry. "Eighteenth-Century Cultural Process in Delaware Valley Folk Building." *Winterthur Portfolio* 7 (1972): 29–57.

––––––. *Folk Housing in Middle Virginia: A Structural Analysis of Historic Artifacts*. Knoxville: University of Tennessee Press, 1975.

––––––. *Passing the Time in Ballymenone: Culture and History of an Ulster Community*. Philadelphia: University of Pennsylvania Press, 1982.

––––––. *Pattern in the Material Folk Culture of the Eastern United States*. Philadelphia: University of Pennsylvania Press, 1968.

––––––. "The Variation of Concepts Within Tradition: Barn Building in Otsego County, New York." In *Man and Cultural Heritage: Papers in Honor of Fred B. Kniffen*. Edited by H. J. Walker and W. G. Haag. pp. 177–235. Baton Rouge: Louisiana State University Press, 1974.

Goddard, Ives. "The Delaware Language: Past and Present." In *A Delaware Indian Symposium*. Edited by Herbert C. Kraft, pp. 103–110. Harrisburg: The Pennsylvania Historical and Museum Commission, 1974.

––––––. "Dutch Loanwords in Delaware." In ibid., pp. 153–160.

Goodfriend, Joyce D. *Before the Melting Pot: Society and Culture in Colonial New York City, 1664–1730*. Princeton: Princeton University Press, in press.

Goodwin, Maud Wilder. *Dutch and English on the Hudson: A Chronicle of Colonial New York*. New Haven: Yale University Press, 1919.

Gowans, Alan. *Architecture in New Jersey*. The New Jersey Historical Series, vol. 6. Princeton: D. Van Nostrand Company, 1964.

―――. *Images of American Living: Four Centuries of Architecture and Furniture as Cultural Expression*. Philadelphia and New York: J. B. Lippincott, 1964.

Grant, Mrs. Anne. *Memoirs of an American Lady*. New York: Samuel Campbell, 1809.

Green, Lucy Garrison. *The DeForests and the Walloon Founding of New Amsterdam*. Lincoln, Neb.: n.p., 1916.

Greven, Philip J., Jr. *Four Generations: Population, Land, and Family in Colonial Andover, Massachusetts*. Ithaca: Cornell University Press, 1970.

Hamilton, Dr. Alexander. *Gentleman's Progress: The Itinerarium of Dr. Alexander Hamilton, 1744*. Edited by Carl Bridenbaugh. Chapel Hill: University of North Carolina Press, 1948.

―――. *Itinerarium*. . . . Edited by Albert Bushnell Hart. St. Louis: W. K. Bixby, 1907.

Hammond, Joseph W. "An Historical Analysis of the Bronck House, Coxsackie, New York." *De Halve Maen* 55 (1980): 5–8, 17–18.

Hand, Wayland D., ed. *American Folk Legend: A Symposium*. Berkeley, Los Angeles, and London: University of California Press, 1971.

Hanson, Frederick Banfield. "The Interior Architecture and Household Furnishings of Bergen County, N.J., 1800–1810," M.A. thesis, Winterthur Museum and the University of Delaware, 1959.

Harvey, Cornelius Burnham. *Genealogical History of Hudson and Bergen Counties, New Jersey*. New York: New Jersey Genealogical Publishing Co., 1900.

Hasbrouck, G. D. B. "The Huguenot Settlement in Ulster County." New York State Historical Association. *Proceedings* 11 (1912): 88–103.

Hasbrouck, Kenneth E. *A Guide to Huguenot Street and Preservation Efforts of the Huguenot Historical Society, New Paltz, N.Y.* New Paltz: Huguenot Historical Society, 1974.

Heilprin, Angelo and Louis Heilprin, eds. *Lippincott's New Gazetteer: A Complete Pronouncing Gazetteer or Geographical Dictionary of the World*. Philadelphia: J. B. Lippincott, 1906.

Hekker, R. C. "De Boerderijtekeningen." In *De Nederlandse Boerderij in het Begin der 19e Eeuw*. Edited by R. C. Hekker and J. M. G. van der Poel, pp. 24–120. Arnhem: Stichting Historisch Boerderij-Onderzoek, 1967.

―――. "Het Hooiberggebied." *Volkskunde* 9 (1950): 31–40.

―――. "De Ontwikkeling van de Boerderijvormen in Nederland." In *Duizend Jaar Bouwen in Nederland*, S. J. Fockema Andreae, E. H. Ter Kuile, and R. C. Hekker. Deel II *De Bouwkunst na de Middeleeuwen*, pp. 195–335. Amsterdam: Allert de Lange, 1957.

―――. *De Zeeuwse Hofstede*. Middelburg: J. C. & W. Alterffer, 1951.

Helbok, Adolf. "Die Deutschen Stamme und die Moderne Volksforschung."

Volkskundliche Gabe. Edited by John Meier, pp. 54–67. Berlin und Leipzig: Walter De Gruyter und Co., 1934.

Henning, Darrell. "Common Farm Fences of Long Island." Friends of the Nassau County Historical Museum. *Bulletin* 2 (1967): 6–13.

Herman, Bernard L. *Architecture and Rural Life in Central Delaware, 1700–1900.* Knoxville: University of Tennessee Press, 1987.

Historic American Building Survey, 1941. New Jersey State Archives. Trenton, N.J.

Holme, Charles. *Old Houses in Holland.* New York: The Studio, 1913.

Hough, P. M. *Dutch Life in Town and Country.* New York and London: G. P. Putnam's Sons, 1901.

Huey, Paul R. *Archeology at the Schuyler Flatts, 1971–1974.* Colonie, N.Y.: Town of Colonie, 1974.

———. "Archeology in Seventeenth-Century Dutch Sites in Rensselaerswyck." A lecture presented at the Seminar on Rensselaerswyck, New York State Library, Albany, N.Y., April 7, 1979.

———. "Dutch Wooden Cellars and Other Evidence of Subsurface Wooden Structures at Seventeenth and Eighteenth Century Sites." Paper read at Conference on Dutch Arts and Culture in Colonial America, 1609–1776. Albany Institute of History and Art, Albany, N.Y., August 2, 1986.

——— and John G. Waite. *Washington's Headquarters: The Hasbrouck House: An Historic Structure Report.* n.p.: New York State Historic Trust, 1971.

Huizinga, Johan. *Dutch Civilisation in the Seventeenth Century.* Translated by Arnold J. Pomerans. New York: Frederick Ungar, 1968.

Irving, Washington. "The Legend of Sleepy Hollow." In *The Sketch Book,* pp. 329–360. 1820. Reprint. New York: New American Library, 1961.

Isham, Norman Morrison. *Early American Houses.* 1939. Reprint. New York: De Capo Press, 1967.

Jackson, John Brinckerhoff. *The Necessity for Ruins and other Topics.* Amherst: University of Massachusetts Press, 1980.

Jameson, J. Franklin, ed. *Narratives of New Netherland, 1609–1664.* New York: Charles Scribner's Sons, 1909.

Jaray, Cornell. *Historic Chronicles of New Amsterdam, Colonial New York and Early Long Island.* Empire State Historical Publications Series, no. 35. 2 vols. Port Washington, N.Y.: Ira J. Friedman, n.d.

Johnson, Alvin Page. *Franklin D. Roosevelt's Colonial Ancestors.* Boston: Lothrop, Lee, and Shepard, 1933.

Jones, Charles W. "Knickerbocker Santa Claus." *The New-York Historical Society Quarterly* 38 (1954): 357–383.

Jones, Robert T. *Small Homes of Architectural Distinction: A Book of Suggested Plans Designed by the Architects' Small House Service Bureau, Inc.* New York and London: Harper and Brothers, 1929.

Kalm, Peter. *Travels in North America.* Edited by Adolph B. Benson. 2 vols. New York: Wilson-Erickson, 1937.

Kammen, Michael G. *Colonial New York*. New York: Charles Scribner's Sons, [1975].

Kelly, John Frederick. *The Early Domestic Architecture of Connecticut*. 1924. Reprint. New York: Dover, 1963.

Kennedy, Roger G. *Architecture, Men, Women, and Money in America, 1600–1860*. New York: Random House, 1985.

Kenney, Alice P. "Dutch Patricians in Colonial Albany." *New York History* 49 (1968): 249–283.

———. "Private Worlds in the Middle Colonies: An Introduction to Human Tradition in American History." *New York History* 51 (1970): 5–31.

———. *Stubborn for Liberty: The Dutch in New York*. Syracuse: Syracuse University Press, 1975.

Keur, John Y. and Dorothy L. Keur. *The Deeply Rooted: A Study of a Drents Community in the Netherlands*. American Ethnological Society Monograph, no. 25. Seattle: University of Washington Press, 1955.

Kim, Sung Bok. *Landlord and Tenant in Colonial New York: Manorial Society, 1664–1775*. Chapel Hill: University of North Carolina Press, 1978.

———. "A New Look at the Great Landlords of Eighteenth-Century New York." *William and Mary Quarterly* 3d ser. 27 (1970): 581–614.

Klopfer, Paul. *Das Deutsche Bauern- und Burgerhaus*. Leipzig: A. Koner, 1915.

Kniffen, Fred. "Folk Housing: Key to Diffusion." *Annals of the Association of American Geographers* 55 (1965): 549–577.

Knight, Sarah Kemble. *Journal of Madam Knight . . .* Boston: D. R. Godine, 1972.

Kouwenhoven, John A. "American Studies: Words or Things?" In *American Studies in Transition*. Edited by Marshall W. Fishwick, pp. 15–35. Philadelphia: University of Pennsylvania Press, 1964.

———. *The Arts in Modern American Civilization*. 1948. Reprint. New York: W. W. Norton, 1967.

Lambert, Audrey M. *The Making of the Dutch Landscape: An Historical Geography of the Netherlands*. London and New York: Seminary Press, 1971.

Laslett, Peter and Richard Wall, eds. *Household and Family in Past Time*. London: Cambridge University Press, 1972.

Leiby, Adrian Coulter. *The Early Dutch and Swedish Settlers of New Jersey*. Princeton: Van Nostrand, 1964.

———. "The Conflict Among the Jersey Dutch During the Revolution." In *New Jersey in the American Revolution: Political and Social Conflict*. Edited by William C. Wright, pp. 26–39. Rev. ed. Trenton: New Jersey Historical Commission, 1970.

———. *The Huguenot Settlement of Schraalenburgh: The History of Bergenfield, New Jersey*. Bergenfield: Bergenfield Free Public Library, 1964.

———. *The United Churches of Hackensack and Schraalenburgh, New Jersey, 1686–1822*. River Edge, N.J.: Bergen County Historical Society, 1976.

Lemire, L'Abbe J. "L'Habitat dans la Flandre Francaise." *Annales du Comite Flamand de France* 20 (1892): 1–18.

Lemon, James T. *The Best Poor Man's Country: A Geographical Study of Early Southeastern Pennsylvania.* Baltimore and London: The Johns Hopkins Press, 1972.

Lessard, Michel et Huguette Marquis. *Encyclopedie de la Maison Quebecoise: Trois Siecles d'Habitations.* Ottawa: Les Editions de l'Homme Ltee, 1972.

Lockwood, Luke Vincent. *Colonial Furniture in America.* 2 vols. New York: Charles Scribner's Sons, 1951.

Loehr, Rodney C. "Self-Sufficiency on the Farm, 1759–1819." *Agricultural History* 26 (1952): 37–42.

Long, Amos J. "Fences in Rural Pennsylvania." *Pennsylvania Folklife* 12 (1961): 30–35.

Lossing, Benson. *The Pictorial Field-Book of the Revolution. . . .* 2 vols. 1850. Reprint. New York: Harper, 1860.

Lowenthal, David. "Age and Artifact." In *The Interpretation of Ordinary Landscapes.* Edited by D. W. Meinig, pp. 103–128. New York: Oxford University Press, 1979.

Lyle, Charles T. "Buildings of the Monmouth County Historical Association." *Antiques* 117 (1980): 176–185.

Lynd, Staughton. *Anti-Federalism in Dutchess County, New York.* Chicago: Loyola University Press, 1962.

———. "Who Shall Rule at Home? Dutchess County, New York, in the American Revolution." *William and Mary Quarterly* 3d ser. 28 (1961): 330–359.

McCormick, Richard P. *New Jersey From Colony to State, 1609–1789.* New Jersey Historical Series. New Brunswick: Rutgers University Press, 1964.

———. *Rutgers: A Bicentennial History.* New Brunswick: Rutgers University Press, 1966.

McKinley, Albert S. "English and Dutch Towns of New Netherland." *American Historical Review* 6 (1900): 1–18.

McLaughlin, William G. " 'Enthusiasm For Liberty': The Great Awakening as the Key to the Revolution." In *Preachers and Politicians: Two Essays on the Origins of the American Revolution*, pp. 47–73. Worcester: American Antiquarian Society, 1977.

McLaughlin, William John. "Dutch Rural New York: Community, Economy, and Family in Colonial Flatbush." Ph.D. dissertation, Columbia University, 1981.

McMahon, Reginald. "The Achter Col Colony on the Hackensack." *New Jersey History* 89 (1971): 221–240.

M'Robert, Patrick. *A Tour Through Part of the North Provinces of America . . . in the Years 1774 and 1775. . . .* Edinburgh: Printed for the author, 1776.

McTernan, Don. "The Barrack, A Relict Feature on the North American Cultural Landscape." Pioneer America Society. *Transactions* (1978): 57–69.

Mather, Eugene Cotton and John Fraser Hart. "Fences and Farms." *The Geographical Review* 2 (1954): 201–223.

Massin, Ch., ed. *Fermes et Habitations Rurales*. 3 vols. Paris: Librairie Generale de l'Architecture et de Arts Decoratifs, n.d.

Maxwell, Perriton. "Some Old Dutch Homesteads of New York." In *The Book of a Hundred Houses: A Collection of Pictures, Plans and Suggestions for Householders*, pp. 140–148. New York: Duffield, 1906.

Meertens, P.J. *Volkskunde Atlas voor Nederland en Vlaams-Belgie*. 3 vols. Antwerpen: Standaard-Boekhandel, 1959–1965.

Meischke, R. and H. Zantkuyl. *Het Nederlandse Woonhuis, 1300–1800*. Haarlem: H. D. Tjeenk Willink & Zoon, 1969.

Meitzen, August. *Das Deutsche Haus*. Berlin: Deitrich Reimer, 1882.

Meldrum, D. S. *Home Life in Holland*. New York: Macmillan, 1911.

Melick, Harry C. W. *The Manor of Fordham and its Founder*. New York: Fordham University Press, 1950.

Merwick, Donna. "Dutch Townsmen and Land Use: A Spatial Perspective on Seventeenth-Century Albany, New York." *William and Mary Quarterly* 3d ser, 37 (1980): 53–78.

———. *Possessing Albany, 1630–1710: The Dutch and English Experiences*. Cambridge: Cambridge University Press, 1990.

Messler, Abraham. "The Hollanders in New Jersey, With Notices of Some of their Descendants. . . ." New Jersey Historical Society. *Proceedings* 5 (1850): 67–89.

Millar, Donald. "A Quaint Dutch Survival: The Jean Hasbrouck House, New Paltz, N.Y." *The Architectural Record* 59 (1926): 229–232.

Miller, John. *A Description of the Province and City of New York . . . in the Year 1695*. New York: W. Gowans, 1862.

Milner (John) Associates. "Historic Structure Report on the Pieter Claesen Wyckoff House, Brooklyn, New York." Preliminary Report. New York City Department of Parks and Recreation and New York City Landmarks Commission, 1979.

"The Minnie Schenck House in Nassau County, L.I." *De Halve Maen* 50 (1975): 11–12.

Mok, Paul. "Folklore of the Netherlands." *New York Folklore Quarterly* 4 (1950): 221–232.

Mook, Bertha. *The Dutch Family in the Seventeenth and Eighteenth Centuries: An Explorative-Descriptive Study*. Ottawa: University of Ottawa Press, 1977.

Morgan, Edmund S. *Virginians at Home: Family Life in the Eighteenth Century*. Charlottesville: The University Press of Virginia, 1952.

Morris, Ira K. *Memorial History of Staten Island, New York*. 2 vols. New York: Memorial Publishing Co., 1898.

Morrison, Hugh. *Early American Architecture from the First Colonial Settlements to the National Period.* New York: Oxford University Press, 1952.

Munsell, Joel, ed. *The Annals of Albany.* 10 vols. Albany: J. Munsell, 1850–1859.

"Names of Settlers in Rensselaerswyck from 1630–1646 Compiled from Books of Monthly Wages and Other Mss." Holland Society of New York. *Yearbook* (1896): 130–140.

Narrett, David Evan. "Patterns of Inheritance in Colonial New York City, 1664–1775: A Study in the History of the Family." Ph.D. dissertation, Cornell University, 1981.

———. "Preparation for Death and Provision for the Living: Notes on New York Wills (1665–1760)." *New York History* 57 (1976): 417–437.

New Jersey Archives. Ser. I *Documents Relating to the Colonial History of the State of New Jersey,* vol. 23. *Calendar of New Jersey Wills,* vol. 1 *1670–1730.* Edited by William Nelson. Paterson: The Press Printing & Publishing Co., 1901.

New Jersey Archives. Ser. I *Documents Relating to the Colonial History of the State of New Jersey,* vol. 11 *Newspaper Extracts,* vol. 1 *1704–1739.* Edited by William Nelson. Paterson: The Press Printing & Publishing Co., 1894.

New Jersey Archives. Ser. I *Documents Relating to the Colonial History of the State of New Jersey,* vol. 12 *Newspaper Extracts,* vol. 2 *1740–1750.* Edited by William Nelson. Paterson: The Press Printing & Publishing Co., 1895.

New Jersey. State Archives. Estate Inventories. Trenton, N.J.

New York State Division for Historic Preservation. *Archeology at the Schuyler Flatts, 1971–1974.* Colonie, N.Y.: Town of Colonie, 1974.

New York State Library. Estate Inventories. Albany, N.Y.

Niemcewicz, Juljan U. *Under Their Vine and Fig Tree: Travels in America in 1797–1799, 1805 With Some Further Account of Life in New Jersey.* Elizabeth, N.J.: New Jersey Historical Society, 1965.

Nissenson, S. G. *The Patroon's Domain.* New York State Historical Association Series no. 5. New York: Columbia University Press, 1937.

Noyes, Anna Gausmann. *Three Petticoats.* Leonia, N.J.: n.p., 1955.

O'Callaghan, E. B., ed. *The Documentary History of the State of New York.* 4 vols. Albany: Weed, Parsons & Co., 1849.

———. *History of New Netherland* . . . New York: D. Appleton & Co., 1848.

"Old Dutch Houses in Bergen County." New Jersey Historical Society. *Proceedings* n.s. 9 (1924): 273–275.

Opdyke, Charles Wilson. *The Op Dyck Genealogy.* Albany: Weed, Parsons & Co., 1889.

Peeters, K. C. *Eigen Aard Grepen Uit de Vlaams Folklore.* Antwerpen: Drukkerij-Uitgeverij De Vlijt, 1947.

Peij, Mario. *The Story of Language.* Philadelphia: J. B. Lippincott, 1949.

Pessler, Wilhelm. *Das Altsachsiche Bauernhaus in Seiner Geographische Verbreitung.* Braunschweig: F. Vieweg & Sohn, 1906.

Pickering, James H. "Fenimore Cooper and Pinkster." *New York Folklore Quarterly* 22 (1966): 15–19.

"Pinkster Ode, Albany, 1803." *New York Folklore Quarterly* 8 (1952): 31–45.

Pirenne, Henri. *Early Democracies in the Low Countries: Urban Society and Political Conflict in the Middle Ages and the Renaissance.* Translated by J. V. Saunders. 1910. Reprint. New York: Harper and Row, 1963.

Piwonka, Ruth Johnson. "Dutch Gardens in the Hudson Valley." *De Halve Maen* 49 (1974): 2–3.

———. "New York Colonial Inventories: Dutch Interiors as a Measure of Cultural Change." In *New World Dutch Studies: Dutch Arts and Culture in Colonial America, 1609–1776.* Edited by Roderic H. Blackburn and Nancy A. Kelley, pp. 63–81. Albany: Albany Institute of History and Art, 1987.

——— and Roderic H. Blackburn. *A Visible Heritage, Columbia County, New York; A History in Art and Architecture.* Kinderhook, N.Y.: Columbia County Historical Society, 1977.

Poesch, Jessie J. "Dutch Taste in Colonial America." New Jersey Historical Society. *Proceedings* 76 (1958): 1–13.

Powell, Sumner Chilton. *Puritan Village: The Formation of a New England Town.* 1963. Reprint. Garden City: Doubleday, 1965.

Prince, John Dyneley. "The Jersey Dutch Dialect." *Dialect Notes* 3 (1910): 459–484.

Prudon, Theodore H. M. "The Dutch Barn in America: Survival of a Medieval Structural Frame." *New York Folklore* 2 (1976): 123–142.

"De Pruttelarij Voerman (The Grumbling Wagoner)." *Olde Ulster* 3 (1907): 136–139.

Ranum, Robert Forster Orest. *Family and Society: Selections from the Annales Economies, Societies, Civilisations.* Baltimore: Johns Hopkins University Press, 1876.

Raup, H. F. "The Fence in the Cultural Landscape." *Western Folklore* 6 (1947): 1–7.

Reynolds, Cuyler, comp. *Albany Chronicles: A History of the City Arranged Chronologically from the Earliest Settlement to the Present Time.* Albany: J. B. Lyon, 1906.

Reynolds, Helen Wilkinson. *Dutch Houses in the Hudson Valley Before 1776.* 1929. Reprint. New York: Dover, 1965.

Rhoads, William B. "Franklin D. Roosevelt and Dutch Colonial Architecture." *New York History* 59 (1978): 430–464.

Riediger, Hans and Johan Ulrich Folkers. *Stammestude von Schleswig-Holstein und Mecklenburg.* Potsdam: Adademische Verslagsge Athenaion, 1942.

Riker, James. *Revised History of Harlem (City of New York): Its Origin and Early Annals. . . .* New York: New Harlem Publishing Co., 1904.

Rink, Oliver A. *Holland on the Hudson: An Economic and Social History of Dutch*

New York. Ithaca and London: Cornell University Press; Cooperstown, N.Y.: New York State Historical Association, 1986.
————. "The People of New Netherland: Notes on Non-English Immigration to New York in the Seventeenth Century." *New York History* 62 (1981): 5–42.

Rodes, Sara P. "Washington Irving's Use of Traditional Folklore." *Southern Folklore Quarterly* 20 (1956): 143–153.

Rose, Peter G., translator. *The Sensible Cook*. Syracuse: Syracuse University Press, 1989.

Rosenberg, Jakob, Seymour Slive and E. H. ter Kuile. *Dutch Art and Architecture, 1600–1800*. Baltimore: Penguin, 1966.

St. George, Robert Blair. "A Retreat from the Wilderness: Patterns in the Domestic Environments of Southeastern New England, 1630–1730." Ph.D. dissertation, University of Pennsylvania, 1982.

————. " 'Set Thine House in Order': The Domestication of the Yeomanry in Seventeenth Century New England." 1982. Reprint, in *Common Places: Readings in American Vernacular Architecture*. Edited by Dell Upton and John Michael Vlach, pp. 336–364. Athens: University of Georgia Press, 1986.

Saltzman, L. F. *Building in England Down to 1540: A Documentary History*. 1952. Reprint. London: Oxford University Press, 1967.

Salwen, Bert, Sarah Bridges, and Joel Klein. "An Archaeological Reconnaissance of the Pieter Claesen Wyckoff House, Kings County, New York." New York State Archeological Association. *Bulletin* no. 61 (1974): 26–38.

"Sancte Claus, Goed Heylig Man." *Olde Ulster* 3 (1907): 235–239.

Schama, Simon. *The Embarrassment of Riches: An Interpretation of Dutch Culture in the Golden Age*. Berkeley: University of California Press, 1988.

Schenck (Jan Martense) House. [Notebooks] 5 vols. Brooklyn Museum, Brooklyn, N.Y.

Schipper, Jan. "Rural Architecture: The Zaan Region of the Province of North Holland." In *New World Dutch Studies: Dutch Arts and Culture in Colonial America, 1609–1776*. Edited by Roderic H. Blackburn and Nancy A. Kelley, pp. 171–184. Albany: Albany Institute of History and Art, 1987.

Schlereth, Thomas J., ed. *Material Culture Studies in America*. Nashville: American Association for State and Local History, 1982.

Schmidt, Bruno. *Das Sachsische Bauernhaus und Seiner Dorfgenossen*. Dresden: Holze & Pahl, n.d.

Schmidt, Hubert G. *Agriculture in New Jersey: A Three Hundred Year History*. New Brunswick: Rutgers University Press, 1973.

————. *Rural Hunterdon: An Agricultural History*. New Brunswick: Rutgers University Press, 1945.

Schwartz, Marvin D. *The Jan Martense Schenck House*. Brooklyn: The Brooklyn Museum, 1964.

Schwartz, Marvin D. "The Jan Martense Schenck House in the Brooklyn Museum." *Antiques* 85 (1964): 421–428.

Scott, Kenneth. "Funeral Customs in Colonial New York." *New York Folklore Quarterly* 15 (1959): 274–282.

Seltzer, Leon E., ed. *The Columbia Lippincott Gazetteer of the World.* New York: Columbia University Press, 1962.

Sewel, William. *A Complete Dictionary Dutch and English.* . . . Amsterdam: Kornelis de Veer, 1766.

Shetter, William Z. "Final Word on Jersey Dutch." *American Speech* 33 (1958): 243–251.

———. *Introduction to Dutch.* The Hague: Martinus Nijhoff, 1975.

Shoemaker, Alfred L. "Barracks." *Pennsylvania Folklife* 9 (1958): 2–11.

Singleton, Esther. *Dutch New York.* New York: Dodd, Mead and Co., 1909.

Slocum, S. E. "Early Dutch Colonial Architecture." *American Architect* 105 (1914): 1–12.

Smith, Agnes Scott. "The Dutch Had a Word for It." *New York Folklore Quarterly* 2 (1946): 165–173.

Smith, George L. *Religion and Trade in New Netherland: Dutch Origins and American Development.* Ithaca: Cornell University Press, 1973.

Smith, Richard. *A Tour of Four Great Rivers: The Hudson, Mohawk, Susquehanna, and Delaware in 1769.* Edited by Francis W. Halsey. New York: Scribner's, 1906.

Stilgoe, John R. *Common Landscape of America, 1580–1845.* New Haven and London: Yale University Press, 1982.

Stokes, Isaac Newton Phelps. *The Iconography of Manhattan Island, 1498–1909.* 6 vols. New York, R. H. Dodd, 1915–1928.

Storms, James B. H. *A Jersey Dutch Vocabulary.* Park Ridge, N.J.: Pascack Historical Society, 1964.

Stoudt, John Joseph. *Early Pennsylvania Arts and Crafts.* New York: A. S. Barnes; London: Thomas Yoseloff, 1964.

Stowell, Marion Barber. *Early American Almanacs: The Colonial Weekday Bible.* New York: Burt Franklin, 1977.

Strickland, William. *Journal of a Tour in the United States of America, 1794–1795.* Edited by Rev. J. E. Strickland. New York: The New-York Historical Society, 1971.

Stuart, James. *Three Years in North America.* New York: J. & J. Harper, 1833.

Sweet, William W. *Revivalism in America.* New York: Charles Scribner's Sons, 1944.

Tallman, Wilfred B. "Death Customs among the Colonial Dutch." *De Halve Maen* 42 (1968): 9–10.

Tanis, James. *Dutch Calvinistic Pietism in the Middle Colonies: A Study in the Life and Theology of Theodorus Jacobus Frelinghuysen.* The Hague: Martinus Nijhoff, 1967.

Taray, Cornell, ed. *Historical Chronicles of New Amsterdam, Colonial New York and Early Long Island.* Port Washington, N.Y.: Ira T. Friedman, n.d.

Thacher, James. *A Military Journal During the American Revolutionary War.* . . . Boston: Cottons and Barnard, 1827.

Trefois, Clemens V. "La Technique de la Construction Rurale en Bois: Contribution a l'Etude de l'Habitat en Flandre et dans les Contrees Voisines." *Folk* 1 (1937): 55–73.

Trent, Robert F. *Hearts and Crowns: Folk Chairs of the Connecticut Coast, 1720– 1840, as Viewed in the Light of Henri Focillon's Introduction to "Art Populaire."* New Haven: New Haven Colony Historical Society, 1977.

Turner, Frederick Jackson. *The Frontier in American History.* New York: Henry Holt & Co., 1920.

Uilkema, K. *Het Friesche Boerenhuis.* Leeuwarden: Friesch Genootschap, 1916.

Upton, Dell. "Vernacular Domestic Architecture in Eighteenth-Century Virginia." 1982. Reprint, in *Common Places: Readings in American Vernacular Architecture.* Edited by Dell Upton and John Michael Vlach, pp. 315–335. Athens: University of Georgia Press, 1986.

Van Berkhey, J. Le Francq. *Natuurlijke Historie van Holland.* 9 vols. te Amsterdam en te Leyden: Yntema en Tieboel, P. H. Trap, 1769–1810.

Van Brunt, Adriances. Diary and Journal Kept on his Farm near Brooklyn, N.Y. 1828 June 8–1830 March 20. New York Public Library, New York, N.Y.

Van Buren, Augustus H. "Wiltwyck Under the Dutch." New York State Historical Society. *Proceedings* 11 (1912): 128–135.

Vanderbilt, Gertrude Lefferts. *The Social History of Flatbush, and Manners and Customs of the Dutch Settlers in Kings County.* New York: D. Appleton & Co., 1882.

Van der Donck, Adriaen. *A Description of the New Netherlands.* Edited by Thomas F. O'Donnell. 1655. Reprint. Syracuse: Syracuse University Press, 1968.

Van Der Lyn, Henry. Diary. New York Historical Society, New York City, N.Y.

Van Hoesen, Walter Hamilton. *Crafts and Craftsmen of New Jersey.* Rutherford, Madison, and Teaneck: Fairleigh Dickinson University Press, 1973.

Van Laer, A. J. F., ed. & trans. *Correspondence of Jeremias van Rensselaer, 1651– 1674.* Albany: University of the State of New York, 1932.

———, ed. *Documents Relating to New Netherland, 1624–1626, in the Henry E. Huntington Library.* San Marino: Henry E. Huntington Library and Art Gallery, 1924.

———, ed. *Early Records of the City and County of Albany and Colony of Rensselaerswyck.* New York State Library History Bulletin 11, vol. 2, *Mortgages 1, 1658–1660, and Wills 1–2, 1681–1765.* Albany: University of the State of New York, 1919.

———, ed. *Early Records of the City and County of Albany and Colony of Rensselaer-*

swyck. New York State Library *History Bulletin 10, vol. 3, Notarial Papers 1 and 2, 1660–1696.* Albany: University of the State of New York, 1918.

———, ed. *Minutes of the Court of Albany, Rensselaerswyck, and Schenectady, 1668–1680.* 3 vols. Albany: University of the State of New York, 1926–1932.

———, trans. *New York Historical Manuscripts: Dutch.* Edited by Kenneth Scott and Kenn Stryker-Rodda. 4 vols. Baltimore: Geneological Publishing Co., 1974.

———, ed. *Van Rensselaer Bowier Manuscripts.* Albany: University of the State of New York, 1908.

Van Liew Papers, 1712–1796. New Jersey State Archives, Trenton, N.J.

Van Loon, L. G. *Crumbs from an Old Dutch Closet: The Dutch Dialect of Old New York.* The Hague: Martinus Nijhoff, 1938.

Van Rensselaer, Mrs. John King. *The Goede Vrouw of Mana-ha-ta: At Home and in Society, 1609–1760.* New York: Charles Scribner's Sons, 1898.

van Wijk, Piet A.M. *Boerderijen Bekijken Historisch Boerderij-Onderzoek in Nederland.* Arnhem: Stichting Historisch Boerderij-Onderzoek, 1985.

———. "Form and Function in the Netherlands' Agricultural Architecture." In *New World Dutch Studies: Dutch Arts and Culture in Colonial America, 1609–1776.* Edited by Roderic H. Blackburn and Nancy A. Kelley, pp. 161–169. Albany: Albany Institute of History and Art, 1987.

Van Winkle, Daniel. *Old Bergen: A History and Reminiscences with Maps and Illustrations.* Jersey City: J. W. Harrison, 1902.

Van Winkle, Edward. *Manhattan, 1624–1639.* New York: G. P. Putnam's Sons, 1916.

Van Wyck, Frederick. *Keskachauge, or the First White Settlement on Long Island.* New York: G. P. Putnam's Sons, 1924.

"Various Versions of 'Trip a Trop a Troontjes.' " *Olde Ulster* 1 (1905): 234–237.

Verplanck Family Papers. Farm Book, c. 1794. New York Historical Society, New York City, N.Y.

Verplanck Family Papers. A Treatise on Agriculture and Practical Husbandry. Farm and Garden Notebook, vol. 1, c. 1800. New York Historical Society, New York City, N.Y.

Vierin, Joseph. *L'Architecture Regionale de la Flandre Maritime.* Brussels: Vromant, 1921.

A Village Guide to the Old Bethpage Village Restoration. Syosset, N.Y.: Friends of the Nassau County Museum, 1975.

Vlach John Michael. *Plain Painters: Making Sense of American Folk Art.* Publications of the American Folklore Society, new ser. Washington, D.C.: Smithsonian Institution Press, 1988.

Vorhees, Ralph. "The Raritan and its Early Holland Settlers." *Our Home* 1 (1873): 53–58, 337–344, 403–410, 467–470.

Voskuil, J. J. *Van Vlechtwerk tot Baksteen: Geschiedenis van de Wanden van het Boerenhuis in Nederland.* Arnhem: Stichting Historisch Boerderij-Onderzoek, 1976.

Wacker, Peter. "Cultural and Commercial Regional Associations of Traditional Smoke-Houses in New Jersey." *Pioneer America* 3 (1971): 25–34.

———. "Dutch Barns and Barracks in New Jersey During the Eighteenth Century." *Annals of the Association of American Geographers* 57 (1967): 806.

———. "Folk Architecture as an Indicator of Culture Areas and Culture Diffusion: Dutch Barns and Barracks in New Jersey." *Pioneer America* 5 (1973): 36–47.

———. *Land and People: A Cultural Geography of Pre-Industrial New Jersey: Origins and Settlement.* New Brunswick: Rutgers University Press, 1976.

———. "New Jersey's Cultural Landscape Before 1800." New Jersey Historical Commission. *Second Annual Symposium*, pp. 35–61. Trenton: New Jersey Historical Commission, 1971.

Wagman, Morton. "The Rise of Pieter Claessen Wyckoff: Social Mobility on the Colonial Frontier." *New York History* 53 (1972): 5–24.

Walker, A. H. *Atlas of Bergen County, N.J.* Philadelphia: C. C. Pease, [1876].

Ward, Christopher. *The Dutch and Swedes on the Delaware, 1609–1664.* Philadelphia: University of Pennsylvania Press, 1930.

Waterman, Thomas T. *The Dwellings of Colonial America.* Chapel Hill: University of North Carolina Press, 1950.

Weinberg, Nathan. *Preservation in American Towns and Cities.* Boulder, Colo.: Westview Press, 1979.

Weiss, Harry Bischoff. *The Personal Estates of Early Farmers and Tradesmen of Colonial New Jersey, 1670–1750.* Trenton: New Jersey Agricultural Society, 1971.

Wendehack, Clifford C. "Early Dutch Houses of New Jersey." *The White Pine Architectural Monographs* 11 (1925–1926): 1–20.

Wenger, Mark R. "The Central Passage in Virginia: Evolution of an Eighteenth-Century Living Space," in *Perspectives in Vernacular Architecture, II.* Edited by Camille Wells, pp. 137–149. Columbia, Mo.: University of Missouri Press, 1986.

Wertenbaker, Thomas Jefferson. *The Middle Colonies.* The Founding of American Civilization. 1938. Reprint. New York: Cooper Square, 1963.

———. *The Old South.* The Founding of American Civilization. 1942. Reprint. Cooper Square, 1963.

Wess, Robert C. "The Use of Hudson-Valley Folk Traditions in Washington Irving's Knickerbocker History of New York." *New York Folklore Quarterly* 30 (1974): 212–225.

Wheaton, Robert. "Family and Kinship in Western Europe: The Problem of the Joint Family Household." *Journal of Interdisciplinary History* 5 (1975): 601–628.

Wheeler, Robert G. "The House of Jeremias van Rensselaer, 1658–1666." *New-York Historical Society Quarterly* 45 (1961): 75–88.

Winter, Heinrich. *Das Burgerhaus in Oberhessen.* vol. 5 *Das Deutsche Burgerhaus.* Herausgegeben von Adolph Bernt. Tubingen: Verlag Ernst Wasmuth, 1965.

Wolley, Charles. *A Two Years' Journal in New York.* New York: William Gowans, 1860.

Woodward, Carl Raymond. *The Development of Agriculture in New Jersey, 1640–1880.* New Brunswick: New Jersey Agricultural Experiment Station, Rutgers University, 1927.

————. *Ploughs and Politicks: Charles Read of New Jersey and his Notes on Agriculture, 1715–1774.* New Brunswick: Rutgers University Press, 1941.

Wright, Langdon G. "In Search of Peace and Harmony: New York Communities in the Seventeenth Century." *New York History* 61 (1980): 5–21.

————. "Local Government and Central Authority in New Netherland." *New York Historical Society Quarterly* 57 (1973): 7–29.

Yerbury, Francis R. *Old Domestic Architecture of Holland.* . . . London: The Architectural Press, 1924.

————. "Old Homes of Holland." *Country Life* 87 (1940): 518–519.

Zabriskie, George Olin. "Bergen County Landmark to be Re-Named." *De Halve Maen* 42 (1967): 11–12.

————, comp. *The Zabriskie Family.* 2 vols. Salt Lake City: George Olin Zabriskie, 1963.

————. "The Zabriskie-von Steuben House." *De Halve Maen* 38 (1963): 11–12.

Zantkuyl, H. J. "De Houten Huizen van Holysloot." *Tijdschrift van de Koninklijke Nederlandse Oudheidkundige Bond* 67 (1968): 11–27.

————. "Het Jan Martense Schenckhuis te Brooklyn." *Tijdschrift van de Koninklijke Nederlandse Oudheidkundige Bond* 63 (1964): 57–80.

————. "The Netherlands Town House: How and Why It Works." In *New World Dutch Studies: Dutch Arts and Culture in Colonial America, 1609–1776.* Edited by Roderic H. Blackburn and Nancy A. Kelley, pp. 143–160. Albany: Albany Institute of History and Art, 1987.

————. "Reconstructie van Enkele Nederlandse Huizen uit de Zeventiende Eeuw." *Tijdschrift van de Koninklijke Nederlandse Oudheidkundige Bond* 84 (1985): 166–179.

Zelinsky, Wilbur. *The Cultural Geography of the United States.* Englewood Cliffs: Prentice-Hall, 1973.

————. "Walls and Fences." *Landscape* 8 (1959): 14–20.

Zink, Clifford W. "Dutch Framed Houses in New York and New Jersey." *Winterthur Portfolio* 22 (1987): 265–294.

Zippelius, Adelhart. *Das Bauerhaus am Unteren Deutschen Niederhein.* Wuppertal: A. Martini & Gruttefien, 1957.

Zippelius, A. "Das Vormittelalterliche Hallenhaus in Mittel-Europa." *Bonner Jahrbucher* 153 (1953): 13–45.
Zwierlein, Frederick J. *Religion in New Netherland: A History of the Development of the Religious Conditions in the Province of New Netherland, 1623–1664.* Rochester: John P. Smith, 1910.

Index

Compiled by KAREN DIANE GILBERT, New Jersey Division, Newark Public Library